GENTLEMAN
GERALD

GENTLEMAN GERALD

The Crimes and Times of
Gerald Chapman, America's First
"Public Enemy No. 1"

H. Paul Jeffers

St. Martin's Press ⚭ New York

Production Editor: David Stanford Burr

Library of Congress Cataloging-in-Publication Data

Jeffers, H. Paul (Harry Paul).
    Gentleman Gerald : the crimes and times of Gerald Chapman, America's first "public enemy no. 1" / by H. Paul Jeffers.
        p.   cm.
    ISBN 0-312-13500-9
    1. Chapman, Gerald.   2. Thieves—United States—Biography.
3. Bank robberies—United States.   I. Title.
HV6653.C42J44   1995
364.1'523'092—dc20
[B]   95-35370
                                                    CIP

First Edition: December 1995

10 9 8 7 6 5 4 3 2 1

This book is dedicated to my friend

Sid Ruderman

who grew up in Connecticut

hearing tales of Gerald Chapman.

Contents

Contents

viii

Author's Note

THIS IS THE TRUE STORY of a brilliant criminal of long ago. It has all the elements of a modern-day thriller: a brazen ambush-robbery that was the biggest in American history to that date, brilliant and dogged sleuthing by dedicated cops, breath-taking escapes, gun duels, murder, a sensational trial that enthralled the nation, a beautiful mystery woman, and a commanding central character abounding with charm and romance—all against the background of the Roaring Twenties.

It is based on the public record and on exploits reported by an astonished and often adoring press, for Gerald Chapman was—and remains—an extraordinary individual whose place in America's criminal annals has been overshadowed by a rogues' gallery of Johnny-come-latelies.

Unfortunately, not all the details of Chapman's life and crimes have survived the seventy-odd years since he paid society's price for being the nation's first "Public Enemy No. 1." For example, New York State prison records of his incarcerations in Sing Sing went up in smoke in 1985, along with all the archives of what was once America's most famous penitentiary. Nor does the federal prison in Atlanta, Georgia, retain a written memory of Chapman, even though he staged one of the most daring prison breaks in history from that facility.

As a result of these and other lamentable gaps in the early years of Chapman's tale, it was necessary for me to create some scenes, actions, and dialogues that may not have happened exactly as depicted. They are drawn from known aspects of Chapman's character and those of his accomplices, adversaries and, yes, admirers.

Because Chapman was the most notorious and hunted criminal in the country for several years, he received considerable newspaper coverage, notably in those cities where he pulled off some of his most spectacular crimes. In researching those events, I relied heavily on the colorful writing and minute details found only in contemporaneous news accounts. I am especially grateful for the exhaustive coverage afforded by the *New York Times*. For invaluable assistance in obtaining copies of the Muncie, Indiana, *Star* and *Evening News* and the *Herald* of New Britain, Connecticut, I am indebted to Laurey Lowery and Ginny Leipold, respectively, for access to those papers' archives on Chapman's escapades in their cities. For contributing immensely to my appreciation of the newspapers and the inspired "ink-stained wretches" who worked for them during the Jazz Age, I am grateful to the greatest living trove of data on the press of the period, my friend Hy Turner.

Enlightenment on the state of American prisons of that time came from the memoirs of the late Warden Lewis E. Lawes, *Twenty-Thousand Years in Sing Sing*. Perspectives on the New York Police Department of the 1920s in general and on Chapman in particular were found in *Night Stick* by Lewis J. Valentine, a lifelong cop who knew Chapman long before becoming commissioner of police in the administration of New York mayor Fiorello H. La Guardia.

Insights into the personalities who took part in one of our

history's most sensational criminal trials came in the form of *The Count of Gramercy Park,* a book by Robert Hayden Alcorn, son of the prosecutor. Published in England in 1955, the book proved to be, unfortunately, erroneous in many facts regarding Chapman's notorious criminal career before and after he arrived in Connecticut in 1924 to deadly effect, becoming the object of a manhunt the likes of which the American people had never witnessed.

I hope that through this book, the first complete and accurate account of Chapman's lifetime of crime, he will be restored to his proper place in the history of the United States underworld in the twentieth century, because it was Chapman who wrote a unique chapter in criminality and blazed the trail for all the public enemies who followed him.

I might have woo'd your liking,
    With chant of choral rhyme,
Made all of blissful singers,
    In new delight of time.

—Gerald Chapman
Connecticut State Prison, 1926

CHAPTER ONE

Night Mail

ON MONDAY, OCTOBER 24, 1921, in the old city hall of Chalons-sur-Marne, France, Sergeant Edward S. Younger, Headquarters Company, Second Battalion, U.S. Fiftieth Infantry, stood at attention before four closed, plain wooden, flag-draped coffins. Because of his distinguished combat record, Younger had been chosen to select one of the caskets by placing a bouquet of flowers upon it. No one could say who lay within. The bodies were those of unidentified soldiers who had lost their lives in the world war. The unknown soldier would be sent to the National Cemetery in Arlington, Virginia, to become, in the words of the Associated Press correspondent who observed the selection, the one who would "forever symbolize the sacrifice of American sons in the war."

That same evening, another person about to make history, Gerald Chapman, was unaccustomedly at home in Manhattan's swank Gramercy Park. A dapper, debonair bon vivant, who spoke with a tony English accent and sported spats, pink gloves, homburg hat, monocle, and silver-capped walking stick, he had missed the war because he had been confined to prison.

Priding himself on being "a man about town," he already had taken in that season's new Broadway offerings: *Blood and Sand* starring Otis Skinner; Marilyn Miller and Leon Errol in *Sally; The Return of Peter Grimm* with David Warfield; Ernest Truex in *Six Cylinder Love;* George Arliss in *The Green Goddess;* Helen Hayes in *The Wren;* Florence Eldridge in *Ambush;* and *A Bill of Divorcement* with Katherine Cornell. Because he had always had plenty of money and a stellar address, Broadway habitués who knew nothing of his past called him "the Count of Gramercy Park." But on this chill and drizzly evening, as he sat in the parlor of his apartment, it was not a night on the town that occupied his mind.

"Settle down, Gerry," said his friend and associate, Dutch Anderson. "Charlie knows his job."

"If Loerber screws up," Chapman grumbled, "I'll kill him."

"Relax, buddy," Dutch said with a smile. "Everything's going to work out fine, just as you've planned it. A few hours from now we'll be rolling in dough." From a vest pocket, he drew a gold watch. "It's only eight-thirty. We have plenty of time."

Chapman rose, crossed the large sitting room to the window, and peered through the mist at the colorful fall foliage of the park and the people walking their dogs despite the inclement weather.

"Looking isn't going to make Charlie appear any sooner," Dutch said with a laugh.

Chapman turned. "Maybe he's got cold feet all of a sudden."

"I can give you a million reasons why that isn't going to happen," Dutch said. "If we're lucky, maybe more! Remember those guys in February?"

"Yeah, but that was in Toledo," Chapman retorted. *"This is New York City!* The cops are smarter here."

"C'mon, Gerry," Dutch said imploringly, "after all the work you've put into planning this caper, it's going to be a cakewalk."

Returning to his chair, Chapman went over the plans in his head. He had thought it out to the last, tiniest detail. He had spent hours rehearsing it. Drawing his own gold pocket watch, he muttered, "This fellow Haveranck should be leaving home for work just about now."

Dutch barked a laugh. "It's going to be a night that he'll tell his grandchildren about."

Chapman smiled. "You know, Dutch, I've watched that guy so much these past few days, I think I know him as well as I know you. I just hope the cops don't give him a hard time over this."

"My hope is that he doesn't try to play the hero."

"Yeah," Chapman said. "It would be pretty bad if we had to get rough with him."

The object of this discussion, Frank Haveranck, had been a driver for the post office for several years. A man of settled ways, he had left his house at 396 Webster Avenue in Long Island City that evening with plenty of time to spare in reaching the main postal facility at Eighth Avenue and Thirty-third Street. Picking up his usual truck, he had set out for his first destination right on schedule.

At ten o'clock he jammed stubby hands into the pockets of his light windbreaker at the loading dock of the City Hall post office on Park Row and leaned his bulky frame against the fender of his green van as Jeremiah Savelli began heaving bulging gray sacks of mail into the back. "You're not forgetting the five bucks are you, Frank?" he asked. "It's been a while.

Night Mail

3

"You'll get it payday, Jerry," said Frank.

"Next time maybe you won't be so hot to bet on the Yankees."

"If Ruth had been in there for all eight games the Yanks would've taken the World Series," Frank replied.

The Yankees had lost to the Giants in the eighth game on a dramatic fielding play. With Aaron Ward on first and one out, Home Run Baker had slammed a ball toward a hole in right field. But Giant second baseman Johnny Rawlings knocked it down and drilled it to George Kelly at first in time to pick off Baker. Meanwhile, Ward, for no good reason, made a try for third, only to be nailed easily by Baker's perfect throw to third and Frankie Frisch. Babe Ruth had hit a homer in the fourth game, but he had been playing with an injured arm and knee and had missed two of the games, watching one of them from the press box.

Jerry flipped the last two bags into the truck.

Chomping the soggy stub of a two-for-a-nickel King Edward Invincible cigar, his second of the evening, Frank asked, "What's the count?"

"Thirty-three in all," Jerry answered, handing Frank a Post Office Department waybill listing the contents of the shipment. Collected throughout the day from a dozen nearby brokerage houses and other Wall Street firms, the list included twenty-eight bags of ordinary mail and five sacks of registered, containing stock certificates, bonds, negotiable securities, money orders, and cash. As Frank closed the wire-mesh doors and locked them, Jerry said, "There's gotta be at least a million bucks in there for you."

Easing the truck away from the loading dock, Frank tapped the horn, blaring a warning to any pedestrians or auto traffic that might impede the start of a nightly journey that would take him from lower Manhattan to the General Post Office.

In making the run, he had developed a finely honed routine. Through careful timing, he could catch the traffic light on green at the intersection of Park Row and Broadway at the southern tip of triangular City Hall Park. Then he made a right turn onto Broadway, its buildings deserted save for cleaning women who shared the night with him. If he missed the green at Park Row and Broadway, he could expect to hit red lights all the way to Canal Street, which meant trouble.

Since work on the new Holland Tunnel had begun exactly one year and twelve days ago, getting across Canal Street could prove to be hell on wheels. According to the publicity surrounding the ground-breaking ceremonies for the ten-million-dollar project, there would be another three years of detours and slow going around Canal Street before the first car made the underwater trip to New Jersey.

Beyond Canal, the only spot where his progress would slow was at Union Square. There, Broadway made a bend known to early-day trolley drivers as "Deadman's Curve," because taking it too fast often resulted in overturned cars and corpses.

Union Square held personal memories for Frank. Before the war he had been taken there for a big rally by the International Workers of the World, only to look on helplessly while his father was beaten with nightsticks by police who had waded into a crowd "to teach the Wobblies and other god-damned Bolsheviks and Red radicals a lesson." The day was coming, his Old Man had vowed, even while being pummeled, when those workers would unite, rise up, and destroy their oppressors as they had done in Russia. However, the Old Man did not go as far as had a group of Reds the previous year. On September 26, 1920, they had planted a TNT bomb across the street from the House of Morgan on Wall Street. It killed thirteen people and wounded hundreds of others on their lunchtime break. Nor had his father approved of sending sixteen paper-wrapped bombs addressed to J. P. Morgan, John D. Rockefeller, and other capitalist luminaries, although his objections had been directed at the irresponsibility of sending bombs through the U.S. Mail and possibly killing or injuring innocent people, such as postal workers. Such as his son. Fortunately, one of them, Charles Caplan, had spotted the suspicious packages and called the bomb squad.

What would the Old Man say, Frank wondered, if he knew that in his son's mail truck on this dank autumn night were five bags stuffed with the paper lifeblood of what the Wobblies called the corrupt capitalist yoke of oppression?

Beyond the memories that passing Union Square invariably evoked, and a slowdown at Deadman's Curve, Frank would find nothing to delay him at Fourteenth Street. The overweening Klein's Department Store and all its neighbors had closed at six o'clock. It was Monday—not a shopping night.

Although New York City's reputation was that of a town for night owls, Frank knew this was a misperception. New York was like every other place in the country: filled with people who worked hard all day and then went home to their families at night. If they stepped out at all, it was to go to the movies for the latest Hal Roach comedy, not to some fancy nightclub or the Ziegfeld Follies, with W. C. Fields and a bevy of beautiful girls in scanty costumes.

Those diversions were for the rich, of which New York City probably had more than its share. But the average New Yorker was working very hard to make ends meet. Most New Yorkers were closer to the people in Sinclair Lewis's *Main Street* than to those of F. Scott Fitzgerald's *The Beautiful and the Damned*, the current best-sellers at the bookstores.

Frank would drive by the shuttered storefronts of Broadway where it slanted in a direct line between Union Square and Twenty-seventh Street, site of Brentano's Book Store. When he passed the Flatiron Building, Madison Square would be on his right. As beautiful a park as New York City had to offer, it lay like a gem between the Fifth Avenue Building and the Metropolitan Life Insurance Company with its imposing tower that copied the campanile of St. Mark's in Venice. Around it rose the somber marble grandeur of the New York State Appellate Court House. Opposite lay the stodgy Manhattan Club edifice at Twenty-sixth Street and Madison Avenue and Madison Square Garden with its graceful tower surmounted by a gilded statue of the naked Diana.

Vividly, Frank remembered the drama that had been played out in the rooftop restaurant of that palace of entertainment, spectacle, and sport on June 25, 1906. He had been in grade school at the time, but not even schoolboys were spared the scandal as journalists blared the news that the love-crazed millionaire Harry K. Thaw had shot and killed Stanford White, the famous architect of the Garden and many other prominent buildings. Thaw's trial revealed that the murder had been over the affections of the beautiful Evelyn Nesbit Thaw and her alleged relationship with White before her marriage. Newspapers had played up stories of sadism and perversion, reporting that White had forced the naked Evelyn Nesbit to divert him on a red velvet swing. Thaw had been found not guilty by reason of insanity, and his impoverished wife had gone into vaudeville with an act featuring a similar swing. Recently, the unfortunate woman's name had been in the papers again—for an unsuccessful suicide attempt with twenty grains of morphine.

The next landmark on Frank's settled itinerary would be the criss-crossing of Broadway and Sixth Avenue at Thirty-fourth Street, site of Macy's Department Store and its archrival, Gimbel's. After a left turn, he would reach his final destination two blocks west: the vast General Post Office, resembling a Greek temple, where the sacks of ordinary and Wall Street mail would be unloaded.

All of this territory was also well known to Gerald Chapman. He had been scouting it for days and observing Frank Haveranck's routines for three consecutive nights, always from a different automobile.

Tonight, flicking the remnant of his soggy cigar through the window, Frank found the first traffic light green and rounded City Hall Park to leave Jeremiah Savelli's post office behind him and swing onto Broadway. He paid no attention to the auto that darted out from a curb and drew up behind him—a green Cleveland touring sedan.

Passing the Woolworth tower, the world's tallest building, Frank honked the horn impatiently, discouraging a fat lady from darting across the street. Watching her scamper back onto the curb, he chuckled at the memory of an item in the morning newspaper. On Sunday, fifty fat women had marched through Central Park in a weight-reduction experiment supervised by Dr. R. S. Copeland, commissioner of the city's health department. At the end of the reducing program, the woman who had slimmed down most would be presented with a certificate of achievement by Mayor John Hylan.

Through autumn-colored trees on his right, Frank saw lights in windows on the ground floor of City Hall and wondered if they were those of the mayor's office. He liked the carroty-haired man everyone called "Red Mike," had voted for him, and planned to vote for him again.

Beyond City Hall Park, windows blazed in the buildings of Park Row. These were the offices and newsrooms of the *New York Tribune* founded by Horace Greeley; the *World*, located beneath the dome of the Pulitzer Building overlooking Printing House Square with its statue of the patriarch of American journalism, Benjamin Franklin; and the *Mirror*, which had moved into the space that recently housed the *Daily News* before that paper relocated to new quarters at Park Place.

Of the seven morning and ten evening papers published daily in New York City, Frank favored the *News* because of its tabloid style of tart headlines, snappy news items, and abundant pictures, all in a size and shape convenient for reading on the subway.

A night worker, he did not have to contend with rush hour crowds during his daily trek from Webster Street by the IRT line across the Queensborough Bridge. "A trip on New York subways is the best buy for a nickel in the world," he liked to say to his wife. "Except for a cigar, of course," he added, enjoying teasing her about her threats that unless he gave up his "smelly stogies" and stopped sprinkling her carpets with those "blasted ashes" she would leave him and take their kids with her.

He had tried giving up cigars at home with no success, but he was making every effort to keep the ashes off the floor.

"I guess I could do worse," his wife always said. "At least you're not a boozer."

Except for an occasional beer, he had never been a drinker. Prohibition, therefore, had not proved a problem, as it had for many of the men who worked with him at the post office. But although unaffected, he thought that the Eighteenth Amendment, which made the country dry, had been a foolish and cruel thing.

Despite the nighttime hours, Frank liked his job and felt proud to have it. Without men like him, he believed, the city could not function. He and his four-thousand-plus fellow employees in the city's post offices handled more than five million pieces of outgoing mail each day and another five million incoming—an annual flow of upwards of three billion items totalling more than sixty million dollars in receipts per year.

It was money well spent. For a two-cent stamp, a New

Yorker knew that when he dropped a letter addressed to Los Angeles into a green mail box on a corner it would be delivered in California in eighty-five hours. A first-class letter going to Philadelphia, mailed in the morning in the Bronx, would be sorted in the City of Brotherly Love that night and delivered in the morning, afternoon at the latest.

Soon, the mail would be going by air. Just eight months ago, on March 4, 1921, a daring pilot by the name of Ernest Allison had flown the mail from San Francisco to New York, stopping only in Chicago, in a total elapsed time of thirty-three hours, twenty minutes. Only yesterday, October 23, 1921, the first aerial delivery ever made in New England had been completed by a plane that had departed Bolling Field in Washington, D.C., at 10:35 A.M. and landed at Framingham, Massachusetts, at 3:35 in the afternoon.

That was quite a feat, Frank thought, considering the fact that trucking mail sacks from the City Hall Post Office to the main facility on Thirty-third Street took almost thirty minutes.

Hearing car horns blaring behind him as he crossed Chambers Street, he glanced into the rearview mirror on the driver's side door to see a Ford flivver swerving to avoid crashing into a big open-topped car gunning through against the light.

"Damned idiot," he muttered.

At the next corner as the automobile that had nearly hit the flivver darted past and cut sharply in front of his truck, Frank counted three men in it—the driver and two men in the rear. "A trio of swells heading for the uptown speakeasies," he thought. Disgustedly, he grunted, "Playboys!"

A block farther, at Broadway and Reade, when the car pulled to the curb and stopped opposite the block-long headquarters of the *New York Sun*, he changed his mind and supposed that its occupants were reporters.

At Pearl and Broadway, he noticed in the mirror that the car had pulled out and was behind him again, perilously close. "What the hell is this?" he muttered. "A game of tag?" A second later it drifted back, only to sprint forward and draw up beside him on the left, so close that he feared it would sideswipe him. "Crazy bastards," he growled.

"Drunks prob'ly," he thought.

Then the car swerved right, nearly hitting the truck's left front fender.

"Watch out!" he shouted, shaking a fist.

As they neared Leonard Street, one of the three men stood up and, with impressive agility, leapt onto the van's running board. Slamming against the door with a dull thud and grasping the strut of the rearview mirror with his left hand, he brandished a pistol with the right.

Jamming the muzzle of the gun against Frank's temple, the man shouted, "Pull it over, pal. There's no use dying for the post office, is there?"

Frank hit the brakes.

"Now, if you please," said the gunman as the van stopped, "pull around the corner into Leonard Street."

The sedan had already made the turn and parked.

"Stop next to the car," the gunman said softly, "and turn off the motor. Then get out with your hands up."

"Anything you say, pal," Frank replied.

As he bounded to the street, two shadowy figures left the car, guns in their hands.

"I promise you that if you cooperate no one will harm you," the gunman said quietly, drawing a laundry bag from a pocket of his gray suit. "I am sorry about this," he said, "but I have to ask you to slip this over your head. I mustn't let you see my associates' faces." Lifting the sack above Frank's head, he smiled. "I know what you're thinking. 'Why worry about them? I've seen *your* face.' " He shrugged. "Well, it doesn't matter. I've got a kisser that could belong to a thousand guys."

Hooded, Frank heard footsteps moving to the rear of the van.

Then, voices:

"Make it quick, Dutch."

"Remember, Charlie! Only the sacks with 'registered' tags."

"That's it, Gerry. Got 'em."

Next: footsteps, slamming doors, and a squeal of tires kicking up grit as the car sped away, westward on Leonard Street.

Removing the hood, Frank estimated that after he had stopped the truck, the robbery had taken less than two minutes.

He had seen the license plate of the car.

He had also gotten a very good look at the gunman with the polite manner. About thirty-five years of age, he was on the short side; maybe five feet, seven; slight build, weighing about 130 pounds; with a high, receding forehead; dark, almost black, hair, greenish blue eyes; a sallow complexion; and high cheekbones.

His voice had sounded funny, like an Englishman's.

School Days

HE WAS IRISH, born in Brooklyn. In the Gay Nineties, there were worse places to be a kid.

Before bridges to Manhattan were built, the poet Walt Whitman boasted, in "Crossing Brooklyn Ferry," that "Brooklyn of ample hills was mine." Several years later, a correspondent of *Harper's Magazine* wrote, "Brooklyn is a city of residences. From a balloon it would look like a sea of them, only broken here and there by parks and factory districts, but so largely made up of so vast an area of dwellings as to have earned for the city the nickname of 'the bedroom of New York.' "

Brooklyn was also a city of churches, many of them Roman Catholic, attended mostly by the Irish. So when Gerald Chapman was born a few years after construction of the Brooklyn Bridge, and before Brooklyn surrendered its municipal independence to become a borough of New York City, Gerald's home of Williamsburg was known as "Irishtown." A flood of immigrants had made it so for more than a generation and would continue to come for decades, filling the ranks of the city's police and fire departments, who marched proudly up Fifth Avenue every March 17 to honor St. Patrick. Newspaperman Lowell M. Limpus, in his biography of another Irishtown lad, Lewis J. Valentine, who would grow up to be a policeman and, eventually, police commissioner, described the Brooklyn of the 1890s as a small-town environment in which barefoot boys and girls cavorted in the streets and wiggled their toes in the dust exactly like kids all across the country.

In this idyllic setting, for some years, Gerald's Irish-born father was a harness maker and his mother tended Gerald and his older sister and brother. She took in washing for extra income. A devout Catholic, she prayed that her youngest child would honor the Chapmans by becoming a priest, an aspiration for which there were encouraging signs. Gerald was smart. Minded by the nuns and priests in school, and by his mother at home, and admonished by both parents to stay away from gangs of toughs who loitered on street corners, he was an obedient, untroublesome child.

Then his mother died, and soon afterward, his father. Taken in by his aunt, Mrs. Catherine Cooper, he moved to 171 East 107th Street in Manhattan. At the turn of the century, there were better places to be a boy.

A mere eighteen blocks north of Gerald's new address stood the infamous Murder Stable. The scene of more killings than any other spot in the United States, it festered in the heart of the domain of Ignazio Saietta, known as "Lupo," Italian for wolf. A vicious killer, he was known for slicing the tongues of victims and stuffing their corpses into trunks and barrels for shipment to other cities. He also demonstrated a talent for the art of counterfeiting. In the middle of Italian Harlem, the Wolf's neighborhood was an expanse of five-story tenements and dangerous streets prowled by gangs known as the Red

Peppers, the Duffy Hills, and the misleadingly named Pansies, commanded by Rags Riley.

An Irish-American version of Fagin, the organizer of the gang of London street urchins in the Charles Dickens classic *Oliver Twist,* Riley gathered around him a group of boys who specialized in burglarizing East Side homes and apartments and East River warehouses. The Pansies were Irish kids, recruited from the streets and the vicinity of Catholic schools. Gerald quickly learned from his new friends that joining the Pansies could offer rewards more satisfying than good marks on a report card and a pat on the head from Aunt Catherine. By running with the gang, he could make easy money. Presently, in addition to readin', 'ritin', 'rithmetic, and the Baltimore Catechism, he was learning about the crimes that older mentors described in a colorful new vocabulary.

A burglar was a *pansy*—hence the name of Riley's gang. One who picked pockets was a *diver, wire,* or *buzzer.* Picking pockets in church made the thief a *kirk buzzer.* To be the robber of a woman's purse was to be a *moll buzzer.* A ring worth the stealing was a *fawney.* Loot was called the *boodle,* money, *gelt* or *gelter.* To rob a house was to *bite the ken.* One who altered numbers on bank notes, as the Wolf did, was called a *figure dancer.* A bundle of bank notes was a *slum,* and if you stole a package of bank bills you went *slumming.* Because a key was called a *screw,* a burglar who worked with a key was a *screwman.* If you got caught and wound up in the city's prison, called "the Tombs," you were said to be "attending City College." To be found not guilty was *music.* A *flat* meant a person who lacked a familiarity with the tricks of crooks. A young apprentice thief such as himself, he learned, was a *kiddie* or an *eriff.*

Eager to test his skills, he attempted to bite the ken, but, failing miserably, he was arrested in August 1902.

He told the police his name was George Chartres.

Sentenced to a year in the House of Refuge, Gerald discovered that the city's boys' reformatory, located on Randall's Island in the middle of the East River, was, in fact, a finishing school for kiddies. Appalled that her young nephew should be in such a place, Aunt Catherine pleaded with authorities to parole Gerald into her custody, promising that he would not repeat his aberrant behavior and assuring them that Gerald would complete school.

Shaken by the daunting experience of the House of Refuge, Gerald hewed to the straight and narrow, completed high school, and, in 1906, enrolled as a student in Cathedral College, all to the relief and delight of his aunt. Pleased to note his employment as a plumber's helper and gas fitter, she could not know that her nephew also had a night job that took him into apartment houses on upper Park Avenue without benefit of permission from the occupants.

Working alone, he scanned newspapers for advertisements of rooms for rent or furniture offered for sale in promising neighborhoods, then called at the addresses to determine whether they were ripe for revisiting. If so, he soon returned to relieve the premises of cash, jewels, silver, and anything else that might prove of value on the city's flourishing market in stolen goods.

Although he was still in his teens, the proceeds of the loot allowed Gerald to partake of the New York life of the early 1900s in high style. Sporting the latest fashion in suits and hats, he dined at Delmonico's, Sherry's, and Cafe Martin. A night on the town included a trip to the theaters on Forty-second Street to see George M. Cohan's *Forty-five Minutes from Broadway,* starring the beautiful Fay Templeton; sixteen-year-old vaudeville star Elsie Janis making her dramatic debut in *The Vanderbilt Cup;* and Edward Abeles's comedy debut in *Brewster's Millions.* After the show, Gerald joined the bubbly crowds of Broadway society for drinks in the roof garden of the new Astor Hotel or supper and a show atop the new Madison Square Garden.

The following spring, Gerald again found himself caught in an act of burglary. Appearing in the Court of General Sessions for sentencing on April 10, 1907, on a charge of grand larceny, he stood in front of Judge Otto Rosalsky. Peering down at the slightly built youth, the unhappy judge, in imposing a sentence of fourteen months, declared, "Chapman, you are a fit candidate for the electric chair."

The Chapman family—sister, brother, and a heartbroken Aunt Catherine—meted out a harsh punishment of their own by publicly disowning him.

Well beyond the age limit for the House of Refuge, Gerald traveled to the New York State Reformatory at Elmira. Founded in 1876, it stood on a high hill above the Chemung River, overlooking the industrial town, which manufactured fire engines. The community would also be known as the birthplace of the famous prison warden Lewis E. Lawes. "The house where I was born stood only a half mile from the Reformatory," wrote Lawes in his 1932 autobiography, *Twenty-Thousand Years at Sing Sing:* "Our crowd, the boys in the neighborhood, grew up with the tradition that the prisoners up there on the hill, behind those walls, were the State's bad boys. Yet, nothing could keep us from there on a Saturday afternoon, when the shooting of the cannon announced the usual weekly military drill. The Reformatory band's martial music was impressive and inspiring. We would listen with rapt attention to the commands of the officers and the steady march of the "soldier boys" and never left until, with the bugle call at sunset, the flag was lowered and the day was done. From the safe distance, I used to watch some of the Reformatory boys work on the front lawns of the institution, or on the farms. They didn't look so dangerous. Nor did they seem unhappy. They joked among themselves and appeared rather neat and clean. I admired, too, the neatly uniformed officers."

Seven months after Lawes donned such a uniform and entered the New York State penal system as a prison guard at Elmira, in October 1906, he saw to his horror that the "military discipline" he had observed from outside had been misleading. While Elmira was nominally a reformatory, it actually imposed more drastic rules of punishment and obedience than other prisons. He believed this was the wrong approach. "You cannot straitjacket good habits into bad men," he wrote in his memoirs. "Fear alone will never develop the desire for decent living."

On the day Lawes began work at Elmira, Gerald Chapman had been an inmate for seven months. Young Lawes found him to be an "ordinary" prisoner, meaning that with each day of incarceration, he grew Less and less likely to become "reformed," he mingled with and learned from older, more experienced, criminals.

Released in 1908, Chapman promptly launched a spree of furnished-room robberies and was just as quickly caught. Found guilty on September 22 of the theft of $115, he arrived at the gates of the most infamous prison in America.

On the east side of the Hudson, thirty miles "up the river" from New York, Sing Sing Prison had been built in 1825 with granite quarried by convicts. Deriving its name from the local Indian tribe "Sint Sinks," a derivation of the older "Ossine, Ossine," meaning "stone upon stone," the bleak and forbidding prison had earned a reputation as the toughest lockup in New York State. It was called "the Big House."

As a second-felony offender, Chapman remained at Sing Sing barely one month before being transferred to Auburn Prison in October. Located on Lake Owasco in Cayuga County, in central New York, twenty-five miles southwest of

Syracuse, the institution had been built in 1816. Described by Lewis Lawes as a "city of silent men," it forced obedience into the hearts and minds of prisoners with clubs and guns. The stringent treatment was supposed to make men over. Through discipline and hard work, new minds were to be exchanged for old, clean thoughts for criminal ones. Prison guard Lawes saw it as one more crime college.

So did Chapman.

On the basis of his high school education and the exemplary behavior he had demonstrated at Elmira, he was assigned to work in the prison library. A few months after his arrival, he returned from a day's work among the books to discover a fresh face among the inmates.

"I am delighted to observe that you read," the new man said, glancing at the books cradled in Chapman's arm, "although I can't say that I approve of your choice in literature. We will have to correct that." Adjusting thick-lensed eyeglasses on a prominent nose, he spoke with a thick European accent. "I shall draw up a list for you."

"And just who the hell are you to criticize me?" Chapman demanded.

"The name is George Anderson." Short, stocky, highbrowed, and with ears sticking out like the handles of a jug, he extended a hand.

"My best friends call me Dutch."

In the age-old tradition of prison inmates, they exchanged biographies. Anderson, ten years older than Chapman, had been born in Denmark in 1880 to wealthy Dutch parents. His real name, he confided, was Ivan Dahl von Teller. He held degrees from Germany's Heidelberg University and Upsala University in Sweden. He spoke five languages. Backed by his family's funds, and their expectations that he would prosper in business, he emigrated to Chicago. There he discovered that Midwesterners were susceptible to his naturally dignified, refined, and aristocratic European demeanor. He abandoned the idea of honorable employment and enjoyed considerable success as a swindler, con man, embezzler, and forger of bank notes. But when he tried his skills in New York, his luck ran out.

"As a consequence, you and I find ourselves in this prison," he said. "I trust it will be a rewarding time for both of us."

Chapman had never met anyone like Anderson. He seemed to know everything. Concerning papers, chemicals, and engraving techniques used in counterfeiting, he relegated Ignazio the Wolf to the ranks of amateurs. No confidence scheme existed that he had not tried, mastered, or invented. He knew precious stones and how to fence them. He had made safecracking an art, specializing in the use of nitroglycerine. There seemed to be nothing outside the law that he could not teach a willing student. In Chapman he had found one. But impressive as Anderson's criminal skills were, what truly fascinated Chapman was that he viewed a life of crime as an intellectual undertaking. While he welcomed the rich proceeds gleaned from burglaries, robberies, and swindles, he explained to the eagerly attentive Chapman, the thrill lay in the planning. Furthermore, if one of his enterprises failed, his reaction was not to bemoan it but to analyze exactly what had gone wrong, scrutinizing elements of the plotting to understand how and why the plan went awry so that the error would never be repeated.

"Anybody can shove a gun under somebody's nose and get away with it," he said, "but where's the intellectual satisfaction? A crime should befit the criminal! If a man has been blessed with brains, he should use them."

Released on parole in the autumn of 1911, Chapman left the prison emboldened, determined to put Anderson's lessons to the test. But nine months later he was back at Auburn on a conviction for grand larceny and the added offense of having attempted to gun down a detective who had apprehended him in the process of burglarizing a Park Avenue apartment house.

Sentenced to ten years, he found to his surprise and delight that he was reunited with Anderson after serving half the time.

In the interim, Dutch had been busy. After completing his sentence at Auburn, he had returned to Chicago, prospering at his con games until he was arrested again. Nabbed under the name Charles H. Heines, he had been sentenced in 1914 to a term of one to ten years in the Illinois State Prison at Joliet. Paroled, he found himself in jail again in Milwaukee and Cleveland for short stretches. Looking for fresh territory, he had returned to New York, only to be collared during an attempted apartment burglary. He now faced a term of two to two-and-a-half years.

In addition to reuniting with Dutch, Chapman struck up the acquaintanceship of another inmate, Charlie Loerber. Like Chapman, Charlie had a string of bungled burglaries. Arrested on May 18, 1907, he was lucky in having the case dismissed, primarily on the basis of his youth. Eight months later, a judge exhibited an unforgiving attitude on burglary by imposing a term of six months in the jail on Blackwell's Island. On June 18, 1913, he was arrested again, fined one thousand dollars, and sentenced to a year. Returning to his crimes, he remained at liberty for three years before receiving a five-and-a-half-year stretch at Auburn.

Observing him, Dutch Anderson judged Chapman's wiry and bushy-browed friend to be slow-witted. "He'd probably be useful in some way," he told Chapman, "just as long as he doesn't have to think."

Claiming to have connections with a Brooklyn gangster by the name of Ciro Terranova, Loerber suggested that when Chapman got out on parole he get in touch with the boss of

Brooklyn rackets. Operating a legitimate groceries' supply business, Terranova held a monopoly on artichokes, an indispensable ingredient of Italian cooking, but the role he enjoyed as "the Artichoke King" was a front for a criminal empire.

"You're from Brooklyn," Loerber pointed out. "I bet you'd fit right in. You also knew John Lupo, right?"

"That was a few years ago," Chapman replied.

"Well, the Wolf is part of Terranova's gang these days," said Loerber. "They're related in some way. You should look him up when you get sprung."

Dutch begged to differ. "Stay away from the guineas," he warned. "My time will be up just a few months after you get out, so just sit still and stay out of trouble. Then you and I will team up. I have some ideas as to what the two of us might do to make some important money."

"What do I do in the meantime?" Chapman asked.

"Do what you have to do," Dutch replied with a wink. "Just be careful. I don't want to find out that you're coming back in just as I'm getting out. Obviously, you and I are destined for one another! Do you believe in destiny?"

"I'm not sure," Chapman answered.

"Well, I do," Dutch exclaimed. "Think about it, Gerry! What else explains this remarkable reunion, if not destiny? There is a Turkish word for it: *kismet*. It means 'fate.' I believe our fates are linked. Separately, we have failed in our enterprises. I see it clearly now. Alone, we are doomed to fail. Together, we shall succeed beyond our wildest dreams. We'll team up. The way I see it, with our brains there should be no limit to our enterprises."

Chapman liked the sound of it.

On March 20, 1919, when he walked out of Auburn Prison a free man at the age of thirty, released three years early for good behavior, he was not the person who had entered the prison as a two-time loser at age twenty-three. Two years of

Anderson's tutoring in crime, culture, and gentlemanly demeanor had altered him profoundly and forever. But the world that he reentered had also changed, beginning a social and moral upheaval that would continue for twenty years.

CHAPTER THREE

Two-Time Loser

SINCE HIS FIRST ARREST at age fourteen in 1902, Chapman had spent most of his life in jail or prison. If the State of New York sent him up the river once more, it would be forever. He would get a life sentence, no possibility of parole. He would be just a number—a permanent nobody. But if he were careful over the next few months, he told himself, he could connect with Dutch and, together, they might reach the top of the world.

At the moment of Chapman's return to New York City in the first year of the postwar era, others of similar stripe and ambition were still unknown. A pudgy thug named Alphonse Capone was mulling over a suggestion from his mentor, Johnny Torrio, that he abandon the notorious Five Points Gang of the Lower East Side and leave New York for Chicago, to lend a helping hand to Torrio's illicit enterprises. In the federal government's lockup on Governor's Island in New York Harbor, with a view of the Statue of Liberty, twenty-year-old John "Legs" Diamond was doing a year for deserting the army during the war. Uptown, a petty thief by the name of Arthur Flegenheimer had adopted the monicker of a deceased thug, Dutch Schultz, while ambitious twenty-two-year-old Louis Buchalter, not yet known as "Lepke," had been making a living through strong-arm extortion of push-cart vendors. Teamed up with another hoodlum, Jacob Gurrah, Buchalter was a member of the "Little Augie" Orgen mob, which included in its criminal ranks a twenty-two-year-old up-and-comer named Charles Luciano, known around the East Side as Lucky. Thousands of miles from New York, Charles Arthur Floyd, eighteen, was an Oklahoma farm boy, so good-looking that some people called him "Pretty Boy." Out in Indianapolis, John Dillinger had reached sixteen years of age and begun dreaming of getting rich without having to do honest work. And in the dust and scrub brush of Telice, Texas, a ten-year-old hell-raiser and incorrigible truant named Clyde Barrow was eleven years away from hooking up with a then eight-year-old tomboy, Bonnie Parker, who already had begun to realize that her Lone Star State hometown of Rowena was much too tame.

When Auburn's iron gates slammed behind Chapman in 1912, the United States had been at peace and quite content to abide by the admonition of George Washington to avoid foreign entanglements. But on the morning of his release, Doughboys streamed homeward across the sea from the battlefields to which they had marched so proudly and cockily in 1917, singing George M. Cohan's plucky "Over There" and determined to validate President Wilson's pledge to "make the world safe for democracy." But now, Woodrow Wilson was in Paris watching his dream of creating lasting peace being dashed against the reefs of Old World rivalries that had thrust America into a world war.

"The boys" returning in triumph faced one more march, this one a glorious star-spangled victory parade up Manhattan's Fifth Avenue arranged by the Mayor's Committee of Welcome, headed by Grover Whalen. A reserved seat in the reviewing stands at the corner of Ninety-fifth Street was selling for three dollars. For forty bucks, big spenders got a box for six from which to applaud the units stepping off to "Mademoiselle from Armentières," "How Ya Gonna Keep 'Em Down on the Farm? (After They've Seen Paree)" and "When Johnny Comes Marching Home."

Among the paraders coming home that spring was the Fighting 69th Regiment. Their overwhelmingly Irish ranks would march the familiar St. Patrick's Day parade route to the brave strains of "Garry Owen," the anthem of General George Armstrong Custer, the Irish war hero of the previous century, and the 69th's own adopted tune, "In the Good Old Summertime." They had done battle on more fronts than any other outfit in the American Expeditionary Force. From Luneville, Baccarat, Champagne, Château-Thierry, the Ourcy, St. Mihel, and the Argonne to the valley of the Rhine, they had suffered 3,501 casualties, including 644 killed.

At City Hall a beaming Mayor John "Faithful" Hylan addressed their commander, Colonel William J. "Wild Bill" Donovan. As brave and daring as anyone in his command, Donovan had been recommended for the Congressional Medal of Honor by the regiment's chaplain, the Reverend Francis P. Duffy. "What you and the men of the Sixty-ninth Regiment did under your command," Hylan declared, "will be one of the brightest pages of our history. In congratulating you on your remarkable achievements, I know I express the gratitude of every race as well as the Irish people in this great metropolis." The thousands of proud New Yorkers of all faiths who cheered them and the other soldiers flowing up Fifth Avenue waved two-by-three-foot woolen flags hawked for the occasion at $2.65 each.

As to the mighty greenback, both an ex-soldier and an

ex-convict found that inflation had reduced its value to forty-five-cents worth of its prewar buying power. The boom fostered by the war had gone bust, forcing overexpanded, overstocked factories to retrench by laying off thousands, while unions refused to go back to prewar working hours and conditions. They took thousands more out to the streets in strikes against railroads, construction companies, meat packers, garment makers, steel mills, and coal mines. Often, strikers on the picket lines found themselves confronted by force, including federal troops.

On the other side of the ledger, the war had increased the number of American millionaires from sixteen thousand to twenty thousand. Some of them participated in a bullish stock market that witnessed astonishing increases in the value of such firms as General Motors (from 130 to 191) and United States Steel (from 90 to 104-¼) between February and May. Trading was up sharply, as much as one-and-a-half-million shares a day—unprecedented in peacetime—causing financial observers to wonder if the traders on Wall Street expected something better in the coming Twenties than the rest of the country.

If the Yank who came marching home looked forward to peace and quiet, he was bound for a deep disappointment. In addition to violence associated with the strikes, Americans were witnessing a rebirth of the Ku Klux Klan. Before the war the Klan had been a phenomenon confined largely to the South, but suddenly the KKK had found adherents in towns and cities of Long Island and New Jersey, as well. Elsewhere, an influx of Negroes looking for work in the biggest cities of the North had sparked race riots.

But nothing in the altered American social fabric of 1919 matched that of the dramatic change in the status of women. The American woman, noted H. L. Mencken, was no longer the naive and charming damsel who had planted a demure peck upon her Doughboy's cheek as he tramped off to war. "The veriest schoolgirl of today knows as much [about sex] as the midwife of 1885," wrote Mencken, "and spends a good deal more time discharging and disseminating her information." Gone were the layers of cotton undergarments, replaced by silk lingerie and black stockings, revealed by the new shorter skirts. Bobbed hair was the fashion. And rouge. And the lady's cigarette.

This "New Woman" also had begun partaking of strong drink in public, and, presumably, was willing to go on doing so had the nation's lawmakers not voted to impose the institution of Prohibition. Already on the books as Chapman left prison, the War-time Prohibition Act was slated to become effective in July.

The rush to temperance notwithstanding, Chapman could look forward to getting a drink. The War-time Act had provided few means of enforcement, and the newly ratified Eighteenth Amendment would not become law until 12:01 A.M. on July 16, 1920. When he stepped from a Greyhound bus at the Dixie Hotel on Forty-second Street, his first swig of alcohol in eight years was available at the hotel bar, paid for out of the ten dollars provided by the State of New York, along with a new suit of civilian clothes and a handshake from a warden who expressed the hope that Chapman would go straight.

Unnoticed among the throngs of Times Square, and hungering to feel like a New Yorker again, Chapman bought all the newspapers and read about the capture of Roy Tyler. Wanted for murdering two bank officials and wounding a detective during the $13,000 robbery of the East Brooklyn Savings Bank the previous December, and for sticking up a bank in Cleveland, Ohio, two years earlier, Tyler had been on the lam until an alert policeman in St. Louis, Missouri, recalled seeing his photograph on a "Wanted" poster. A reward of $3,500 was offered for his capture. Although he denied the charges, Tyler had elected not to fight extradition and would be returning to New York City with Brooklyn detectives William Roddy and Bernard Dowd.

Such a man, according to Dutch Anderson, had to be a fool. If facing arrest on a charge of murder, Dutch believed, the only reasonable action was to go for one's gun and shoot it out with the cops. "I would prefer a slug to a hangman's noose anytime," he said. "And I'd take at least one of the cops along with me!"

Pondering Dutch's words as he nursed his drink and scanned the papers in the Dixie Hotel bar, Chapman recognized that if his immediate dilemma, getting cash, led to a misfortune like Tyler's, the arrest would send him to prison for life. To avoid such an outcome, he decided, he would have to get a gun, which required a lot more money than the rest of the ten dollars he had gotten from the warden, already dented by the cost of his drink.

Leaving the bar, he strode to Eighth Avenue, long known for its pawn shops.

"Good afternoon," he announced cheerily as he entered the first place he saw. "I'm in need of a pistol. I've just arrived from upstate, and I deal in precious gems. I think I should have one for self-protection while I'm here on business."

The clerk shook his head. "To buy a gun in New York City you gotta have a license," he said from behind a counter. "That's the Sullivan Law."

"I'm on my way to get one," Chapman said with a smile, "but I thought I'd first have a look at what's available, but not too expensive. The desk clerk at my hotel, the Astor, suggested I try your shop. May I see your selection?"

The clerk opened a drawer. "I've only got three," he said. Examining two long-barreled Remingtons and a nickel-plated Colt revolver that would fit snugly into a jacket pocket, Chapman tapped the Colt. "This is the one for me, I think."

"It's the most expensive, sir," the clerk warned. "It's five dollars."

Chapman slapped the sum on the counter. "I'll pay you now," he said, "and pick it up when I have the license. Say, tomorrow?"

"I'll be glad to hold it for you, sir."

Chapman stroked his chin. "I'll need bullets, won't I? Do you have them? If so, might you, please, teach me how to load it?"

"Oh, this one's already got bullets in it," the clerk said. "I keep it loaded in case anybody should try to stick me up."

"Very wise," Chapman said. "And quite convenient," he added, plucking the gun from the clerk's hand. "Now, if you please, put the other guns in a bag, along with all the paper money in your cash drawer. And don't try anything foolish," he added, pointing the gun. "I wouldn't hesitate to blow your head off. You should also know that I have a friend outside who will be watching the shop for ten minutes after I'm gone. I assure you, if you raise an alarm in that time, he will gun you down. Now, be quick about it."

"You don't have to worry about me, Mister," the clerk said, stuffing cash into a bag. "I don't own the place. I just work here."

Leaving the shop, Chapman walked briskly but calmly to the subway entrance at Forty-second Street, slipped a nickel in the turnstile, and dashed onto an uptown train just as the doors were closing. Two minutes later, he left it at Columbus Circle, where he bought a *New York Times*, proceeded into Central Park, and found a bench. Opening the bag containing the guns and cash, he found sixty dollars in tens and fives.

Turning to the newspaper's classified advertisements, he found exactly what he needed:

ATTENTION!—APARTMENTS, furnished, two and three rooms and bath. $17.50 weekly and up; full hotel service, one block from subway. HOTEL ST. LOUIS, 34 East 52nd St.

Leafing through the paper, he came upon a large ad for men's clothing. Gimbel's offered new spring and summer suits in plain blues, grays, and striped worsteds, attractively sale priced at $29.95. Combined with a hat for three dollars, such an outfit would be exactly the attire that would permit him to enter and move around in the city's finest hotels, like the Astor and the Waldorf-Astoria.

Catering to businessmen from out of town, the city's best hotels were always easy pickings for someone who knew how to inveigle the confidence of a visitor who desired nothing more after a day's work than a drink at the bar and someone friendly to talk to. Having met such men, one could readily lighten, if not empty, their wallets.

Should these tactics fail, Chapman reasoned, he could always fall back on burglary and, thanks to his newly acquired guns, holdups. With skill and care, he could accumulate a considerable amount of cash before Dutch Anderson got out of prison—certainly enough to finance whatever enterprises Dutch had in mind for them. Meanwhile, he would also acquire a personal bankroll more than sufficient to pay for living in high style.

With caution uppermost in his thoughts, Chapman moved frequently, changing his name as often as he found new addresses. Settling, at last, into an apartment in Greenwich Village, he went out at night instilled with a confidence engendered by Dutch's prison-cell lectures. Inspired by Dutch's *savoir faire,* he transformed himself into a person of gentlemanly appearance and demeanor as he plunged into all the heady enticements that postwar Manhattan offered a man with plenty of money to spend.

As always, the theater fascinated him. Playing on Broadway the week he came out of Auburn was Al Jolson in his last two weeks as *Sinbad* at the Forty-fourth Street Theater; the ads promised that "Mr. Jolson will positively appear at every performance." Victor Herbert's musical comedy *The Velvet Lady* was at the New Amsterdam. Other attractions included Otis Skinner at the Globe, starring in *The Honor of the Family;* Fay Bainter in *East Is West* at the Astor; and William Gillette, not in his trademark role of Sherlock Holmes, but in James Barrie's *Dear Brutus.* At the movies were, Charlie Chaplin in *A Dog's Life* at the Broadway Theater, Fred Stone in *Johnny Get Your Get Gun* at the Strand, and *A Man in the Open,* starring Dustin Farnum, at the Plaza.

If a man just out of prison wanted a drink, he had a choice of fifteen thousand bars, from the opulence of midtown hotels to the cozy lounges of Greenwich Village to saloons that were nothing more than dives, but offered criminal, companionship like the Golden Swan, known as "the Hell Hole. Of all the available spots, Chapman preferred those in the Village, which offered intellectual stimulation. Polly Holliday's bohemian *boîte* stood on the north side of Fourth Street between MacDougal Street and Sixth Avenue. Intellectuals also gathered at the Samovar, Sam Swartz's, TNT, Purple Pup, Pirate's Den, and Romany Marie's. At Bertolloti's, on West Third Street, a little coterie of Village residents ate Italian food and dawdled over Mother Bertolloti's cappuccino to talk about philosophy, the arts, poetry, and literature. There he was known as Charles Colwell.

Finally, as he and Dutch had arranged, he received a note

addressed to Mr. Alexander Jones, care of General Delivery at the main post office on Eighth Avenue. Dutch told him the date of his release from Auburn, concluding, "If all is well with you, I trust you will come upstate to meet me."

On the day preceding the date of Dutch's freedom, Chapman left his Village apartment to shop for an automobile. Dressed to the nines in a homburg hat, a black suit with a gray waistcoat, a gold watch chain with a diamond-studded fob, and spats, he settled on a Lexington Minute-Man Six. Examining various models at the salesroom at Broadway and Sixty-first Street, he found a convertible sedan that cost $1,985.

"Before I expend such a sum," he said to the salesman in a clipped English accent, "I wonder if you would be kind enough to permit me to try out the machine on the road?"

"I'd be delighted to accompany you, sir," exclaimed the eager salesman. "May I suggest a drive through Central Park?"

Entering the park at Columbus Circle, Chapman turned east on a curving roadway that would carry them to an exit at Fifth Avenue and Seventy-second Street. Stopping well before he reached the spot, he slipped his hand into his inside coat pocket. "This is indeed a fine automobile, and I have enjoyed your company," he said, drawing his Colt revolver and poking it into the salesman's ribs, "but this is where you get out."

The next morning, after driving all night, he greeted Dutch at the prison gate. "Where to?" he asked as Dutch climbed into the car.

Dutch answered without hesitation, "Chicago!"

"What's in Chicago?"

"It's the gateway to the Midwest," Dutch replied enthusiastically, "and the Midwest is lush with green fields that are ripe for the picking, green being the color of money, of course!"

Two-Time Loser

CHAPTER FOUR

Enterprises Unlimited

TO FINANCE THEIR WESTWARD ODYSSEY, the proprietors of Enterprises Unlimited left their stolen car long enough to use the guns Chapman had appropriated on Eighth Avenue to make a cash withdrawal at a bank in Canandaigua, New York. A string of hotel burglaries in Ohio added to their coffers, as did a cracked safe belonging to the Veatch automobile dealership in Crawfordsville, Indiana. Settling in Chicago, they devoted the first three months of 1920 to fleecing businessmen in confidence games. Come March, they plowed through the "American Breadbasket" towns of Illinois, Iowa, Missouri, and Nebraska, hitting banks on Friday evenings and Saturday mornings, when their safes bulged with payrolls intended for farmhands hired for spring planting. With the farmers' crops seeded, and their own pockets bulging, they headed for Oklahoma and Texas to carry out a con-game spree among the oil fields, swindling rig workers and petroleum company executives alike. Richer than either had ever been, they headed toward Chicago in late July by a route that took them through Muncie, Indiana.

Located on the White River in the east-central region of the Hoosier state, the seat of Delaware County had been named for the Munsee Indians and incorporated as Muncie in 1847. In 1876 a crew boring for coal eleven miles to the north struck natural gas. The find set off a land rush that, in turn, attracted new industry. Among the early entrepreneurs were five brothers named Ball, who moved the family glass manufacturing firm from Buffalo, New York, and promptly established the Ball name among the leading lights of the community. Within a short time, they had breathed new life into the faltering Indiana Normal University, renaming it Ball State Teachers College, and built the Ball Brothers Company into a nationally known producer of glass jars. Their product became indispensable to women who preserved garden produce and fruit, not to mention the growing numbers of Americans who were defying Prohibition by bottling home-brewed booze.

Crossing one of the seven bridges that spanned the White River, Chapman asked, "What the hell's in Muncie, Dutch? A fat bank for us to knock over, or another bunch of patsies with so much greed in their eyes they can't see when they're being taken?"

"A friend of mine lives here," Dutch replied. "And a friend to others whom fortune and fate have placed on the other side of the tracks and the law. He is Dr. Harry Spickermon. The good and kindly sawbones patched me up once. For a price, of course."

Small, middle-aged, and beady-eyed, wearing a neatly trimmed mustache and goatee and round wire-rimmed eyeglasses, Spickermon welcomed them. He had a roomy gray frame house with a gabled roof and numerous bay windows at

123 Mulberry Street, at the corner of Washington Street. Its vestibule and long dark hallway smelled of antiseptics, but when the doctor's surprise guests arrived, the big house was empty of patients.

Unimpressed by the sleepy town, Chapman asked, "What does a guy do in this burg for excitement?"

"Don't be fooled by the peace and quiet," Spickermon said, his gray eyebrows arching. "Muncie isn't what it seems to be. In fact, it's got an exciting criminal history."

Chapman cracked, "Yeah, I'll bet."

The first truly sensational crime, Spickermon said, had been committed in 1911, when Norman Black, owner of a paint and wallpaper store on East Main Street, arrived at a High Street livery stable and was shot to death in his horse-drawn buggy by a sniper on the roof of a nearby building. "The police thought he was having an affair with another man's wife," said Spickermon, "but they couldn't prove it. Then, in 1913, Charlie Taylor ran amok over at Elm and Willard, gunning down five people. The years In 1914 and '15, there were at least thirty-three killings, most related to drugs. You see, when Louisville ordered all its drug addicts out of town, they descended on Muncie. Center Street, from Howard to Willard Streets, is still called 'Cocaine Alley.' You can take my word for it, Muncie is what you could call a Saturday-night town, especially now, what with Prohibition coming in and closing down the town's only brewery. As a result, there's a lot of illicit liquor being peddled, just like everywhere else in the country. If I were younger, I'd do it myself. Bootlegging appears to be the latest way—and surely the easiest—to get rich quick."

When the Eighteenth Amendment took effect on July 16, with the Volstead Act to enforce it, Prohibition had become law. Welcoming its advent, the evangelist Billy Sunday had staged a funeral for John Barleycorn, despatching the condemned "Demon Rum" in a twenty-foot horse-drawn coffin while ten thousand people cheered. "The slums soon will be only a memory!" Sunday cried. He predicted that with alcohol outlawed, prisons would be turned into factories and jails into corncribs. "Good-bye, Barleycorn," he intoned. "You were God's worst enemy and you were Hell's best friend. But now the reign of tears is over."

As they left Muncie, with Chapman behind the wheel of a Cole Aero-Eight roadster they had stolen in Kansas City, Anderson said, "You know, Chappie, the doc has a point about bootlegging. It could be an easy way to make a buck." With a dubious sidelong glance, Chapman replied, "Dutch, are you suggesting that we quit what we've been doing and go into the hooch business?"

"What I'm proposing," Dutch said, lighting a cigar, "is that it's worth exploring. If it works out, that'll be fine. Should it not, you and I can return to what we've been doing. But remember the name of our undertaking: Enterprises *Un*limited."

Chapman smiled. "How do we get started?"

"How else?" Dutch said with a laugh. "We begin in Chicago!"

Already, the Windy City had moved to the fore in capitalizing on America's thirst. An hour after Prohibition began, six men wearing masks had invaded a railway switching yard, bound and gagged a watchman, and pillaged two freight cars full of whiskey that had been legally reserved for medicinal use. It was valued at $100,000. At about the same hour, another gang stole four barrels of grain alcohol from a government warehouse and a third group hijacked whiskey trucks from a rival gang. Eleven days later, federal agents raided the Red Lantern, a North Side speakeasy, and arrested forty violators of the new law.

In a country whose yearning for strong drink appeared to

be unquenchable, these events signaled the start of a far different era than that which the Prohibitionists had envisioned. The American people, noted newspaperman Herbert Asbury, had expected the new age to be heralded by a covey of angels bearing gifts of peace, happiness, prosperity, and salvation. Instead, they were met by a horde of bootleggers, moonshiners, rumrunners, and hijackers, along with gangsters, racketeers, trigger men, venal judges, corrupted police officers, crooked politicians, and thousands of speakeasy operators.

Since Chicago proved to be crowded with men of similar bent, who were violently unwilling to share the rich spoils of bootlegging, Chapman and Anderson decided to try their luck elsewhere. Dipping into capital raised during their farmstates spree, they bought into fledgling smuggling operations in Detroit that specialized in spiriting liquor over the border from Canada.

"The illegal traffic about Detroit is well organized," wrote U.S. Prohibition Commissioner Roy A. Haynes. "Stocks of whiskey are usually on hand in warehouses along the river docks on the Canadian side, having been shipped there direct from distilleries in the province of Ontario. The rumrunners' boats load up, slip across the river under darkness, and unload at any of a thousand places along the Detroit River. There is no secret handling of the liquor on the Canadian side. It may be ordered at a brewery or distillery and consigned 'for export' to a certain man in the United States. Of course the name is fictitious."

Gerald Chapman had always exhibited a talent for coming up with names.

By the end of 1920, when their investment had nearly quadrupled, he told Dutch that he wanted to go back to New York. "We've got plenty of dough," he argued, "so why not spend some of it?"

Determined to live in high style, Chapman turned his attention to Gramercy Park. One of Manhattan's wealthiest neighborhoods, the area had been created out of marshland that the Dutch settlers of New York had called *Krom Moerasje,* meaning "the little crooked swamp." By 1692 the term had been transformed to "Crommashie" and eventually into "Gramercy." In draining the swamp in 1831, real estate developer Samuel B. Ruggles envisioned building a fenced park patterned after residential squares he had seen in London. To ensure privacy, a gold key would be provided to the purchasers of the sixty-six surrounding lots. The square, built between Third and Fourth Avenues, ended Lexington Avenue at Twenty-first Street on the north and formed the top of Irving Place on the south. Originally lined by rows of red brick townhouses with spacious rooms and high windows, the square had witnessed the incursion of several twentieth-century apartment buildings, including No. 12. The building had large windows behind black-painted iron grilles and a redbrick facade with a green door, It stood (and still stands) adjacent to the former mansion of Governor Samuel B. Tilden, now the home of the National Arts Club, on the downtown side opposite the intersection of Gramercy Park West and South. Each floor had one apartment.

The third-floor apartment into which Chapman moved with Dutch Anderson in the early spring of 1921 offered a large modern kitchen, ample dining room, bathroom, two bedrooms, and a well-proportioned drawing room overlooking the park. Its slightly arched ceiling seemed higher than it was. The walls were painted white and gold, and the window hangings were a deep, lustrous emerald green. The rooms were already furnished in a style suitable to the man about town with impeccable clothing, a monocle, and a feigned English accent who had signed the two-hundred-dollar-a-month lease with the name "G. Vincent Colwell."

Among the advantages of a Gramercy Park residence was the proximity of Brentano's bookstore at Broadway and Twenty-seventh Street, where Chapman alleviated his appetite for books. Out of walking distance were familiar Greenwich Village haunts like Polly Holliday's, Brooks Brothers midtown haberdashery, and the theater district. But a taxi cost only thirty cents for the first half-mile. After the theater, habitués of the Great White Way had a bewildering choice of places to eat and, Prohibition notwithstanding, drink. The best were Shanley's at Forty-third Street, the Little Club on West Forty-fourth, and the Knickerbocker Grill and Murray's, both on Forty-second Street. All operated with little concern about violating the Volstead Act. "In order to enforce Prohibition," quipped Congressman Fiorello H. La Guardia (a "wet"), "it will require a police force of two-hundred-fifty-thousand men and a force of two-hundred-fifty-thousand men to police the police."

Downtown, also undaunted by the possibility of prosecution, saloon-keeper Barney Gallant continued to serve liquor at his West Third Street oasis, the Greenwich Village Inn. It catered to the literary crowd, including Eugene O'Neill, Theodore Dreiser, and Edna St. Vincent Millay.

Chapman lost no time in returning to the spots he had favored while awaiting Dutch's release from prison, especially Bertolotti's. There, a few weeks after returning to the city, his eye caught an attractive, dark-eyed, diminutive, and expensively dressed young woman who had left her home in Indianapolis for the excitement of New York City. An aspiring actress, she was introduced to Chapman by Florence Bertolloti as Betty Bales. He was intrigued. Betty was a child of the times. She smoked cigarettes, wore rouge and short skirts, loved dancing to jazz music.

Chapman had been startled upon his return to New York by the rage for jazz, though he did not share the alarm of the

Catholic Telegraph: "The music is sensuous, the embracing of partners—the female only half-dressed—is absolutely indecent," the scandalized newspaper declared. Even the *New York Times* noted that skirts had been lifted far beyond any modest limitation. Not only did legs show, but stockings were often rolled below the knee. And hemlines were not the only aspect of women's clothing that shocked the older generation. Youngsters had abandoned corsets and layered undergarments to drape themselves in thin dresses with short sleeves—if they had sleeves at all.

Every girl, it seemed, was determined to become like the characters surrounding Amory Blaine, the protagonist of a sensational first novel that came out in April 1920. "Amory saw girls doing things that even in his memory would have been impossible," wrote twenty-three-year-old author F. Scott Fitzgerald in *This Side of Paradise:* "Eating three-o'clock after-dance suppers in impossible cafes, talking of every side of life with an air half of earnestness, half of mockery, yet with a furtive excitement that Amory considered stood for a real moral let-down."

Pretty Betty Bales was just such a girl. Not only did she catch Gerald Chapman's fancy, she soon moved into No. 12 Gramercy Park. She was introduced as Mrs. Colwell and found nothing extraordinary about Chapman's ominipresent friend Dutch Anderson, or their occasional, sometimes lengthy, absences. She told Chapman that what he did for a living was not her business—or as she put it, "none of my beeswax."

Had she asked, it was unlikely that he would have told her what he and Dutch were doing. In the months after she moved in, they had cracked a safe on Long Island, stuck up a Canal Street diamond dealer, hijacked a truckload of whiskey from Brooklyn bootleggers, and carried out a series of burglaries. These included the Langwell Hotel at Times

Square, the Pennsylvania, opposite Penn Station, the Waldorf-Astoria on Thirty-fourth Street, the Hotel Marion at Lake George, New York, and, on July Fourth, Galen Hall and the Chalfonte on the Atlantic City Boardwalk.

Chapman passed the balance of July resting during the heat of the day, often reading a book beneath the shade of Gramercy Park's trees, and squiring Betty around the city's clubs at night. Rising early in the afternoon on Sundays, he settled down by the window overlooking the park to plunge into a thick pile of newspapers. Engaged in this routine one rainy day in early August, he thrust one of the papers toward Dutch. "Have a look at this item," he said, stabbing the page with a finger.

A brief article datelined Washington, D.C., reported that United States Postmaster General Will Hays had expressed alarm about the increase in mail robberies. During the previous year, the proceeds of these crimes had amounted to $6,300,000, of which only half had been recovered. The biggest theft had been in February, in Toledo, Ohio. The bandits had made off with close to $2,000,000 dollars in cash and negotiable paper.

"Very interesting," Dutch said, putting down the paper.

"It's more than interesting," Chapman said, grinning. "It's a *challenge*. If the Toledo post office hauls around a couple of million bucks, what's being handled here in New York?"

The Big Haul

ON TUESDAY, OCTOBER 25, 1921, purchasers of the *New York Times* were startled by the headline:

U.S. MAIL HELD UP
IN BROADWAY:
LOOT MAY BE $1,000,000

THREE BANDITS IN AUTO FORCE TRUCK DRIVER
INTO LEONARD STREET, STEAL 4 POUCHES

ROBBERY UNDER ARC LIGHT

"As soon as the bandits disappeared in a westerly direction through Leonard Street," the item reported, "the chauffeur of the mail truck drove to the Beach Street Police Station, where he told detectives of the robbery."

Moments after Frank Haveranck's report to the police, the phone rang in the home of John Coughlin. After listening to the sketchy report of the stickup from Desk Sergeant Floyd Davis, the head of the New York Police Department Detective Division began, as usual, with the assumption that the crime had been committed by someone who was already known to the police. "Put out the word to all the duty stations," he ordered. "Round up every crook we have in the 'hijack' files, anyone with a record for mail heists, and anybody who uses an automobile for stickups. I guess it's too much to hope that the truck driver got the license plate number?"

"Haveranck saw the first three digits," Floyd replied, "but he isn't sure if they were two-oh-three or three-two-oh."

"Put out both numbers on a general alarm. Meantime, I want to question the driver, so keep him around. I'm on my way in."

As he rolled out of bed to dress for a trip into the city from his Brooklyn home, the Cleveland touring car with its trio of bandits, having crossed the Brooklyn Bridge and left behind the eastern boundary of "the borough of homes and churches," was on the way toward a hideout that had been suggested by Charlie Loerber. During an evening of nightclubbing in late August, financed by the proceeds of the summer's escapades, Chapman had run into Loerber. Since his release from Auburn Prison in 1919, a few months after Chapman's and several weeks after Dutch Anderson's, Loerber had barely scraped together a living by burglary and small-potatoes armed robberies. Always an unlucky gambler, he found himself deeply in debt to bookmakers.

"Since you seem to be rolling in clover," he said, fingering the supple lapel of Chapman's Brooks Brothers suit, "how's chances of me putting the arm on you, a few bucks to tide me over for a few days?"

"I'll do better than that, Charlie. I'll hire you."

Loerber chuckled. "To do what?"

"You've always been good with cars," Chapman said. "I think you might be just the man Dutch Anderson and I will need behind the wheel on a little job we've got in mind."

The plan had always anticipated a third man to acquire a car for use during the robbery and to do the driving. But Loerber also proved to be invaluable in one of the most important aspects in planning the holdup. Since the biggest payoff was likely to be gleaned from the post office branch that handled the mail of Wall Street firms and the Stock Exchange, the partners of Enterprises Unlimited had decided that they needed to know more about the workings of the Park Row branch. They would watch the facility day and night for days, possibly weeks, and gather information from an employee.

Loerber's job was to frequent the diners and speakeasies visited by Park Row branch workers. He had succeeded beyond Chapman's hopes. "There's a guy down at Park Row," Loerber reported, "who's in deeper to the bookies than me. Name of Savelli. I think if we cut him in on the action, this character will open up like an oyster!"

Finally, Loerber had provided the answer to the question of an immediate hideout, where the loot could be evaluated, divided, and, if necessary, stashed.

"I've got an uncle who owns a farm out in the sticks of Long Island that will be perfect," Loerber had proposed. "I've used it a couple of times with no questions asked."

On inspection, the old red barn on the farm at Lake Ronkonkama proved to be ideal for their purpose, Chapman, Anderson, and their new partner began observing the routines of a mail-truck driver pointed out to Loerber by Savelli—cigar-smoking, portly, good-natured, middle-aged, and, most importantly, docile, Frank Haveranck.

Still shaken by having had a gun jammed into his ribs, he was drinking a third cup of black coffee as John Coughlin arrived at Beach Street. The police station was crowded not only with uniformed cops and detectives, but with investigators from the post office, including their boss, William E. Cochrane, known as Colonel Cochrane because of his wartime service.

Having worked with him on holdups of other post offices and mail trucks, Coughlin knew the tall and mannerly chief inspector well enough to be blunt. "Whoever pulled this off must have had help from inside, Bill," he said. "These fellas knew exactly what sacks to look for. If there's to be a quick break in this case, it's most likely to come from whatever your people can turn up in questioning your employees. Meantime, we'll be doing our best to track down the gang. It's not going to be easy. These boys were smart—too smart to hang around in town. How much did they get?"

"We won't even begin to know until we get in touch with the firms that sent out mail yesterday," Cochrane said. "At least a million, I'd guess."

Dumped into heaps on the dirt floor of the red barn on Long Island, the loot consisted of negotiable securities, bonds, travelers' checks, and other paper bearing the addresses of Wall Street's most thriving enterprises. Among the pile were gold bonds issued by Chase National Bank on behalf of the government of Argentina and valued at more than $400,000; Canadian Northern Railway Company bonds worth $5,000; securities belonging to customers of Hitt, Farwell and Parks in the amount of $8,000; and bundles of negotiable instruments in the names of the Goodyear Tire and Rubber Company, Aluminum Company of America, American Telephone and Telegraph, and scores of Wall Street firms, including Guaranty Trust Company ($62,000); Seaboard National Bank ($52,150); White, Weld and Company ($28,800); Edward B.

Smith & Co. ($13,200); and Doremus & Co. ($56,000). Other sacks disgorged packets of money orders and thick sheaves of currency. The heftiest package of cash came to $27,000. By Chapman's count the contents of all the sacks came to $2,643,720.

Colonel Cochrane's inventory proceeded more slowly, but as dozens of banks, brokerages, and other financial institutions reported losses, the official figure surged upward. In disclosing the figures to the press, Cochrane announced that the Post Office Department was offering a reward for any information leading to the arrest of the robbers.

Despite multiplying evidence that this robbery had been the biggest not only in post office annals but in American history, the money available as a reward—$15,000, or $5,000 for each of the three robbers—was no more than had been authorized in lesser lootings during the rash of U.S. Mail holdups that had attracted the attention of Chapman and Anderson.

As the vast dimensions of the Leonard Street robbery became apparent, the man who had established the reward system in May, Postmaster General Will Hays, informed Colonel Cochrane that he was coming to New York City to take charge of the investigation. Asked by reporters if he favored the death penalty for mail robbers, Hays replied, "I draw the line on nothing that would prevent further outrages against the sacred mails of the United States."

Appointed by President Warren G. Harding to head the Post Office only seven months earlier, Hays had come to the government with a reputation as an astute politician who brought to his work the same righteous fervor that had made him an elder in the Presbyterian Church. (The year after the great mail robbery, his reputation as a defender of decency would result in his appointment as head of the new Hollywood Motion Picture Producers and Distributors of America.

It was created by the moguls of the film industry to improve Hollywood's image after several scandals had erupted. What many considered a censorship organization became known to the film industry and the public alike as "the Hays office." Its rigorous code would prevail until the 1960s.)

Born and raised in Indiana, Will Hays was a teetotaler, a nonsmoker, and a rock-ribbed Republican who rose to the chairmanship of the Republican National Committee and had been regarded as a darkhorse possibility for the party's nomination for president in 1920. After the delegates at the Republican National Convention settled upon another dark horse, Harding, Hays turned his efforts to the job of electing the first Republican president since Teddy Roosevelt. For this he had received a traditional reward for political operatives—appointment as postmaster general.

A short man with big ears that were not a matched set (one triangular, the other gracefully rounded) and with a surprisingly booming voice for a little man, he thundered to the reporters at Washington's Union Station as he stepped aboard the Pennsylvania Railroad's midnight express to New York: "I am not coming back to the capital until the robbers are caught."

In addition to his moral indignation about the robbery, Hays realized angrily that if orders he had issued in April regarding postal security had been carried out, the robbery might not have been attempted. Alarmed over the increase in mail robberies, he had instructed all post offices to require that drivers of vans transporting registered mail be armed, or be accompanied by armed guards. Weapons for that purpose had been sent to New York. The question of why the guns had not been issued would be high on his list when he arrived in New York. Another grievance was the likelihood, suggested by a story in the *New York Times*, that the stickup men might have had assistance in their planning of the robbery from a venal and traitorous post office employee. "It was not unusual," said the *Times,* "for former employees to meet regular employees in restaurants near City Hall Post Office, where the activities of the station were discussed. Through such discussions, it would have been easy for representatives of the bandits to have learned that Frank Haveranck was unarmed and that his truck contained money and securities worth hundreds of thousands of dollars."

As Hays's train departed from Washington, Haveranck, who had been dismissed as a suspect after a quick but thorough check of his background and work record, was studying photographs in the police department's Rogues' Gallery. Among the array of mug shots was one that, he said, resembled one of the thieves. But the faint candle of hope flickered out when a detective on Coughlin's staff recalled that the man in the photograph was confined to Sing Sing.

Awaiting the arrival of Hays, Colonel Cochrane passed the hours in his office at the Main Post Office on Eighth Avenue in conference with Post Office Department investigators, including three additional officers who had been rushed from Washington to New York by airplane hours after the holdup. Keenly aware that they had turned up not a single clue to the identity of the perpetrators, they met in an atmosphere as gloomy as the cold mist outside the windows. But by Thursday, he was able to tell Hays that the Cleveland touring car used in the robbery had been found abandoned in Brooklyn. With nothing more substantial than this to go on, he told the city's newspapers with abounding confidence that the manhunt would lead the police to a band of local gunmen instead of professional mail robbers from the West, as had been widely rumored.

Satisfied that the investigation was proceeding as well as could be expected, Hays turned his attention to the shocking lack of security in the New York postal area. What he discovered made him furious. Although four hundred pistols had been received soon after his order in April, only a few of them had been distributed. The rest were locked in a closet at the General Post Office, he was informed, but had now been given out. "In other words," he said, icily, "now that a horse has been stolen, we have locked the barn door." He also learned to his dismay that fifteen motorcycles that he had authorized in May to guard every postal truck containing valuable mail had never been delivered from a warehouse in Newark.

Demanding that the post master for New York City, Edward M. Morgan, discover and punish those responsible for the failure to implement his orders, Hays announced that he was assigning the day-to-day supervision of the investigation to Third Assistant Postmaster General W. Irving Glover and was, himself, returning to Washington.

As Hays settled into his berth on the midnight express from Penn Station, and the train crossed the New Jersey Meadowlands beyond the Hudson River, a thick fog drifted out of the swamps and bogs and spread like a gray blanket across the Pennsy right-of-way, especially around a tangle of tracks and switches known as the Manhattan Transfer. Confronted by near-zero visibility as the train slowly negotiated the intricate maze of tracks, the engineer gaped in horror as, out of the wall of fog, appeared the red lanterns on the rear of a local train en route from New York to Long Branch, New Jersey. The trains collided.

Catapulted to the floor of the darkened Pullman, Hays found people piled around him as other passengers groaned and struggled to get up. Making their way toward doors at opposite ends of the upright but tilted car, none had suffered serious injury. Taken back to New York on another train, he was examined by a doctor. Though bruised and aching, he was pronounced fit.

On Sunday, October 30, before going back to Washington,

CHAPTER SIX

A Trip Upstate

PACING THE PARLOR of Chapman's Gramercy Park apartment on a slate-gray mid-December evening, Charlie Loerber was miffed. Although most of the loot from the robbery amounted to millions of dollars worth of negotiable stocks, bonds, securities, and checks, none of it could be redeemed immediately. In the publicity surrounding the most spectacular stickup in the nation's history, the sources, names, registration information, and serial numbers of the instruments had become known everywhere. Before any of the items could be disposed of, Dutch would have to alter them. This required time. Besides, the atmosphere had become so hot in the six weeks since the robbery that persons who dealt in such items were far too nervous to even talk about making deals.

Cash from the robbery totaling $125,000 had been divided four ways—Chapman, Anderson, Loerber, and their post office ally, Savelli. "Patience, Charlie," counseled Dutch Anderson. "The worst thing any of us could do right now is to be impetuous. I promise you that in due course we will convert he met with newspaper reporters at the Waldorf-Astoria. "A part of my check-up, X-Ray pictures were taken," he said "As a result, the men who carried out this outrageous robbery should know that the X-Rays show that I have a backbone. So does every man working on this case. We'll never give up. These infernal gangsters *will* be caught."

everything into cash. You'll be rolling in money."

"Maybe so," Loerber grumbled, "but at the moment I'm plenty short."

Chapman bolted from his chair. "Whose fault is it if you're short?" he demanded. "You've been spending your share of the take like a drunken sailor on Saturday night."

"That's not true, Chappy," Loerber pleaded. "I had to pay off my bookies. With what's left I can't even afford a place of my own. I'm living in a damned two-room dump of my brother's in the goddamned slums of East Forty-fourth Street. And Christmas is coming!"

"What do you want," Chapman groaned, "a loan?"

"All I need is something to tide me over till Dutch unloads the paper, so I was thinking that since we're such a good team, maybe we could pull another job."

Chapman strode to the window. "The town's too hot," he said, looking down at snow-crusted Gramercy Park "We can't run the risk of being pinched and winding up back in stir while we've all got a fortune buried out on Long Island."

"Why not go out of town for a job? Someplace in Jersey, or maybe upstate? What with the heat on, it might be a good idea to make ourselves scarce. We could all take—" he smiled impishly—"a working vacation."

"I think Charlie's got a point," Dutch said. "Getting away from New York might be the wisest thing for all of us right now. Frankly, I could stand an infusion of fresh capital myself." With a laugh, he added, "And how long has it been since you bought a new suit, not to mention something in diamonds for Betty?"

Chapman told Betty that he had to go away on business for a week or two. As always, she asked no questions. She responded that she would go away too, on a visit to her family in Indianapolis. Both promised to return to New York for Christmas.

A Trip Upstate

After escorting Betty to Penn Station to take the Broadway Limited, Chapman settled beside Dutch in the backseat of a gleaming black Packard sedan purchased out of his proceeds from the mail robbery. Outfitted in chauffeur's livery, Loerber started the engine, turned, and asked, "What's our destination, gentlemen?"

"Over to Broadway for a farewell look and then uptown," Chapman answered. "I've always wanted to see where this town's main stem leads to."

"I think you know," Dutch said teasingly. "It becomes U.S. Route Nine and goes to Ossining, where the State of New York runs a little spa called Sing Sing."

"I've been there," Chapman replied, laughing. "Didn't care for it, though. Take a different route, Charlie!"

Boating across the thinly iced Hudson at Dobbs' Ferry, well south of the Big House, they followed New Jersey Route 17 northward into the wintry Catskill Mountains of New York State and west to Binghamton.

Built at the confluence of two rivers, the Susquehanna and the Chenango, the small but thriving industrial city had a busy post office. Quite wisely, neither customers nor employees challenged the two nattily dressed men waving guns who walked in at midday and departed moments later with a few hundred dollars in cash and bundles of blank money orders. However, at a much larger main post office in Syracuse, the presence of a guard with a highly visible Smith & Wesson pistol strapped to his right hip provided a compelling and eloquent argument against an attempt at robbery.

Whatever disappointment Chapman, Anderson, and their capable driver may have experienced was assuaged a few miles to the north. A holdup at the Fulton post office yielded almost a thousand in cash and money order blanks equivalent to those taken in Binghamton.

Moving south again, the executives of Enterprises Unlimited set aside unpleasant memories to pause for lunch at a raodside diner on the edge of Auburn. It provided a view of the hillside prison so familiar to them. Entering the town, they stopped again, leaving Loerber in the car with the engine running while they entered a bank a few minutes before its three-o'clock closing. Unresisted, they left the bank and the town at high speed, nearly seven thousand dollars richer.

Following Route 20, they arrived early that night at Niagara Falls. They stopped at a "honeymooners' hotel" that was merely half a dozen clapboard-sided cabins clustered around a diner. Unhappy with what he called the "chicken feed" garnered from two post offices and a bank, Anderson anticipated a better haul in the city. "We'll take our time," he said. "This is a big tourist town, even in the winter, so we're sure to score a big haul if we case the place properly."

In the aftermath of the Leonard Street robbery, with rigid adherence to Hays's orders, the post offices of America's scenic honeymoon capital were well protected. So were several banks whose officers had tightened security when they learned of the Auburn holdup. But on the third afternoon of their painstaking exploration of the city, Anderson poked Chapman in the ribs. "I think we've hit the jackpot," he exclaimed, nodding in the direction of a small green truck bearing the name AMERICAN EXPRESS COMPANY.

Tapping Loerber on the shoulder, Chapman said, "Follow it, Charlie."

"There's just the driver and one guard," Anderson noted as the truck stopped in front of a bank. "Making deliveries," he added, as the men unloaded two heavy canvas sacks. "That means those bags must contain money order blanks."

Returning to the truck, one of the men carried a small but heavy-looking sack.

"There's money in that, for sure," muttered Chapman.

"I think you're right, Dutch," chuckled Loerber. "This is a real jackpot!"

After two more stops, the truck lumbered into a street that appeared as deserted as Leonard Street had been.

"No time like the present," Chapman said, drawing his gun. "Let's do it, fellas. Cut him off, Charlie."

Within five minutes they were on their way back to New York City, some seventy thousand dollars richer.

CHAPTER SEVEN

Ain't We Got Fun?

THE NEW YEAR OF 1922 came in to the tune of a popular song of the Old Year—"Ain't We Got Fun?" Betty played it over and over again on a new Victrola. It had been Chapman's Christmas gift, paid for from the proceeds of the Niagara Falls job. Though he liked popular music, Chapman played records of symphonies and grand operas, especially the familiar arias performed by Beniamino Gigli, Amelita Galli-Curci, and the late Enrico Caruso, whose Victor Red Seal records continued to earn a gross income of $2,500,000 a year. But what "G. Vincent Colwell" enjoyed most was Betty playing the piano and singing the new songs from sheet music purchased on nearby Twenty-eighth Street, known as Tin Pan Alley. Other evenings with Betty were spent at popular nightclubs, or the theater.

Other evenings were spent with Dutch Anderson, either at No. 12, or at Dutch's new apartment just down the block at No. 20. Dutch had found it just the quiet spot required for the painstaking work of altering the bundles of financial instruments acquired in the mail holdup and their upstate robbery spree.

Identifying himself to the landlord as Charles Heines, he had offered in advance an explanation for the unusual odors that neighbors might notice emanating from his rooms. "I'm a chemist," he said, "lately associated with the Kodak Company of Rochester. I'm in New York temporarily, as a visiting professor of science at Columbia College." Thick glasses and a German accent added credibility to his story.

Through diligent application of his skills in the arts of counterfeiting and forgery, Dutch changed the serial numbers on stocks, bonds, and other papers that would amount to hundreds of thousand of dollars. He took into account the fact that in fencing the items, Enterprises Unlimited would receive only a fraction of their real worth. Many trips were taken to meet trusted dealers in such stolen goods in Philadelphia, Detroit, Chicago, Milwaukee, and, finally, Indianapolis, to deal with a fence who had been highly recommended by Dr. Spickermon. Yet in April, with the police still trying to solve the Leonard Street robbery, more than half of the loot remained untouched, some of it stored in the two Gramercy Park apartments, the bulk still buried on the farm at Lake Ronkonkoma, to be tapped when the in-town supply dwindled. On trips to Long Island, Chapman and Dutch were driven by the man whom Chapman's Gramercy neighbors knew as "Mr. Colwell's chauffeur."

Charlie Loerber's impatience about converting the mail robbery loot into cash worried Chapman, who hired him as a chauffeur and bought him a resplendent uniform. Perfectly tailored in gray Norfolk-back mohair duster coat, riding breeches, gleaming knee-high boots, kidskin driving gloves, and a jaunty cap with patent-leather visor, Loerber basked in the envy of other drivers when he drove up to a ritzy restaurant or club and stepped from Chapman's Cadillac to open the door for Mr. G. Vincent Colwell and his lady. Even so, and despite the fact that his share of the loot from the Niagara Falls heist had provided him with plenty of cash, Loerber bridled at being told that Dutch's "doctoring" and the necessary fencing would delay the final payoff. Nor did he want to wait before using his share of the postal money orders and American Express checks garnered in December's raids upstate.

"One of the things that gets under Charlie's skin," Chapman suggested to Dutch, "is that our inside man on the Leonard Street job, Jerry Savelli, took a much smaller cut and opened up a nifty little cabaret in Rockaway. Charlie doesn't understand that if he didn't let himself get so deep in hock to bookies, he would have enough dough to hire somebody to drive him around town, instead of chauffering me and you."

With a shrug, Dutch replied, "I told you years ago in prison that Charlie Loerber was no genius. But when we've unloaded all the goods, he'll see that it was worth the wait. In a few months the heat will be off, you and I will say good-bye to Enterprises Unlimited, and we'll all be able to let go and have some real fun."

"What about you?" Chapman asked. "Have you made plans?"

"I shall return to the Continent. And you?"

"I might visit Europe, but New York's for me. It's the best spot in the world. As long as you have the money, of course! In this town, it's all that matters. If you have it, nobody cares where it came from. I've yet to meet a headwaiter who asks about the origin of the dough you slip him to seat you at the best table in the joint, or bring you his best bottle of pre-Prohibition booze. And is there any dame who really cares where you got the cash, as long as the fur coat she's wearing when you take her to dinner at the Waldorf-Astoria or lunch at the Algonquin came from Arnold Constable?"

Nothing pleased him quite so much, Chapman told Dutch, as being able to patronize the Algonquin. "I pulled a few of my best burglaries there," he said with a twinkle in his eye, "so it's a hell of kick, now, to breeze into the lobby without a cautious look-round to see if the house detective is giving me the fisheye!" The fact that the hotel on East Forty-fourth Street, between Sixth and Fifth Avenues, might be a lucrative hunting ground had been suggested to him inadvertently in 1919, when he read a a newspaper column praising "a little unpretentious hotel, tucked away on a side street" that catered to a theatrical and literary clientele. Pondering the item by Alexander Woollcott, he envisioned a place busy with the entrances and exits of persons whom other hotels would regard as so bizarre and flamboyant as to be unwelcome. In such an atmosphere, he calculated, the comings and goings of a young man who might very well be an actor or a playwright might pass unnoticed. The most important factor in being a successful hotel thief, he had learned, was the ability to appear to belong, to fit into the surroundings.

This situation had not changed in the three years since his first foray into the Algonquin, as Chapman discovered in his role as the Count of Gramercy Park. With his shoulders draped in an opera cape, and swinging a silver-tipped walking stick, he blended in with tubby, beak-nosed, bespectacled Woollcott and a retinue of literary wits including Dorothy Parker, Franklin P. Adams, Mark Connelly, Robert Benchley, George S. Kaufman, and Heywood Broun.

Referring to the gatherings of these sophisticates at the table reserved for their Algonquin lunches, George M. Cohan said it was "a round table without a square at it." Smarting over the theatrical criticisms offered by members of the group, the Irish actor J. M. Kerrigan suggested tartly, "If you don't like the plays you go to see, why don't you put on a show yourselves?" Taking up the challenge at the 49th Street Theater on April 30, 1922, the Algonquinites presented, for one night only: "NO SIRREE! An Anonymous Entertainment by the Vicious Circle of the Hotel Algonquin"

Manhattan offered many other places in which Chapman was welcomed in 1922, including the glittery new silver-and-chrome Park Avenue Club. "In this luxurious setup," wrote the fledgling Broadway reporter Louis Sobol, "host George LeMaze served lobsters that brought them galloping from Sutton Place—and even in from Southampton." Lunch cost a dollar. Dinner was two-fifty. But at the grandiose bar, the minimum charge for a drink was a buck.

In the two years since the advent of Prohibition, the number of New York City establishments offering liquor for sale had doubled. In attempting to stamp out widespread drunkenness, the temperance laws had produced a vast criminality. Efforts to control human conduct by statute, observed Harold J. Laski, "meant that a group of men would arise to supply those wants [and] the more widespread the want, the greater would be the profit in supplying it, and the more earnest would be the zeal of those responsible for applying the law to see that it was enforced."

In their effort to enforce Prohibition laws that spring, no one proved more zealous or resourceful than Isadore Einstein and Moe Smith, nor more entertaining. A former salesman and clerk at Station K of the New York Post Office, fat-and-forty Izzy, and the even fatter Moe, a cigar-store owner and fight-club manager, had become the nation's most successful Prohibition agents and the darlings of newspaper reporters and editors.

"What the newspapers enjoyed most," observed Herbert Asbury, "was their ingenuity." Challenged by a Brooklyn speakeasy that other agents had been unable to close down, Izzy stood in front of the establishment in shirtsleeves on a freezing winter night until he was shaking with cold. Half-carrying him inside, Moe shouted, "Give this man a drink. He's frost-bitten." When the kind-hearted bartender complied, Izzy arrested him. To enter a speakeasy that featured music, they carried instrument cases. In working-class neighborhoods, they dressed in overalls and toted full grocery bags, as if they were laborers who had stopped to shop on their way home from work. Carrying a pail of pickles, they raided half a dozen illicit saloons in Brooklyn. "Who'd ever think a fat man with a bucket of pickles was a federal agent?" Izzy asked amused reporters.

Quickly discovering that the slowest day of the week for news was Monday, Izzy and Moe scheduled most of their raids for Sundays. "A few more Izzies scattered over the the country," asserted the Brooklyn *Eagle,* "and the U.S. would be bone dry, parched and withered." However, most newspapers thought that the entire effort to enforce the unpopular and almost universally ignored law belonged on the vaudeville stage. Of the antics of Izzy and Moe, the *New York Herald* wrote, "They never made prohibition much more of a joke than it has been made by some of the serious-minded prohibition officers."

Although numerous restaurants and clubs fell victim to the energies of law enforcement, many more opened their doors and in so doing brought together elements of society who otherwise might never have met. "At popular night spots," said Polly Adler, who was on her way from owning a lingerie shop to becoming New York City's most famous bordello operator, "you saw bankers and safe-crackers, lawyers and boosters, publicists and con men, politicians and beer barons, artists and brokers, film stars and jockeys, dowagers and kept women, butter-and-egg men and pimps, exiled royalty and out-of-work chorines, millionaire playboys and penniless gigolos—and, always, of course, visiting firemen of varying degrees of sophistication and prominence and prosperity."

Through this bubbling brew of the Jazz Age, as the summer of '22 began, moved elegant, big-spending G. Vincent Colwell of Gramercy Park, relishing every moment of it, basking in his role as the Count.

CHAPTER EIGHT

The Mick Dicks

A PILLAR OF TASTE AND REFINEMENT opposite the luxurious Waldorf-Astoria Hotel at Fifth Avenue and Thirty-fourth Street, B. Altman & Co. had spearheaded an invasion. In 1906 Benjamin Altman abandoned his original location at Third Avenue and Tenth Street to move uptown, leading the way for other monuments to merchandising with a New York City flair. Soon, Franklin Simon's, Oppenheim Collins, Best and Company, Lord & Taylor, and Arnold Constable arose on Fifth Avenue, forming "the ladies' mile," while the more proletarian Macy's and Gimbel's arrived a block away on Sixth.

In making the move, Altman took over an entire block of a midtown neighborhood that since the last quarter of the nineteenth century had been dominated by the mansions of wealthy New Yorkers whom society's arbiter of fashion, Ward McAllister, defined as "the Four Hundred." This was the number of guests who could fit into the ballroom of the opulent house of Mrs. William Backhouse Astor, née Caroline

Schermerhorn. (At No. 350 on the southwest corner, it was combined in 1890 with No. 338 to form the Waldorf-Astoria Hotel, which was demolished in 1931 to make room for the Empire State Building.) To assuage the consternation of snooty neighbors, the mundane purpose of Altman's building was masked by a facade resembling that of a Florentine palace. In a further concession to the genteel sensibilities of 1906, he omitted signs.

Into this staid and respectable emporium, on March 4, 1922, long after the Astors had moved away, marched Martha Fuller.

A frequent customer, she expected that in paying for her purchases with a five-dollar American Express Company Traveler's Check she would have no problem. To her astonishment, she found herself detained by a polite but insistent store detective.

Mortified, she learned that the police had been called.

Then she discovered herself being placed under arrest.

Trembling with fright, she arrived in a squad car at police headquarters, where the only detective she had ever met, Inspector John O'Brien, demanded that she tell him where she had obtained the traveler's check.

"A young man gave it to me as a rent payment," she replied tearfully. "I run a boarding house. The man said he had just come to New York from out west."

"Is this man still a tenant?"

"No," the woman sobbed. "He stayed only a week."

"What was his name?"

"As I recall, it was Lambert."

"Had you ever seen him before?"

"No."

"Did he give you any more of these checks?"

"That was the only one."

"Until we have searched your house and verified your

story," O'Brien advised, "you'll have to remain in custody."

Soon satisfied that Fuller had committed no crime, O'Brien explained that the check had been stolen and that, should they find the man who had given it to her, she might be called upon to identify him. Should Lambert, if that were his name, stand trial, he added, she might be called as a witness against him.

Presently, a copy of O'Brien's report on the incident, along with the check, landed on the desk of Gordon T. McCarthy. A burly figure with a face as Irish as his name, and a former investigator with the Pinkerton Detective Agency, he had been a special agent of the American Express Company's Buffalo district for more than five years. Since December 21, he had been preoccupied with the armed robbery of the firm's delivery truck in Niagara Falls.

Within an hour of receiving O'Brien's report, and the check that was part of the seventy thousand dollars in loot, he booked a berth on the New York Central's eastbound 20th Century Limited, arriving at New York's Grand Central Terminal at nine o'clock the next morning. Half an hour later he stepped from a taxi at 240 Centre Street—a profusion of carved-stone ornament designed by architects Hopkin and Koen in the French Baroque style. The headquarters of the New York Police Department had moved to that location from its original site at 300 Mulberry in 1906. In a cramped and untidy third-floor office, McCarthy introduced himself to John O'Brien.

"You didn't waste any time getting here," the detective said with a laugh.

"I've been after these bastards for nearly three months," McCarthy replied. "When a couple of the checks from the heist turned up in Indianapolis, Milwaukee, and Cleveland back in January, I figured I was dealing with a gang from the Midwest. So I hightailed it out there. But nothing else turned up. Now it looks like these boys might be from your neck of the woods."

"Finding one check passer in this town is looking for the needle in the proverbial haystack," O'Brien said. "And believe me, New York is one hell of a pile of straw."

"If I come across the boys who stuck up our truck I'll know them. The driver gave excellent descriptions, especially of the gang's leader: thick-lensed glasses, sunken eyes, bushy eyebrows, high cheekbones, on the short side, a snappy dresser."

"That could be lots of guys. Just where do you expect to start looking for him?"

"What's that old saying?" McCarthy said, smiling. " 'Set a thief to catch a thief?' " The smile stretched into a grin. "I'd like to set myself up to do some trading on the hot-paper market. I'll need guidance and advice from the best fellows in your Safe and Loft Squad, of course."

"That'll be Fred Steppat and Johnny Riley."

"When may I meet them?"

"No time like the present!"

The strategy for catching his quarry had planted itself as the train left Buffalo, McCarthy explained to the detectives over a spaghetti-and-Chianti lunch in nearby Little Italy. It germinated during a sleepless night while the 20th Century Limited sped east through the Mohawak River Valley and had come into full blossom by the time he had stepped onto the Limited's red carpet at Grand Central.

"The surfacing of the check that wound up in the hands of the unfortunate Fuller woman indicates that these crooks might have decided that the heat is off," he continued. "If they've figured that it's safe to unload the loot, they'll probably be eager to dump it all at once. They'll be looking for a buyer. Well, why shouldn't I be that man?"

"I like it," said Detective Riley, his green eyes wide and lit in a round, ruddy face. "How can we help?"

"What I need is the dope on where to go to rub elbows with the New York City underworld. Their hangouts and the like."

"Most of them are Broadway joints around Times Square," said Detective Steppat, an intense young man with a hawkish nose that brought to mind the fictional sleuth Sherlock Holmes.

"It would be nice if the word got out to their circle that you fellas were looking for a fence specializing in hot paper," McCarthy said. "Someone of my description who just blew in from out of town."

"Detective Riley can handle that," O'Brien said. "He's got a pipeline into the Broadway bunch."

McCarthy turned to Riley, a short redhead with the build of a prizefighter. "Spread the word that this guy has a bundle of cash and is offering top dollar if he can get the right deal on negotiable paper," McCarthy said to him. "Then leave it to me."

"What's the name of this out-of-towner?" Riley asked.

"It's always awkward using an alias," McCarthy replied. "I might forget who I'm supposed to be! Now, which hotel do you propose I check into? One that suits a successful fence looking to make a big score in the big town."

The three detectives answered as one: "The Astor."

The hotel had opened in 1904, when Mayor George B. McClellan, the Civil War general and failed contender for president of the United States, signed the resolution that changed the name of the confluence of Broadway and Seventh Avenue from Longacre Square to Times Square, in honor of the newspaper's splendid new triangular tower at the crossroads. In the eighteen years since its debut, the hotel had been taken to the hearts of the Broadway crowd. During that period, the carriages that had once conveyed patrons to Rector's, Shanley's, the Metropole Cafe, and other fashionable bistros had been superceded by autos, hack drivers by chauffeurs.

The World War had killed nearly everything that was the old Broadway, observed newspaperman Gene Fowler in *The Great Mouthpiece,* a biography of the 1920s' most famous criminal lawyer, William J. Fallon. "Prohibition, the mockturtle soup of purists, provided the *coup de grace,*" Fowler wrote. "Before the war, one might walk Broadway and meet friends. There were men and women worth being pointed out. It was Cohan's Broadway. One might have a drink, openly arrived at. But Prohibition shot the heart out of Broadway and its people. Crime was ceasing to be mere enterprise. It was becoming an industry."

To encounter a bewildering assortment of criminals, McCarthy had been told by his friends at headquarters, he need not wander far from the Astor. Men of the stripe he sought would be found at Shanley's, Murray's, the Little Club, and "the city's country club," the Grill of the Knickerbocker Hotel. On Forty-second just off Broadway, it had been built at the turn of the century and claimed to possess the world's second longest bar, graced by Maxfield Parrish's mural of Old King Cole. (The painting survived the old hotel and found a new home in the bar at the St. Regis Hotel.)

In addition to these hunting grounds, dozens of speakeasies, restaurants, and other establishments frequented by persons who could never have been invited to dance in Caroline Astor's ballroom offered McCarthy ample opportunities to meet characters with a penchant for peddling stolen goods to anyone whom they believed could be trusted. Confident that once information got around that someone named McCarthy had blown in from out of town looking for deals, he used his natural gregariousness and detective's wiles to establish himself as a familiar face and to make his name known. "My monicker's been blared around Broadway so much," he told Inspector O'Brien when he telephoned to keep him apprised of his activities, "I'm getting to be as famous as George M. Cohan!"

Unfortunately, he reported to O'Brien in late April, no one had approached him about the commodity he sought. "I could have made some sweet deals in jewelry, furniture, fur coats, and truckloads of hijacked booze," he griped, "but when it comes to what I'm here for, I'm batting zero. One guy offered me a bundle of paper and I thought I was onto something, but the son of a bitch never showed up. Who knows why? Maybe he thought he smelled a cop. Some people say they can, you know."

"Cheer up! Have patience, pal," O'Brien answered. "Babe Ruth strikes out more often than he homers."

McCarthy advised his superiors at the American Express Company about his lack of progress and conceded that he might be on the wrong track. He offered to call off the investigation. "I agree that it doesn't look good at this point, Gordon," said his boss.

"I'm running up a pretty fancy hotel bill down here."

After a long pause, the voice from Buffalo said, "The cost of your work is a pittance compared to the seventy grand they got from us. Give it a couple more weeks."

"I'm positive that gang is in New York."

At that moment, however, Chapman and Anderson were hundreds of miles away, aboard the Cunard White-Star's flagship *Aquitania* and bound for New York. Known as "the grand old lady," the four-stack liner had been built immediately before the war, a sister ship to the ill-fated *Titanic* that had gone down in the Atlantic, killing 1,503 passengers. The *Aquitania*, enthused the Cunard Line's publicist, offered its passengers Harris tweeds, Chanel jerseys, indolent conversation, and energetic sport by day; at night, "a sudden increase in tempo . . . a blaze of jewels . . . gowns of rose, gold and green . . . men and women wearing formality with the perfect ease that is the distinction and delight of aristocratic English life."

As G. Vincent Colwell, Chapman had basked in the sumptuous glories of ocean voyaging. In company with Dutch Anderson, he had left New York aboard the Holland–America Line's *Nieuw Amsterdam*. Landing at Rotterdam, they toured the capitals of Europe in search of buyers for a half-million dollars' worth of securities packed in Anderson's bags. But after more than a month of Dutch's negotiations in Paris, Berlin, and London, they parted with only a small portion of the Leonard Street loot. Debarking in New York, they carried barely more in profits than the costs of the journey.

Wearing his uniform, Charlie Loerber greeted them at the White Star's Pier 59 at Sixteenth Street. Informed of the slim pickings, he flew into a rage. "You guys wouldn't be trying to hold out on me, would you?" he demanded. "You wouldn't be pulling a fast one?"

"Charlie, Charlie," replied Anderson, "you break my heart. I have never cheated on an associate in my life. As for Chappy, he has gone out of his way to see that you are content. Why, if it hadn't been for him, you would not have been part of the greatest robbery in American history! I have to tell you, Charlie, that I was against bringing you in. Chappy insisted. I believe you owe him, at the very least, an apology."

"I guess you're right, Dutch," Loerber conceded grudgingly. "Maybe I was off base in what I said. It's just that it's been six months since we pulled that job and I'm still waiting for the big payoff. All I've got is a pile of so-far worthless paper. It drives me nuts everytime I look at it."

"Soon, Charlie," Dutch murmured consolingly. "Soon."

Later, back at his Gramercy Square apartment, Chapman

erupted. "What I ought to do is blast the ungrateful son of a bitch!" he roared. "If Loerber does anything to queer this setup of ours, I'll strangle him with my bare hands."

"No you won't, Chappy," Anderson said with a smile. "If he crosses us *I'll* kill him."

Delighted to be home, Chapman returned to his role as the Count. To all who would listen, he extolled the charms of postwar Europe as though he had known the Continent before 1914. But as he toured favorite Broadway haunts, he listened with increasing interest to gossip that an individual by the name of McCarthy was trying to obtain exactly the sort of merchandise that few in Europe had been prepared to buy. While Dutch Anderson agreed that McCarthy appeared to be as he advertised himself, caution dictated discretion.

"Once you've met him," Anderson counseled, "just treat him like your other Broadway friends. Even if he appears to be on the up-and-up, let's not rush things. As far as he's concerned, you are just another Goodtime Johnny. When the time is right for us to talk business with him, we'll know it. Then we give him enough to hold his attention until we're really sure of him."

The following evening, at the Knickerbocker Grill's long bar, Chapman plucked a cigarette from a gold case. In lighting it, he knocked over the cocktail of the man beside him.

For a moment, McCarthy stared into the clumsy man's face. A most interesting visage: Deeply set eyes. Bushy brows. High cheekbones. No thick eyeglasses, however. Instead, pince-nez perched on the bridge of his nose. Could this well-dressed man be the one he was looking for? Or was he simply a dead ringer?

"I do beg your pardon," the man exclaimed. "How embrassing."

"Think nothing of it," McCarthy said. "In my lifetime I've spilled almost as much of the stuff as I've drunk."

"I insist you allow me to buy you another."

Stepping back, Chapman looked at McCarthy studiously.

"Something the matter?" McCarthy asked.

"I just wanted to be sure," Chapman said with a laugh, "that you're not one of those crazy federal agents, Izzy and Moe!"

"The bane of my life," McCarthy answered, "is that people think I'm a copper. It's because I'm big, you know? And Irish. It gets to be a pain in the ass, because the truth is, I don't care much for cops, on account of my being arrested a couple of times just because I wanted a drink. Whoever pushed through Prohibition ought to be taken out and shot, in my opinion."

"*Meum est propsitium in taberna mori!*"

"Beg pardon?"

"Latin," Chapman said. "*De Nugis Curialium,* by Walter Map, a Welsh author and favorite of King Henry the Second. 'I intend to die in a tavern; let the wine be placed near my dying mouth, so that when the choirs of angels come, they may say, God be merciful to this drinker.' "

"You're quite an educated fellow," McCarthy said.

"I owe it all to my mother," Chapman replied. "And to one especially inspiring teacher by the name of Anderson."

Over the next two weeks, seemingly by chance, McCarthy kept encountering this remarkable man, who gave his name as Charles Brown and delighted in flourishing thousand-dollar notes whose source was not disclosed. Soon McCarthy had had enough of the chance meetings. Encountering Brown at the Knickerbocker, he demanded, "How long are we going to continue this gavotte, Brown? Are we or are we not going to do business?"

Chapman smiled teasingly. "What sort of business?"

"Look, the whole damn town knows by now that I'm in the market for paper. You know it, too. You knew it before we even met. It's *why* we met. So what do you say?"

Chapman rolled a Havana cigar between a manicured finger- and thumbnail. "You surely appreciate that one does not rush in where angels fear to tread," he said. "I have to be certain that you're on the square."

"Well, I am," McCarthy grumbled, "so either shit or get off the pot."

Chapman flicked cigar ash into a tray. "Securities," he said softly. "The cream of the crop. Easily disposable."

"Oh yeah? Then how come you haven't disposed of them long before now?"

"They were hot. Now they're cool. Downright cold, in fact."

"When can I see them?"

"You can take a gander at one of them now," Chapman said, slipping his hand into an inside coat pocket. "If you're satisfied, there are plenty more where this one came from."

Studying an Argentine Republic government gold note in the amount of one thousand dollars, McCarthy recognized its validity immediately. "This looks like good stuff," he said, noting the registration number. "What are you asking for?"

"Sixty cents on the dollar."

"I'll give you forty. Of course, I don't have four hundred on me right now. I could have it tomorrow evening. Shall we meet at my hotel? In the bar at seven o'clock?"

"That's fine with me."

Next day, over a bowl of chop suey in Chinatown, blocks from police headquarters, McCarthy recounted the conversation to O'Brien. "Of course, this isn't the case I've come down here to solve," he concluded, "but it'll do for now."

O'Brien had listened with mounting excitement as McCarthy described the material that had been offered to him. Now, with a shake of the head, he exclaimed, "You don't realize what you've stumbled onto, my friend. I believe that Argentine gold bond you held in your hands is part of the biggest mail robbery ever! Of course, I can't say for sure until I see it myself. If it is, you may have accomplished what the New York Police Department and an army of postal inspectors have been trying to do for eight months. If this Brown is a member of that gang, we'll have to be careful reeling them in."

"I'm just a visiting fireman," McCarthy said. "From here on, it's your show, Mike."

"Have you got the four hundred?"

"I was hoping you could help me out on that score."

"No problem. The department has a fund for things like this. It's a small price if we end up nailing that mob. C'mon with me. I think you'd better meet my boss."

In a cluttered second-floor office of the Detective Division on East Seventeenth Street, Commander John Coughlin was a deeply frustrated man. Eight months after being awakened by a call from the Beach Street Station about the stickup of Frank Haveranck's mail truck, he was no closer to making an arrest than he had been in October. Countless leads had been followed. Scores of "the usual suspects" had been questioned. Now, here was a tale told by Gordon McCarthy. Might it be the big break, at last?

"Like they say, one robin doesn't mean it's springtime," he said wearily, "and one Argentine gold note doesn't mean this guy pulled the Leonard Street heist."

"On the other hand he might have," McCarthy said. "I'll do whatever you think is best."

"Go through with the deal," Coughlin said. "Play out the string as far as it goes. If this man was involved in that damned mail robbery, he could lead us to the whole gang. Of course, when you go to that meeting, O'Brien will have his men there. Don't take any foolish risks. If the deal goes sour, McCarthy, get the hell out and leave it to us."

When McCarthy walked into the Astor Bar precisely at

seven, he found Brown waiting. "Do we have a deal?" he asked.

"I'm a man of my word," McCarthy said, taking an envelope containing four one-hundred-dollar bills from his coat pocket.

Chapman handed him the bond. "As am I," he said. "And now that we've shown our good faith, let's go for a walk and a talk."

Leaving the hotel, they turned down Broadway, already bustling with Friday night theatergoers.

"I've got eighty grand worth of those bonds," Chapman said as they strolled past the Edison Hotel, where three years ago he had gotten off a bus from Auburn with a ten-dollar bill to his name. "I'll let you have the whole lot for half a buck on the dollar," he said. "That's forty thousand."

"I don't walk around town with forty grand on me," McCarthy said.

"But you *can* raise it?"

"The most I'd go for is twenty-five on the dollar. That's twenty thousand."

"Make it twenty-one. I've got a girlfriend who wants a new fur coat."

McCarthy laughed. "In *July* she wants a fur coat?"

"Dames," Chapman said, throwing up his arms. "Who can ever explain them?"

"All right, if an extra grand will make her happy and get you laid, I'll make it twenty-one."

"How soon can you have the cash?"

"It'll take me a couple of days. How do I contact you?"

Chapman smiled. "I'll call you."

The following morning, McCarthy met with O'Brien.

"This thing is moving pretty fast," O'Brien said. "Twenty-five Gs is not in our budget. I think the time's come to have a chat with our federal brethern." Picking up his snap-brim hat, he slapped it against McCarthy's chest. "Come on. You'd better meet Bill Cochrane, Joe Doran, and Jim Doyle. You'll like 'em: they're just like you—pigheaded, never-give-up Mick dicks."

The federals had not been idle.

Two weeks after the Niagara Falls robbery that sent Gordon McCarthy on a long visit to New York, and three months after the stickup of Frank Haveranck's mail truck, the embarrassed and outraged loan department of the Quaker City Bank, in Philadelphia, had informed post-office inspectors in the City of Brotherly Love that it had accepted one-third of a million dollars in securities as collateral for a loan in the amount of $250,000. The problem was, the bank pointed out, it had discovered on closer inspection that the serial numbers of the securities had been altered to disguise the fact that they were part of the loot from the Leonard Street robbery.

Realizing that the robbers had begun disposing of their ill-gotten goods, the chief of the New York investigation, William Cochrane, saw an opportunity, albeit a long shot. Calling in his top man, Inspector Joseph J. Doran, he announced, "Joe, you are going into the stock-brokering business." Overnight, the naturally quiet and conservative Doran found himself in an office on Lower Broadway, on the fringes of Wall Street, transformed into a loud, shifty, overdressed, blue-sky stock-and-bond dealer named Rose who was not above dealing in hot paper. But after five months of the masquerade, he had nothing to show for it.

Suddenly, in Colonel Cochrane's office sat a fellow from Buffalo by the name of McCarthy, relating what just might be the break in the case. There was the evidence of the Argentine gold bonds. But most significant was the American Express driver's description of one of the men who had held him up—an exact match for the description that had been provided by Frank Haveranck.

"What do you make of it, gentlemen?" asked Colonel Cochrane.

"I think McCarthy's onto something," Joe Doyle answered.

"I agree," said Doran. "Thanks to our friend from upstate, Mr. Gordon McCarthy, I think we can finally make use of that office I've been hanging around in for months."

"What do you propose?" McCarthy asked.

"If we set you up with the twenty-one grand so that you can make the deal with Brown, and then arrest him, we get just one of the Leonard Street gang. I want all three. Why not let Brown lead us to them?"

"I hand over the cash," McCarthy said, "and then you fellows tail him?"

"Exactly. But let's not go off half-cocked. There's always a chance that Brown could give us the slip. I think we should pin a tail on him *before* you fork over the dough. When he gets back to you, Gordon, tell him that you've got a partner. Your bankroller. Tell Brown that before he comes across with the money, he wants to meet Brown to talk about future deals."

"That could scare Brown off."

"That's where my little brokerage office comes in. You tell Brown that your money man is a Wall Streeter. Give him my address and phone number."

"What if he doesn't go for it?"

"You proceed with the deal for the twenty-one thousand and we take our chances that Brown will lead us to his accomplices. When do you meet Brown next?"

"He'll let me know," McCarthy said.

Two days later he found a note slipped under his hotel-room door: "Astor Bar, six P.M. today. B."

He found Brown waiting. "You got the cash?" he asked.

"Before I can get my hands on it," McCarthy said, "the man who actually bankrolls my deals wants to meet you."

"What the hell for?"

"What can I say? He's a nervous guy. Wouldn't you be if you were a respectable Wall Street broker who's dabbling in hot paper on the side?"

Chapman's eyes went wide. "Your associate is a broker?"

"Yeah. It's a perfect setup. It's been a real sweet deal for me. And it could be for you, too, Charlie. If he likes you."

"When can I meet him?"

"Anytime. I'll give you his address and phone number. Call him, or drop in at your convenience. During regular business hours, that is. He's strictly a nine-to-five, little-wife-and-kiddies type of guy. Like in that song that Eddie Cantor sings, 'Makin' Whoopie.' "

Three days passed before the man McCarthy and Doran knew as Brown walked into Doran's bogus brokerage office. Satisfied that Doran was a bona fide dealer, he left envisioning lucrative future deals. Hailing a taxi on Broadway, he did not observe that he was being followed, as he would be, day and night, from that moment.

From a public phone at Grand Central Terminal, Chapman told McCarthy that he was eager to complete the twenty-one-thousand-dollar deal.

"Let's meet next Monday, six o'clock," McCarthy said excitedly. "Dinner on me at the Astor Roof. And bring your girlfriend."

"Oh, no. Betty's not involved in my business. When it comes to dames, I follow the advice of Sherlock Holmes: 'A woman is not to be trusted, not the best of them.' As to a meeting, let's make it elsewhere, somewhere out in the open. How about the corner of Broadway and a-Hundred-second Street?"

"That's fine with me."

"Good. So it's there at three o'clock on July third. We'll take care of business and go on our merry ways and have a good old-fashioned Fourth of July."

"I wouldn't think you'd care to celebrate Independence Day."

"Why the hell not?"

"Your accent," McCarthy said. "I took you to be English."

In a conference with O'Brien, Doran, and Doyle, held while walking in Central Park, McCarthy said, "This is pretty funny, isn't it? I came down here to look for American Express traveler's checks and suddenly I'm up to my ass in stocks and bonds!"

"When you meet him on Monday," O'Brien said, "shake his hand. That will be our signal to move in on Brown, or whatever his name is."

"It's not the name he uses in Gramercy Park," Dolan said.

O'Brien pulled up short. "Are you telling me that the son of a bitch lives in that ritzy neighborhood?"

"He goes by the name of G. Vincent Colwell."

"That's an alias, too, I'll bet," O'Brien said.

"You know, I'm not surprised that he's got a swank address," McCarthy said. "It suits him. Charming as all get-out. A snazzy dresser. Foreign accent. Quite well educated, too. We've shared some wonderful evenings while we were feeling each other out the past few weeks. He's quite the man about town."

"I'll say," grunted Doran. "He's had a dozen of my men on a real merry-go-round. Slippery cuss. Very careful in everything he does. Changing cabs frequently. Ducking on and off subways and trolley cars. This guy is a real pro. He knows all the tricks."

"Well, he may be a man about town," O'Brien said, resuming their walk, "but if he keeps his appointment with

McCarthy on Monday, he's going to be quite the man around Sing Sing."

"Correction, please," said Doran. "After we nail him, he'll be checking into the United States Penitentiary in Atlanta. Robbing the U.S. Mail is a *federal* offense."

CHAPTER NINE

The Big Leap

DURING GORDON MCCARTHY'S YEARS as a detective, he had become an expert at killing time. It seemed to him that half of all he did was wait. And the secret to waiting, he had learned, was in keeping busy. On Saturday morning he boarded a Royal Blue Line Motor Tours bus at the McAlpin Hotel for Tour No. 1, which promised to show him "New York, Uptown, Downtown and over the great bridges to Brooklyn, from the Statue of Liberty to Grant's Tomb." After a steak dinner at the Hofbrau, at Broadway and Thirtieth Street and a leisurely stroll up to Forty-second, he took the advice of the *New York World*—"Go see it!"—and bought a balcony seat at the Cameo Theater for a "busman's holiday" in the form of a play about a detective. Written by William Gillette, and based on stories by Arthur Conan Doyle, it starred John Barrymore in the title role of Sherlock Holmes.

Beginning with Mass at St. Patrick's Cathedral, McCarthy whiled away Sunday in Central Park and the American Museum of Natural History, where he lingered over the fifteen hundred gems of the Tiffany collection, a gift of J. P. Morgan. Returning to the Astor, he had dinner sent up by room service and retired to bed, reading himself to sleep in the pages of the pulp magazine *Black Mask*, founded in 1920 by H. L. Mencken and George Jean Nathan.

On Monday morning McCarthy got a haircut in the hotel and a shoeshine at a stand on Forty-second Street. He saw the movie "While Satan Sleeps" at the Rialto, then returned to his room to fetch his Colt .45 automatic pistol. Tucked into an inside pocket of his coat, its slight bulge might easily be seen as an envelope stuffed with twenty-one thousand dollars in currency.

Arriving five minutes early at Broadway and 102nd Street, and realizing that Brown, alias Colwell, had not specified which corner, he chose the northwest. Waiting in the hot, glaring sunlight, he was confident that O'Brien and his men were already in position to act. But he felt no such faith in Brown. Despite his own threats to take his business elsewhere, and Brown's assurances that the deal was firm, he could think of compelling reasons for him not to appear. McCarthy could turn out to be a cop after all. Was there a law that said a cop couldn't lie? And if McCarthy were not a lawman, as he said, what guarantee was there that he was not a clever con artist? He might be a stickup man planning to pull a gun and help himself to the goods. A man with a fondness for quotations might remember that "there's no honor among thieves." Also on McCarthy's mind as he glanced at his pocketwatch and noted that Brown was three minutes late was the possibility that the man had found another customer since Friday.

Returning the watch to its pocket, he heard the beep of a horn. Looking up, he watched a black, open-top Packard touring car pulling to the curb. At the wheel, Loerber looked

The Big Leap

fancy in green chauffeur's livery. Seated in the rear, Anderson appeared dapper and cool under a straw boater. Hatless on the curb side, in a white linen suit, Chapman raised a hand in greeting. Clasping and shaking it energetically, McCarthy boomed, "Mr. Brown, I was afraid you'd forgotten our appointment!"

Through all that occurred in the next instant—the slap-slap of running feet, a police squad car cutting in front of the Packard, the dark blue of policemen's uniforms with the sun glinting off their badges, drawn guns—Chapman's attention was riveted on McCarthy. Polite and firm, as Chapman had been in addressing Frank Haveranck under an arc light on deserted Leonard Street, McCarthy said, "Brown, you and your friends are under arrest."

Chapman stood, shaking a fist: "On what charge?"

"Robbing the mail," barked O'Brien, shoving Chapman down in the seat and plucking a bundle of Argentine government gold notes from his inside coat pocket.

In the twenty years since he had first felt the bite of handcuffs at the age of fourteen, Gerald Chapman had become accustomed to the plodding and meticulous routine that would now unfold. He knew that his captors would discover his real name and, with it, his record. On the eve of the 146th anniversary of national independence, he had become a three-time loser who faced the certainty of spending the rest of his life in prison. But he didn't have to make the policemen's job an easy one. Asked to identify himself by the booking sergeant at the West 100th Street Police Station, he gave the name on his driving license and other papers contained in his wallet.

"I am Edward Bryce," he said. "Spelled with a Y. But as the Bard, William Shakespeare, asked, 'What's in a name?' "

Claiming to be a professor of languages from Rochester,

New York, Dutch Anderson identified himself as Charles Heines.

Stating that he currently resided with his mother at 802 Amsterdam Avenue, Charlie Loerber said he was Charles Lambert. "I don't know what's going on here," he pleaded. "I haven't done a thing wrong. I'm just a chauffeur."

With a glint of triumph in his green eyes, Gordon McCarthy recalled that the name of the man who had paid his rent at Martha Fuller's boarding house with a stolen American Express travelers' check had been Lambert.

"Is this your true address?" asked the booking sergeant as he examined the contents of Chapman's wallet. "It says here that you live at Number 12 Gramercy Park."

"The world is my address," Chapman answered, smirking. " 'The earth, that is sufficient.' "

The sergeant frowned impatiently. "What was that?"

"That," Chapman laughed, "was Walt Whitman."

"Are you saying your name isn't Bryce but Whitman?"

Chapman howled with laughter.

"There's no use stalling," declared Detective O'Brien. "We know you're the one who stuck up a mail truck in October. We know you're the Count of Gramercy Park. And at this very minute, some of my men and inspectors of the Post Office Department are on their way to your house."

Abruptly, Chapman's demeanor became subdued. Betty was at home entertaining a friend from out of town who knew her as Mrs. Colwell. Everyone believed they were married. "Tell them to go easy," he said softly. "My girlfriend is there. She has nothing to do with any of this, so no rough stuff, okay?"

Opening the door, Betty was astonished to find the hallway crowded with men holding guns. Inspector James J. Doyle of the U.S. Post Office Department stepped forward. "Police," he said. "You're under arrest, lady." Entering the parlor, he discovered another woman, wide-eyed and trembling. "You're under arrest, too, honey," he said. "Both of you sit down while we search the premises."

The task of examining the bedroom fell to Post Office Inspector Joseph Vick. Opening a steamer trunk, he found bundles of papers.

The first consisted of $3,000 in American Express traveler's checks—all that remained of the $70,000 stolen in Niagara Falls. The second batch bore the names of the Argentine Republic. Others consisted of common stock certificates of the Puget Sound Light and Power Company, the Mexican Petroleum Company, the Anaconda and Braden Copper Companies, and the Duluth and Iron Range Railway Company.

"Hey, Jim!" Vick shouted. "Bingo!"

A moment later, Doyle was on the telephone to his boss, Chief Inspector Cochrane, at the Main Post Office building on Eighth Avenue.

Colonel Cochrane immediately phoned Detective O'Brien at the 100th Street Statoin. "Congratulations on your department's outstanding work on this investigation, Bill," he said, "but now this is strictly a federal case. How soon can your boys bring those guys over to my office so we can question them and find out where they've stashed the rest of the loot?"

Reluctant to yield his quarry, O'Brien consulted with his boss. "I'm sorry, Bill," said Chief Coughlin, "but the federals have priority on those guys. We can book 'em and hold 'em, but this case is bound to wind up in federal court. I'd guess that Sam Hitchcock, the U.S. Commissioner, is already at work drawing up the papers. So as soon as you've completed booking 'em, turn that gang over to the mailmen."

Directly across Eighth Avenue from Pennsylvania Station, above the railroad's maze of tracks, was the New York General Post Office, designed by the architectural firm of McKim,

Mead, and White. The nation's largest post office stood on steel stilts over the Pennsy's tracks, yet it appeared to have been hewn from the granite bedrock of Manhattan Island. In its vast basement an intricate system of belts, chutes, and sorting tables handled 45 percent of the city's mail.

Delivered to the third floor on the Thirty-first Street side, the short, sweating, handcuffed man standing before Cochrane represented an affront to the vow chiseled in granite above the building's majestic facade. Stretching for almost two blocks in the frieze above a Corinthian colonnade, the words were those of the Greek historian Herodotus: NEITHER SNOW NOR RAIN NOR HEAT NOR GLOOM OF NIGHT STAYS THESE COURIERS FROM THE SWIFT COMPLETION OF THEIR APPOINTED ROUNDS.

"So you're the man who pulled off the biggest robbery in the history of the country," Cochrane said, looking Chapman up and down. "You're nothing but a pip-squeak. A runt." Coming around his desk, he fingered Chapman's linen lapel. "A *dandified* pip-squeak."

Chapman shrugged off Cochrane's hand. "Sir, you cut me to the quick. I may not be as tall as you and your minions, but, to paraphrase the Bard of Avon, hath not a short person senses? If you prick a short man, does he not bleed? If you tickle him, does he not laugh? If you wrong him, shall he not revenge?"

"You're a wiseguy, too, I see," Cochrane said, turning his back. "Well the jig's up, Mister. My men have been to your home and found the evidence that will put you and your gang away for a long, long time."

"Found?" Chapman said. "Don't you mean 'planted?' "

Separated from Anderson and Loerber, Chapman recognized an old police device. His interrogators hoped to divide and conquer. Playing one against another, they looked for the weak link that, once broken, would provide a confession and information that allowed them to recover the loot as well as their pride. The Leonard Street robbery had been profoundly embarrassing. What had Postmaster General Hays said in vowing to catch the robbers? "I draw the line on nothing that would prevent further outrages against the sacred mails of the United States."

Sacred!

Sticking up Frank Haveranck's mail truck had been worse than a crime. It had been a sacrilege.

But if his interrogators expected him to blurt out a *mea culpa,* if they wanted him to kneel penitently as he had in the confession box of his mother's church in Brooklyn, and his Aunt Catherine's in Harlem, Gerald Chapman intended otherwise. He was, he insisted, innocent. A mistake had been made. How could they believe that a person of his culture and breeding had taken up the life of a common criminal?

As the questioning continued, a breed of men in pursuit of their own line of work learned of the drama that unfolded at the corner of Broadway and 102nd Street—reporters. Ensconced in the "press shack" across Centre Street from police headquarters, they had listened eagerly to a detective with a remarkable tale to tell. "Remember that big mail-truck stickup last October?" he had asked. "Well, the gang that pulled it was pinched this afternoon. They're now in custody up at the post office on Eighth Avenue."

By nine o'clock, Cochrane could not ignore them: they crowded the front steps. "I can confirm for you that we are questioning suspects in the recent robbery," he told them. "We haven't gone half through this case, but we expect to know a great many more facts in the morning."

Had they confessed?

"They have talked a blue streak, but not about the crime," he replied with chagrin. "One of them was quoting Walt Whitman to us at length this evening, and two of them exchanged remarks that showed more than a casual knowledge of medieval history."

Laughing, the reporters scrambled to telephone their city desks. What had been shaping up as a holiday short of news had become the occasion for a blaring headline in every New York newspaper, and, quite possibly, a Fourth of July "extra."

Returning to his supervision of frustrating interrogations, Cochrane found that Inspectors Doyle and Frick had returned from Gramercy Park. In addition to the material discovered in the bedroom, they had brought the two women. In questioning them at the apartment, Doyle reported, he had come to the conclusion that the woman he had arrested in the parlor knew nothing of the affair and had simply had the bad luck to be visiting. "She was just in the wrong place at the wrong time," he said. "I also think that the first woman, who says she's Mrs. Bryce, is in the dark about her husband's activities. She's done nothing but cry and ask about her husband. I gather that she's heard a lot of stories about the 'third degree' and thinks we're using a rubber hose on him. She's been begging to see him."

"Maybe that's not a bad idea," Cochrane said. "It could be the little woman will persuade her lover-boy to wise up and level with us. Or maybe when he sees that she's in custody and thinks that we're charging her as an accomplice, he'll get so upset that he'll crack."

Electing to follow the latter strategy, Cochrane escorted Betty to the room where Chapman was being held, surrounded by a dozen men.

"What the hell kind of a man are you, Bryce?" Cochrane demanded. "Here's this woman whom you say is your wife and she's facing a stretch in prison because of you. You're nothing but a cad and a cur."

"You sons of bitches," Chapman yelled as he leapt to his

feet. "I told you to leave her out of this."

With a cry of "Oh, Gerry!" Betty fainted.

Catching her, Cochrane shouted, "Get her some water!"

The scene resembled that described in Pope's *An Essay on Man, Epistle II*—"Chaos of thought and passion, all confused." And Chapman seized the moment. Like a panther, he sprang toward an open window. To jump meant instant death eighty feet down on the sidewalk of Thirty-first Street. But three feet below stretched one of Stanford White's decorative copings. Two feet wide, it circled the building like a cornice.

Grasping the windowsill, he climbed over it and lowered himself to the coping. Pressing his back to the wall, he eased to the left and turned the corner. Looking down on Eighth Avenue, he found it busy with traffic, mostly taxis picking up passengers streaming through the rear doors of Penn Station. Directly below, a small crowd of men appeared to be lounging on the post office steps. If anyone glanced up, he was likely to be seen. Finding an open window, he scampered through it into a darkened office.

Out of breath, sweating in the stifling heat and hearing an eruption of voices and footfalls in the corridor, Chapman knew that the door to his hiding place would soon swing open and his break for freedom would be over. At best, it had been a very dangerous act. He might have been shot in the back. One slip and he certainly would have plummeted to the pavement. Furthermore, what chance did he have even now? How could he make his way out of a building full of people?

Why had he done it? Had it been prompted by anger at seeing Betty in custody? Was it doubt that he could go on resisting the probing of relentless questioners? Somewhere in his mind, did there lurk a suspicion, even fear, that Dutch or Charlie would sell him out? Or had it been simply the spectre of spending the rest of his life in prison that drove him to risk death?

Whatever motivated him, he decided that he must never again allow himself to be driven by emotion. In all that he might do from this moment onward, he would follow a clear, concise, and logical plan. No more would he be so stupid as he had been in falling into McCarthy's trap. He had gone to meet him unarmed. In future, should he find himself free again, he would never be without a gun. And, most assuredly, he would never hesitate to use it.

Hearing voices in the corridor, he scrambled into hiding atop a bulky wardrobe. Lying motionless, he looked down from the perch as the office door opened. Silhouetted in the light of the hallway, two men gripped pistols. Inspector Doyle flipped a light switch. "Nice try, Bryce," he said, pointing his gun at Chapman, "but it's over now, so come on down."

Returned to the interrogation room, Chapman found Inspector Dolan in conversation with a police captain. "You've got him, I see," said the cop. "So I can send my men back to their post." Alerted to the possibility that their prisoner had escaped from the post office, a squad of officers had rushed from the Thirtieth Street Station to search the vicinity—an arrival witnessed eagerly by the reporters on the post office steps. The fact that arrests had been made in the greatest robbery in the city's history was an important story. But that one of the culprit's had nearly escaped from a room full of policemen by leaping through a third-story window was more than any crime reporter could hope for, except in a stage or movie melodrama. Who was this desperado who exhibited such daring?

Presently, they had their answer. He was Gerald Chapman, also known as Bryce, also known as Colwell, also known as Gerald Chartres, also known as "the Count of Gramercy Park."

Chapman read the newspaper headlines and stories in his jail cell the next day and exulted in every one of them.

The Big Leap

CHAPTER TEN

Postmark: Atlanta

"IT'S OVER THERE under that tree," said Charlie Loerber as the sun came up. "A tin box. About a foot down."

He stood beside Jim Doyle of the Post Office Department as earnest men with shovels scraped the hard, dry ground of the farm at Lake Ronkonkoma where not so long ago he had observed Chapman dividing the spoils of the mail truck job and dreamed of becoming a wealthy man. But the golden vision had turned into dross. Out of the haul he had only six thousand dollars in cash and promises that he would share in the sale of securities and other paper valued in the millions.

"All it takes is a little doctoring of the registration numbers," Dutch Anderson had told him. "We ought to be able to get eighty cents on the dollar."

Yet after nearly nine months, he had received nothing but more promises.

Instead of wearing silk shirts and squiring beautiful women around New York in his own automobile, Loerber had found himself in a chauffeur's uniform behind the wheel of Chapman's new Packard, being ordered around by Chapman's woman, then under arrest and being grilled by Doyle. Why? Because Chapman had not heeded his warning about dealing with McCarthy. "I got a bad feeling about that guy," he had pleaded, only to be brushed aside as if he didn't have a brain in his head.

As a result, they had found themselves looking down gun barrels and having to sweat all night, hit from all sides by questions from guys gleefully gulping glasses of ice water while his mouth and throat were as dry as sandpaper.

"You pulled that big mail robbery, didn't you?"

"We know you're the brains behind it, so why not admit it?"

"Wasn't it you who stuck a gun into that driver's ribs?"

"Your two pals tell us that it was you who thought up the plan. What do you have to say about that?"

"Do you know what your pals are doing to you, Charlie? They are selling you out."

At midnight, Doyle had walked into the interrogation room. "Let me tell you what I think about all this, Charlie," he had said, handing him a glass of water. "The way I see things, you've been played for a sucker. We went down to that apartment in Gramercy Park. What a layout! That guy Chapman or Bryce, or whatever his true name is, sure has been living high on the hog. And what a swell that Anderson is! Yet here you are, Charlie, a poor sap in a chauffeur's outfit. Now that doesn't seem right to me. Unfair, you know? Here you are, one of the three fellows who pulled off the biggest stickup in U.S. history, and you're no better off than any of the working slobs in this town. Know what I think, Charlie? I think those guys have been taking *you* for a ride. How old are you, Charlie?"

"Thirty-two."

"So here you are, a young man, facing a stretch of hard

time in the federal pen down in Atlanta. Minimum of twenty-five years is my guess. When you get out, you'll be pushing sixty. The best years of your life will be behind you. And for what? Nothing! So wise up, Charlie. Look out for yourself. Why should you give up a life for a pair that's done nothing but cheat you and mock you? Cooperate with me, and I'm sure the judge will listen to me and go easy on you. What do you say?"

That Loerber had talked became evident to Chapman later that morning, when Loerber did not appear with him and Dutch Anderson in a police lineup. "The bastard squealed," he whispered to Dutch. "I should've killed the son of a bitch when I had the chance."

In the dark at the rear of the lineup room, Frank Haveranck studied seven men awash in light. "Of course, it was nighttime and it all happened fast," he said softly to the detectives at his side, "but I'm pretty sure that the little one on the left is the guy who jumped onto the running board and the heavyset one in the middle was in the car. There was three of 'em, only I don't see anyone up there who looks like the third one."

Seven miles from police headquarters, an Independence Day crowd basked in the hot afternoon sun and cavorted in the cooling surf as Policeman John Eagan left the Rockaway Beach Station for a short squad-car drive to the Clarendon Hotel. Minutes later, he stepped onto the porch to arrest Jeremiah Savelli, putting an end to the former postal employee's flourishing cabaret enterprise. Booked at New York City Police Headquarters for aiding and abetting the mail robbers pending an arraignment hearing, Savelli was taken a few blocks south to join Chapman, Anderson, and Loerber in separate cells of the city's jail on Centre Street. The prison occupied the site of the former Halls of Justice that had been erected in 1838. Because its architecture was modeled on that of an ancient Egyptian mausoleum, it became known as "the Tombs," a name that stuck.

Chapman had seen its interior several times, but on this occasion, as he waited for the unfolding of the criminal justice system, he considered the irony that he had carried out the greatest enterprise of his life only a few blocks away. The courtroom where he would stand trial for it was a stroll of under five minutes, although his bold attempt to escape ensured that he would not be permitted to get there on foot.

Surrounded by armed guards, and in handcuffs and leg chains, Chapman traveled to the Federal Building by automobile on Wednesday, July 5. Standing before U.S. Commissioner Samuel M. Hitchcock, he listened to Post Office Inspector Joseph Vick present charges of theft of stocks, bonds, jewelry (there had been a few baubles in the mail sacks) and cash, and "a murderous attack on the driver of the mail truck, Frank Haveranck." Under Section 197 of the United States Code, conviction on the robbery charge carried a maximum sentence of ten years. If he were found guilty of sticking a gun into Haveranck's ribs, it meant a maximum of twenty-five. Pending action by a Federal Grand Jury, Hitchcock set bail for Chapman, Anderson, and Loerber at $125,000 each. Savelli's was put at $35,000.

Unable to post the cash, and certain that there would be a speedy indictment, Chapman and Anderson engaged attorney William Baker to defend them and waited for trial.

It began on Wednesday, August 17, with the calling of the government's star witness. Pointing a steady finger, Loerber declared, "It was Chapman and Anderson who were with me in the robbery."

Spellbound, reporters from the city's newspapers and members of the public who considered themselves lucky to get into the courtroom were transported to a drizzly October night when a stolen Cleveland automobile followed and then cut off Frank Haveranck's mail truck. "Chapman pulled a gun on him," Loerber said. Then, the turn into Leonard Street. The laundry bag pulled over Haveranck's head. Grabbing the five bags of registered mail. The Long Island hideout. The barn. Examining the loot. Dividing it by four, alloting their inside man his fair share. Burying most of it. Then, waiting for the payoff that never came because Chapman and Anderson double-crossed him, cheated him. Finally, a man calling himself McCarthy who turned out to be their downfall.

Opening his defense, Baker told the jury a different story. "These men have a past," he said, pointing to Chapman and Anderson. "They have lived lives that are prone to criticism, but they are not stickup men; they are not robbers."

Wearing the white linen suit in which he had been arrested, Chapman assumed the witness chair.

"On the night of October twenty-fourth of last year," asked Baker, "were you in the vicinity of Broadway and Leonard Street?"

"I was not," Chapman replied. "On that evening my wife and I dined at a restaurant in Sheridan Square, went to the movies, and returned home to retire early."

"Do you know the man who testified that you were with him in the robbery of a mail truck on that occasion?"

"Yes, I do."

"Did there come a time when Loerber asked you to assist him in disposing of some bonds?"

"Last November Loerber came to me with the suggestion that I help him and two associates, "Slim" and "Schmitty," by taking thirty thousand dollars in bonds to Chicago, where they knew a man who would sell them."

"Did you take the bonds to Chicago?"

"I did. The man in question agreed to handle the bonds at a 40 percent commission, but he refused to advance any money. I left the bonds with him and returned to New York."

"What happened then?"

"Loerber flew into a rage. He said, 'Didn't you get any money at all? Do you think my people will believe that?' I told him I couldn't help that."

"What were you doing for a living at that time?"

"I was dickering in whiskey," Chapman said. "I have a very fine clientele of bootleggers and make a good living at it. It is a reliable way to earn a living. I tried investing in stocks and bonds but lost my shirt. Handling bonds is just too risky."

The courtroom erupted in laughter.

When it subsided, Baker turned to Chapman's attempted escape from the post office. "If you are not guilty of the charges that have been leveled against you, please tell the jury why you did such a dangerous thing."

"It was because of my wife," he said, his voice choking. "I saw what they were doing to her and . . ."

With a sob, he buried his face in his hands.

The judge declared a recess.

Composed, Chapman returned to the witness stand. "The police officers had taken my wife and a woman visitor to the post office building," he continued, dry-eyed. "An inspector told me of their presence. I worried that they were going to be grilled all night and it drove me nearly out of my mind. I felt that I had to get out of that place."

As the trial neared an end, Chapman brought in another lawyer—a criminal specialist with a reputation for saving seemingly lost cases through spirited summations. His name was Frederick J. Groehl. Appoaching the jury on Wednesday, August 24, Groehl faced a formidable task. Addressing Haveranck's identification of Chapman and Anderson, he asserted that it should be discounted, because the mail-truck driver feared he would be fired if he did not identify them. "Haveranck was a poor boob who wanted to keep his job," said the lawyer. "On the night of the robbery, he was so scared that all he saw was the gun."

As to Loerber's testimony: "This man is a vacillating, low-life coward whose only interest is in saving himself."

"Whom to believe?" asked U.S. Attorney William Cahill in his concluding remarks, "Loerber or the two defendants? I say to you that the story Loerber told was so clear, simple, and connected that it cannot be controverted. And what was that story? That these brilliant men, Chapman and Anderson, are the men who robbed the mail truck and that Loerber merely acted as the chauffeur."

Jumping up, Chapman shouted, "That's a lie!"

Rebuked by the judge, he apologized.

"I didn't mean that Mr. Cahill was lying," he said. "I meant that Loerber was a liar."

How could anyone believe that Loerber was a criminal mastermind? demanded Cahill. "It is absurd," he said, "to think that these shrewd men of full experience were being led and deceived by such a dub as Loerber. For Loerber is a dub, a criminal dub."

The jury retired for deliberations at 1:45 P.M. Returning three hours later, they found Chapman and Anderson guilty on all charges.

The next day, Gordon McCarthy sat beside Bill O'Brien as Judge Holmes sentenced Chapman and Anderson to a term of twenty-five years, to be served at the federal penitentiary in Atlanta.

"You know, Gordon," said O'Brien as they left the court-room, "the post office put up a reward for the capture of that gang—five grand each. It seems to me that the money rightly belongs to you. I hope you'll put in a claim to it."

McCarthy shrugged. "We'll see. You're a cop. You know

how it is. If money were important, none of us would carry a badge. It's the work that matters."

"Speaking of work," O'Brien said with a laugh, "do you know what Chapman is going to be doing in Atlanta? That prison has a knitting mill that makes cotton canvas. And do you know what they do with it? They sew it into sacks . . . for the U.S. Mail!"

CHAPTER ELEVEN

Lights Out

LIKE THE BIG HOUSE on the Hudson at Ossining, the granite walls of the federal penitentiary erected at McDonough Road and South Boulevard in Atlanta, Georgia, had been hewn by prisoners, but from historic Confederate ground, Stone Mountain. From two to four feet thick and between 28 and 37 feet high, they ran 4,178 feet, encompassing 28 acres. Entrance was through an overweaning steel gate of the administration building that had been built in two stages, the east wing in 1915, the west in 1919. From windows of offices on the second floor Warden J. E. Dyche and deputies Looney J. Fletcher and George S. Hughes looked out on four cell houses, each five tiers high and with a capacity of three thousand inmates; workshops, including the mill that wove Georgian cotton into canvas; and a well-equipped hospital with a separate facility for treatment of inmates suffering with tuberculosis.

At frequent intervals in the bleak gray perimeter which enclosed Gerald Chapman and Dutch Anderson in July 1922 watchtowers equipped with machine guns afforded guards an unobscured panorama of walkways between cell blocks, lawns and gardens maintained by inmates, and an exercise area. At night floodlights on the walls kept everything below as bright as day.

Although he had lived half his life in reformatories, jails, and prisons, Chapman had never encountered anything like it. Yet much of what he found within the walls of the federal lockup was familiar. Drab denim garb. Silent files of sullen faces. Eagle-eyed and wary guards at every turn, enforcing strict adherence to the rules. Appointed hours for baths, meals, work, exercise, and sleep.

Locked in his cell from six in the evening to six in the morning, he spent hours engaged in the timeless obsession of all men in prison—thinking of ways to escape. The history of penology in America was replete with spectacular attempts. In 1788, thirty-three highwaymen of the Doane gang had broken out of the Walnut Street prison in Philadelphia, requiring a battalion of infantry to track them down. In 1808, at least sixteen men got loose from a Baltimore jail, twelve of them permanently. In 1864 the entire population of San Quentin escaped, resulting in a ragging gun battle in which fifty of them were killed. In escaping from jail in Mesilla, New Mexico, in 1881, William H. Bonney, "Billy the Kid," had the help of a beautiful Mexican girl who smuggled him a gun. Train robber Oliver Curtis Perry cut his way out of the State Hospital for the Criminally Insane at Mattewan, New York, in 1895 with a saw sent to him in food by a woman who had fallen in love with him during his trial. At Leavenworth federal penitentiary in Kansas in 1910 dozens of inmates commandeered a small locomotive to smash out. And in 1913 Herbert Respold cut short his term for burglary by pulling the main switch at the San Quentin power station, plunging the prison into darkness while he scaled a wall and got into a rowboat. To ensure that the blackout of the prison continued, he carried the fuses away with him. But the bid for freedom foundered when the boat hit a rock and sank in San Francisco Bay. His body washed ashore the next morning. As for Atlanta, the only attempts at escape in its relatively brief history had occurred at the institution's outlying work farms. Had he been assigned to one of them, Chapman might simply make a run for it. But his leap through the window of the post office and the sensational coverage given to the exploit by the newspapers had put him in Warden Dyche's "high risk for escape" category, meaning that he must be kept under close observation at all times, and under no circumstances be permitted outside the perimeter of the prison.

Escaping, therefore, required getting over the walls, which meant that were he to attempt an escape it would have to be during the night. But how could he cross the floodlit yard without being observed from the guard towers? And even if he could, how to get over those forbidding walls? Furthermore, should he manage these miracles, what next? Once outside, how could he remove himself from the vicinity of the prison without a weapon?

Obviously, breaking out would be a lot easier if he had help from outside. According to prison rules, visitors were limited to "immediate relatives and to those having business to transact" with inmates. Chapman could claim neither, save for Betty.

To his surprise she came. But his delight in seeing her quickly dimmed. "I've met a very nice man," she told him. "He's a businessman from Rhode Island. He knows nothing about you and me. He's asked me to marry him and I've accepted."

"After the scrape I got you into," Chapman said, "what you do with your life is none of my. . . ."

"Beeswax?" she asked, half laughing, half in tears.

"Exactly," he said.

"I won't be coming down again," she said, "but that doesn't mean I won't be thinking about you. If you ever want to get in touch with me, I've made arrangements with the Biltmore Hotel in Providence. I want to keep in touch with old friends. I told them to write to me as Betty Colwell. You may do the same. If there is anything I can do for you, just let me know."

Could Betty help him in escaping? Though she might be willing, he decided, she would not even know where to begin.

If Dutch Anderson were on the outside, there would be no problem. Dutch would know exactly what to do.

He had not spoken to him since their arrival at the prison. Under orders of Warden Dyche they had been housed in different cell blocks and during exercise periods the guards had kept them at a distance.

Yet there were means of communicating, as there had been in all the jails and prisons in which Chapman had served. Connecting him with Anderson was an intelligent, cool-headed and personable young forger named John Gray. Regarded by the prison authorities as a "trusty," he had been assigned duties as an orderly in the hospital, where he had met Dutch while Anderson was being treated for a fainting spell brought on by heat prostration while working in the metal shop.

Sidling up to Chapman during an exercise period, he passed him a note from Dutch: "Johnny's a good guy. Trust him. Dutch."

Told of Anderson's fainting, Chapman laughed. "Dutch never fainted in his life," he said to Gray. "It was probably an excuse to get into the hospital so he could case the joint with an eye to escaping. I've been thinking of going on sick-call myself for the same purpose."

"Lots of guys check out the hospital," Gray said. "Nobody ever figured out how to do it. I've thought about it myself. But, as you can see, I'm still here."

Of all buildings within the prison compound, the two-story hospital stood closest to a wall, separated from it by only a few feet of lawn and flower beds. But directly above this area loomed a guardtower and beneath it a floodlamp that illuminated the entire space from dusk till dawn. To make a break via that route, Chapman speculated, a man would have to first find a means to put out the light, as Herbert Respold had done at San Quentin's power station by removing fuses. Atlanta's electrical station, however, was out of bounds to inmates.

In brief whispered moments over the next few weeks Chapman and Gray continued what Chapman considered merely an amusing and diverting intellectual exercise, with Gray subsequently relating the items discussed to Dutch, who sent Gray back to Chapman with comments and ideas.

"We'd need some kind of ladder," Chapman declared as Gray listened raptly.

"Where the hell do we get a thirty-five foot ladder?" Gray asked.

"We don't get one," Chapman said. "We make it."

"Out of what? And where would we keep it till you need it?"

"We string one together from that heavy cord that they use in the textile mill to bundle up sheets of canvas. Use the cord to connect the rungs. Those could be made out of the iron rods that are lying all over the place in the metal shop. As to where to conceal it, there must be lots of spots in the hospital where you could stash it."

Endorsing the concept of the ladder, Anderson envisioned no difficulty in procurement of the materials with the assistance of mill workers whom he supposed would be delighted to be a part of such an escape, although they would not be going over the wall themselves. Anderson allies in the metal shop, he informed Chapman through Gray, would happily provide a saw for cutting through window bars that existed even in a hospital, plus a file and a small hand drill. Furthermore, Anderson advised, an especially enthusiastic life-termer knew of a loose flagstone in a pavement near the prison where, years ago, an associate had buried two revolvers wrapped in oil cloth in the hope that his interned friend might one day retrive them during his own escape. Presumably the guns were still there. Like other dreamers, the lifer never resolved the dilemma of scaling the wall.

Confident that he had a plan worth attempting, Chapman set out to investigate the problem of the lights. On a chill February afternoon he sauntered alone across the exercise yard to the corner of the hospital nearest the wall, a dogleg rectangle of lawn edged with flower beds and a line of shrubs planted against the wall itself. Sitting on the grass, he lit a cigarette. Tilting his head backward as if he were sunning himself, he peered toward the top of the wall but with his eyes fixed on the stanchion supporting the floodlight that bathed the area throughout the night.

Having never been so close, he had not noticed a feature that now held him transfixed. The lamp's electrical line ran straight down the wall, plunged behind the shrubs, turned in a 45-degree angle and then stretched at a height of four feet above the ground to a transformer box on the wall of the hospital.

Finding Gray among the milling prisoners, he whispered, "I have three more items for you to get for us, Johnny. It should be a piece of cake for a hospital orderly."

"Name 'em, Chappy, and you got it," Gray said.

"A small, sharp knife, tied-together sheets that will reach from the second-floor hospital window to the ground . . . and a pair of rubber gloves."

The next day Gray reported, "I've got those items you asked for. They're stashed with the rest of the stuff—ladder, hacksaw blade and drill. Now what?"

"I have a feeling my health is about to take a turn for the worse. I think you'll be seeing me in the hospital tomorrow."

Chapman rolled from bed before dawn. Taking a bar of soap from a shelf above the cell's sink, he bit off one corner, chewed and swallowed. Dressed, he sat on the cot, took a deep breath and screamed as if he were in severe pain. By the time a guard looked into his cell, he was clutching his belly. Tumbling to the floor, he vomited. "It's my gut," he cried. "It's killing me. You've got to get me to the hospital."

Cursorily examined, he was diagnosed as suffering grippe. "This man will be confined for at least a week," the doctor informed the guard. "If he goes back to the population now the entire prison will come down with it."

Genuinely ill, Chapman spent most of the day retching, but by dusk when Gray delivered a supper of chicken consume and bread a slight fever had subsided and the vomiting had stopped.

"Is everything ready?" Chapman asked.

"The stuff's in a closet down the hall, near the window."

"How many bars in it?"

"Just two."

"You've got the sheets?"

"Yes. Plenty of 'em, all tied together."

"The rubber gloves?"

"Yep."

"Be ready to go at four o'clock," Chapman said. Unable to resist a joke, he added, "If I'm asleep, be sure to wake me."

Throughout the night, aware of the distant guttural coughs

of men in the tuberculosis ward in a separate wing of the hospital and the murmurings, snores, and creaking of beds as other patients turned in their sleep, he considered the escape plan again and again, looking for anything that could, and probably would, go wrong.

This was, after all, not a post office on New York's Eighth Avenue where the men who would come looking for him did not have standing orders to shoot to kill. This was the United States Penitentiary in Atlanta, complete with machine guns and bloodhounds and men who not only knew how to employ them but would not hesitate to do so.

At four o'clock on the dot John Gray pushed open the door of the ward.

Moments later they stood at the barred window. Opening it, Chapman whispered, "Hacksaw."

To minimize the rasping bite of the blade into a steel bar that was not as thick as expected he cut slowly while Gray worked just as silently with the drill, boring into the window frame to loosen the top of the bar.

"Hold onto it," Chapman said. "Don't let it fall outside. We are going to need it." As the bar came out, he said, "Okay, now tie the sheets to the other bar."

With the same agility with which he leapt onto the running board of Frank Haveranck's mail truck and out a third-floor window above a Manhattan street, Chapman scrambled down the ladder of sheets, clutching the severed window bar. As he landed, Gray followed with the cord-and-steel-rod ladder that Anderson had provided and, a flourish of yellow hanging from a hip pocket, a pair of rubber gloves.

Chapman quickly donned them. Grasping the steel bar, he whispered, "Where's the blade?"

From a pocket Gray produced a jackknife.

Taking it, Chapman edged toward the electrical trans-former box. Holding the wire that led from it to the floodlight with one hand, he cut shallowly into its black insulation. Gently slicing and peeling it back, he revealed copper wiring. Pocketing the knife, needed for digging up the guns, if they could be found, he lifted the steel bar and raised it above his head. "Stand back, Frank," he said breathlessly. "And cross your fingers."

As the bar slammed upon the bared wires, sparks flew in a brilliant flash, smoke puffed and a bang split the night as if a gun had been fired, aimed at the floodlight.

The entire prison went dark.

Crouching, Chapman and Gray scampered to the foot of the daunting granite wall rising like a sheer cliff. "The ladder," Chapman barked. "Quick!"

Grasping a metal hook that formed the top of Dutch Anderson's ingenius rope-and-steel stairway, Gray drifted back from the wall, planted his feet and heaved. Trailing the ladder, the hook snared the railing of a walkway with a satisfying clink of metal against metal.

Within seconds Chapman and Gray stood atop the wall.

Though only a few feet from a guardhouse, they pulled up the ladder unnoticed, unfurled it against the outer wall, descended it and touched the ground running.

▨

CHAPTER TWELVE

Marching through Georgia

BECAUSE HIS SHIFT at the South River shops of the Southern Railway began at seven in the morning, W. H. Edwards sat down to breakfast with his wife and six-year-old son at six o'clock. In his ten years as maintenance shop foreman, he had earned enough to buy a cozy little house in Lakewood Heights not far from Lakewood Park. The largest municipal amusement park in Atlanta covered an area of 366 wooded acres. The land had once been a reservoir and waterworks, but in 1895 it had been acquired by the Lakewood Park Company. Since 1915 the annual Southeastern Fair had been held there in several large stucco buildings, under the sponsorship of the Atlanta Chamber of Commerce.

Also near the Edwards' home on tree-lined Lakewood Avenue stood the federal penitentiary. Though Edwards had been anxious at first about its proximity, he had been assured by the real estate agent that the prison was a good neighbor. There was little likelihood that any of its inmates would escape, but, if so, he would be quickly apprehended. Alarm bells would sound and search teams would deploy with blood-hounds.

Indeed, in all the time Edwards had lived on Lakewood Avenue, no one had escaped, although the prison staged regular escape drills, forewarning residents of the dates and times. Consequently, on the morning of March 27, 1923, when Edwards heard sirens wailing without warning, he knew it could not be a drill. Observing the concern on his wife's face, he sought to reassure her. "Something must have gone haywire with their system down there. It's probably a short circuit," he said, resuming his meal.

Finished with his bacon and eggs, he heeded his wife's plea that he put on his jacket, picked up the brown paper bag containing his lunch, kissed her and his son, and left for work by the back door. Approaching the corner of the front porch, he noticed two men in blue denim bib overalls.

Appropriated by Chapman and Gray from a clothesline a block away, the loosely fitting dungarees covered their trousers but did not conceal their gray shirts. Chapman was sure that Edwards recognized the shirts as prison uniform. "One peep out of you, Mister, and you're dead on the spot," he said, brandishing a small silver-toned automatic pistol, hidden years ago with a U.S. Army Colt .45.

"You'll get no trouble from me, fellas," Edwards answered, raising his hands.

"Nobody's going to be hurt," Chapman said quietly. "I see you've got your lunch bag. On your way to work, eh? Since you're obviously a decent hard-working guy, I'll give you one thousand bucks if we can hide out in your house for awhile."

"I can't be mixed up in a business of that kind," Edwards said. "I have a wife and a kid to think about."

"Then I'm afraid you'll have to come with us."

At that moment Mrs. Edwards appeared at the front door. "It's all right, honey," Edwards shouted. "Go back inside."

A neighbor, John Jordan, came out onto his porch. "Anything wrong, Edwards?" he called.

Chapman shoved the gun into Edwards' ribs. "If you speak to that man," Chapman growled, "or make any kind of trouble for us, we'll blow your brains out. Do you own an automobile?"

"No. I go to work by trolley."

"Then you're walking with us to the nearest stop. How far is it?"

"At the next corner."

As a car approached, Chapman said, "I doubt if the motorman will have change for a grand note, so you'll have to give us the fare. Hand over whatever money you've got on you."

As the trolley stopped, Edwards withdrew a dollar bill.

"Get on," Chapman said. "No heroics. Remember, I'll have this gun pointed at you."

"Good morning, Mr. Edwards," said the motorman as Chapman handed him the dollar.

Wordlessly, Edwards moved to the rear of the car, empty save for a man whom he did not recognize as a regular rider at that early hour. Uniformed as a taxi driver, the stranger paid no attention to the three men who passed him to take seats at the back of the car as it lumbered to the next stop, McDonough Street.

"This is where you get out," Chapman whispered to Edwards. "If you're smart you won't call the police. Remember, we know where you live. Leave your coat."

As the trolley pulled away, Edwards broke into a run, his destination the house of a friend, Bob Wells, who was an Atlanta police officer. Wells, in turn, telephoned Madison County police officer Alfred Hornsby. Speeding to the Wells house in a Lincoln sedan, Hornsby picked up both men and raced to catch up with the trolley. Forcing it to halt, they discovered that Edwards' kidnappers were not aboard.

"They got off two stops back," the motorman reported. "Them and the fellow in the cab driver's uniform. One's wearing overalls and the other a black jacket."

"It's mine," grumbled Edwards. "I don't suppose I'll ever get it back. What a lousy day this turned out to be."

For C.W. Nychols, the day's work of driving his yellow taxi appeared to be getting off to a promising start, as two passengers on the trolley asked him if he could drive them to Decatur. But when they arrived, the men told him to proceed to Lawrenceville, paying him in advance with a fifty-dollar bill.

"We've changed our mind," Chapman said when they arrived at Lawrenceville. "How about taking us to Athens? We'll pay you another twenty bucks."

Increasingly curious about his passengers, Nychols kept an eye on them in his rearview mirror.

Six miles short of the Athens city line, he observed what appeared to be the grip of a pistol protruding from the pocket of the younger man's coat.

Sensing a sudden rigidity in the driver's formerly pleasant and relaxed demeanor, Chapman blurted, "This is far enough. We'll be getting out here, driver."

The seat of Clarke County, surrounded by cotton country, the City of Athens was home to the University of Georgia, the state's oldest institution of higher learning. It boasted a fine library, but books were far from Chapman's mind as Nychols sped away.

"Odds are," he said to his companion, "that guy is going straight to the police."

"So where do we go from here?" Gray asked, looking around. "It seems to me we're stuck in the middle of nowhere."

Through the glare of the midmorning sun, Chapman observed a column of white smoke rising against the pale blue sky above the city. "They've got manufacturing plants in that town," he said.

"So what?"

"I don't suppose you've ever heard of a poetess by the name of Edna St. Vincent Millay, have you, Frank?"

"Books are your department, Chappy."

Chapman put an arm around Gray's shoulder. "Then listen to Miss Millay and learn, my friend:

> My heart is warm with the friends I make,
> And better friends I'll not be knowing;
> Yet there isn't a train I wouldn't take,
> No matter where it's going."

Gray's eyes went wide. "Ah, I get it," he said, grinning. "We hop a train!"

On a siding on Athens' outskirts, they found a line of cars packed with cotton bales and flatbeds piled with Georgia Pine lumber coupled to a northbound locomotive of the Seaboard Air Lines railway. Pulling open the doors of the boxcars, they found one with sufficient room to accommodate them comfortably. Presently, with a toot of the engine's whistle, the clang of couplers, and a shudder of their car, they relaxed for the first time since four o'clock that morning.

Against all odds, through a combination of good planning, patience, the assistance of selfless others, luck, and, most important of all, the guidance of Dutch Anderson, they had escaped the toughest prison in the country. With caution and a little more luck, Chapman believed, he would never be found. But should brains and luck fail him, he would not permit himself to be taken back to prison.

As the train picked up speed, he regretted that Dutch was not at his side. Yet might it not turn out, he wondered, that in time Dutch, too, would find a way to freedom? Sometime and somehow, he felt, he would be in touch with Dutch again to let him know that his partner in Enterprises Unlimited was eager to resume business—bigger and better than ever.

John Gray's voice intruded into his thoughts. "Whatcha thinkin' about, Chappy?"

"The future."

"Any idea where you'll be going? Back to New York?"

"Hell, no. Every flatfoot in uniform and every dick in the detective squad's going to be carrying my picture in his pocket. I'm going to have to lie low. There's a man I know in Indiana. I plan to drop in on him. What about you?"

Before Gray could answer, the train lurched to a stop.

"That was a short ride," Gray joked.

"Quiet," Chapman said, pressing an ear against the side of the car. "Somebody's coming."

The door slid open.

"Okay, you bums," boomed the voice of conductor Harvey Lee. "Unless you have a Seaboard ticket," "get your asses out of there and off railroad property. I ain't kidding. I got a gun, and the law says I can use it against trespassers. So move it fast, boys."

Gray drew his pistol.

"Don't be stupid," Chapman said, pushing the Colt aside. "He's just a railroad dick. If we shoot him all the cops in the State of Georgia will know it was us . . . and where we are."

Raising his hands, he stood in the doorway.

"We're going," he said, bounding from the car.

"Mind telling us where we are?" Gray asked as he came out.

"A little ways north of Athens," said the railwayman, his hand resting on the butt of his holstered pistol. "About halfway between Hull and Colbert. The road to either one is just over there. Plant your feet on it and keep 'em off Seaboard property."

Gentleman Gerald

114

As the railwayman climbed onto the caboose and the freight resumed its journey, Chapman stepped onto the two-lane blacktop and turned north. After barely four miles, he heard the motor of an automobile approaching rapidly from behind. He slipped his right hand into the bib of the overalls. "I don't like the smell of this," he said, gripping his pistol. "Get ready for trouble, Johnny."

The driver of the black car, County Policeman David Butler, had listened to Harvey Lee's account of putting two men off his train. Neither of them looked at all like the usual hoboes. They were dressed funny, too, Lee said. One had on a black winter jacket, the other, a gray shirt. Both wore bib overalls. And each of them was wearing the same kind of black shoes. They weren't Southerners, either, but Yankees, from the way they talked.

Having just received a telephone call from the police in Athens, Butler wondered if these men might be the escapees from Atlanta. If so, the Athens police warned, they were to be considered armed and dangerous. If these men were the convicts, Butler thought as he ran for his car, they had traveled a long way in a few hours.

Slowing the car, he drew up beside the two men. If they were not the escapees described by the Athens police, they sure were their spitting image. Drawing his pistol, but holding it in his lap, he shouted through the window, "Hey, you two, just stay where you are. I want to have a word with you."

Drawing their guns and firing simultaneously, Chapman and Gray riddled the car, spun round, and dashed for the woods as Butler, unhurt, emptied his revolver toward their backs with no effect. Out of ammunition, Butler turned and sped away to enlist assistance.

The round trip consumed fifteen minutes, but when Butler got out of his car at the site of the brief gunbattle, he had the company of Sheriff W. H. Hall and County Policeman P. L.

McCaneff. Minutes behind them, recruited by the sheriff through the town of Colbert's telephone operator, was a posse of townspeople carrying rifles, shotguns, and revolvers, some of them dating back to the Civil War.

Assessing the situation, Sheriff Hall ordered the men into the woods. "Don't take any chances," he declared gravely. "If you see the sons of bitches, shoot to kill."

Emerging from the woods to face a field of cotton, Hall signaled the posse to form a line, much as their ancestors had done in what these hardy men called "the War Between the States." With guns cocked and ready, they advanced slowly, alert for any sound, any movement.

"Remember men, they shot at one of my men," Hall shouted, "so "shoot to kill!"

Hunkered down amid the cotton, Chapman heard him clearly.

He had no idea where Gray was, nor did he care. It was each man for himself now. Good luck to him.

Although the men of the posse did their best to be quiet as they advanced across the field, it proved impossible. Dry earth crunched beneath their boots. Waist-high cotton swished with the passage of their bodies. Guns shifting in their grasp rattled and clinked. Soon, it seemed, he could hear their breathing, shallow and tense. Inevitably, one of them would appear before him, looming above, discovering his hiding place.

Then what? Would the posseman shoot to kill? Or ignore the sheriff and try to reap a different kind of glory by capturing him?

Bolting up, Chapman screamed, "Never!"

Instantly, bullets slammed into him. One in the right leg. One in the right side of his hip. A third in the gut, left side, passing through and out the back.

Others shot at him, but by then he had collapsed, falling backward into the cotton.

Bleeding profusely.

Unconscious.

But alive.

CHAPTER THIRTEEN

⊠⊠

The Impatient Patient

CHAPMAN WOKE UP to the worst pain he had ever felt, opening his eyes upon a woman's face.

"What's your name, sweetheart?" he asked, groggily.

"Shirley."

"Shirley what?"

"Shirley Simpson. I'm your night nurse."

"When I saw you in that white outfit, Shirley, I thought you were an angel and I was dead and in Heaven. Since I'm not, would you kindly tell me where I am?"

"You are in a hospital in Athens, Georgia."

"Am I going to live?"

"For a while we thought you wouldn't," she said, adjusting the pillow behind his head. "But I haven't lost a patient yet, and I don't plan to start with you."

"How long have I been out?"

"Two days."

His eyes drifted to a window without bars.

"There was a man with me," he said, turning to the nurse.

"Do you know what happened to him?"

"He's fine. He was taken back to prison."

"Too bad. John was a good guy."

"The two of you caused quite a sensation in town."

"I'll bet."

"The Atlanta newspapers were full of it. And there've been lots of calls from all over the country, reporters asking about you and wanting to talk to you. You must be the most famous man in the United States by now."

"Well, you shouldn't believe all you read in the papers."

"One of them called you an escape artist. It said you broke out of a jail in New York City once."

"See? That proves my point about not trusting the papers. It wasn't a jail. It was a post office."

He looked again at the window. "What floor am I on?"

"The second. There are only two."

"I'm not as bad a man as you may think," he said, looking her in the eyes. Blue ones, he noted. A nice face; not as pretty as Betty's, though. "You look a lot like my wife," he said. "Her name's Betty." Tears welled. "She must be awfully worried. Did she call about me?"

"Not that I know of."

"I guess I can't blame her, can I? I've made a pretty bad mess of things. She probably doesn't want to have anything more to do with me. I suppose I'll never see her again." Now tears glinted in the nurse's eyes. "Nor my kids, either, most likely."

"You're a father?"

"A boy, five years old, and a girl of three. What about you? Are you married?"

"No I'm not."

"Excuse me, but I find that hard to believe. It seems to me the men would be wooing you all the time. I know that if I were a single guy I would."

Blushing, she turned away. "You must be mighty hungry. Shall I bring you a tray?"

"That would be lovely, Shirley. Thanks."

As she opened the door and stepped into the hallway, he saw a policeman tilted back in a chair against the opposite wall.

"How's the guy inside?" the cop asked. "Is he awake yet? We'd like to get him the hell out of here."

"Mr. Chapman's condition is far too serious for him to be moved," she said, curtly. "I expect he'll be with us for several more days, at least."

When she returned with a meal of beef broth and toast, she found Chapman propped up on his pillows. "Is that true, what you said to that cop?" he asked. "About me having to stay here for a few more days?"

"Oh yes. I can't imagine you leaving that bed for quite some time. You suffered a very serious abdominal wound. We were afraid a bullet had damaged your liver. Lucky for you it didn't."

"Some luck," he said, sipping the broth. "I think I'd rather be dead than go back to that hell hole. Excuse my language! But a nice lady like you can't imagine what it's like. Believe me, this soup is a full-course dinner compared to the swill they feed the men in that place. There's no counting how many times I went to sleep at night trying to remember the taste of beefsteak." He winked and gently touched her hand. "What are the chances that I could have a juicy T-bone at least once before they drag me back to the pen?"

"You're much too weak for solid food," she said, "but when you're improved, in a couple of days, I'll see what I can do."

"Look, Shirley, do you think you could do me a favor? I've got an uncle who's probably read all about me in the newspapers. He's my mother's brother. He and I have always been close. In fact, he became both a mother and a father to me after my parents were killed in a train wreck when I was a little kid. He's my only relative, except for Betty and the kids, and quite elderly. I'd like to write to him and let him know that I'm okay."

"Oh, I don't think they'd allow you to write anybody."

"They?"

"The sheriff's men."

"Yeah, they're probably afraid that I'll send word to my *gang* to come and get me out of here. Utter nonsense, of course! I have no gang. The truth is, I never committed any crimes. I was framed. Railroaded! That's why I tried to escape up in New York. I thought if I could get away I could find the guy who framed me and turn him over to the police. That's also why, when the man I was with told me he was breaking out of prison and wanted me to go with him, I went along. It probably sounds crazy, but I still believed that if I could find that fellow who framed me, I could prove my innocence. How could I know that Frank would take it into his head to shoot it out with the police? Now, of course, I'll never get a chance to see my uncle before he . . . passes away. That's why I'd like to write him. You know, to tell him that I'm innocent and that I'm sorry about all the trouble I caused for him."

"I'm sure if you told the authorities who it is you want to write to that they'd give you permission."

"Maybe you're right, but I can't do that. I don't want them reading anything so personal. They'd probably look on it as a big joke. Or, worse, they might get it into their heads that my uncle is part of my *gang*."

"They wouldn't!"

"Look, forget the whole idea. It was wrong of me to ask you. I shouldn't be putting you on the spot."

"It's outrageous that somebody would actually read someone's letter. Why, the mail is, is—private. Sacred!"

"I agree, but what can you do? So forget I ever asked you.

And thanks for the soup and the bread. It hit the spot!"

Taking the tray, she said, "Is there anything I can bring you? Magazines? Books?"

"Books! Yes, I'd love to have a good book to read. And do you think you could find a Bible for me? Ever since I was a kid living with my uncle, I've read from Holy Scripture every day."

Tears trickled down her cheek. "I'll bring my own from home, and tomorrow I'll go to the library and get you some books."

"No novels, please. I prefer history."

The next evening she brought a Bible, a thick biography of General Robert E. Lee, a Waterman fountain pen, three sheets of plain white stationery, and an envelope.

"I couldn't get to sleep last night, worrying about your uncle," she said. "Write to him tonight and I'll mail it in the morning."

He began a letter immediately.

Two days later a mailman deposited it in the letter box of Harry Spickermon at 123 Mulberry Street, Muncie, Indiana.

Within an hour, in the company of Charles Wolfe, an all-around scoundrel known as "One Arm" because his right hand had been mangled in a farm-machinery accident and replaced with a steel hook, the doctor was behind the steering wheel. His Indiana-built Auburn phaeton sped toward the red-clay heart of Dixie.

CHAPTER FOURTEEN

Heigh Ho, the Derry Oh

THROUGH A TORRENT OF TEARS, Shirley Simpson explained how it happened that Gerald Chapman had vanished while under her care.

"I thought he would die in a few days. I couldn't help looking at him, he was so pitiful. One day he told me he was a Yale graduate. Then he began to cry, and afterward he asked me for something to read. He wanted the Bible, and I wondered if he was guilty. Every morning he would cry, and it got on my nerves, so I asked him please to quit, but he said that his wife and children were mistreated because he was in prison. Then one day he asked me would I mail a letter for him? Well, I did. Later someone called me on the telephone and wanted to see me. He said that he was in Athens to get Chapman out of the hospital. I wanted to call the police, but they scared me, and that's all I know. Then he escaped."

He did it through the window, grimacing with pain all the way to the ground on a ladder of bed sheets, in the early hours of April 4, 1923. He descended into the caring arms of Dr.

Spickermon, as One Arm Wolfe stood lookout.

Moments later, wrapped in a blanket and lying across the backseat of the Auburn, Chapman drifted to sleep. When he awoke a few hours later, a welcome and healing sun shone upon Blue Ridge Lake, hard by the Georgia-Tennessee line. Sitting up, he patted Spickermon on the back. "I knew if anybody could get me out of that dump it would be you, Doc," he said. "I'm grateful, and one day I'll make it up to you."

Turning to face Chapman, Spickermon saw him wincing with pain. "I gave you a dose of morphine," he said. "Do you want One Arm to pull over so I can give you another? I don't believe you have met Charlie Wolfe, who despite his misfortune is one of the best wheel men there is."

"I'm fine, Doc. Just keep this machine on the road, One Arm. I want to put as many miles behind me as fast as you can. Where are we, by the way?"

"Passing into Tennessee," One Arm replied.

"We'll be in Muncie tomorrow," said Spickermon. "Then I'll take a proper look at you. Later on, I'll introduce you to some discreet friends who have a farm up near Eaton, where you'll be welcome to stay until you're completely healed."

"You're a wonder, Doc. I'm glad Dutch brought us together."

"Too bad he didn't make the break with you."

"I regret it, too. I couldn't have pulled it off without his help, believe me."

"The way you broke out of Atlanta was pure genius," Spickermon said. "It was in all the newspapers along with stories about your life, some of 'em pretty wild. I doubt if there's anybody in the country who's more famous right now than you. They all wrote that you were the mastermind of that big mail robbery, and how you got away right under the noses of the guards. One of the big shots in Atlanta said the rope ladder you used was the finest specimen of its kind that he'd ever seen. Another article called you the Rudolf Valentino of Crime."

Chapman grunted, half in laughter, half in pain. Lying down again, he muttered, "Maybe I should start keeping a scrapbook."

The next day, at nightfall, the Auburn rolled into Muncie. In the four years since Chapman had first arrived in the city (1919), it had been the focus of a sociological study by Robert S. Lynd and his wife, Helen Merrill Lynd. Hoping to show how accelerated industrialization changed people's values and priorities, they took up residence in Muncie for the project. It was an ideal place in which a significant sample of citizens could be interviewed, and which did not have a dominant ethnic group, or a domineering "first family" (The Ball brothers and their kin notwithstanding). Having created a basis for comparison, the Lynds planned to return in several years to see what changes had occurred. Their findings would be published in 1929 as a best-selling book, *Middletown,* followed by a Depression-years' revisit and a second report entitled *Middletown in Transition.* They found that Muncie, like most American towns and cities, underwent a dramatic transformation from an agriculturally rooted economy to urban-based manufacturing, and that the nation's prewar Christian morality had been affected by a social and cultural revolution as profound as that which Gene Fowler discovered on postwar Broadway.

One advance in the lifestyle of Muncie residents since 1919 was the introduction of a bookmobile, extending the services of the public library to those for whom travel to the library itself was difficult or impossible. For a book-hungry, convalescent Gerald Chapman, confined to a second-floor bedroom in Spickermon's house, the service was a welcome amenity. One Arm checked out the books for him.

To improve his strength and stamina, Chapman borrowed money from Spickermon and enlisted One Arm to drive him to Indianapolis. There he bought a set of golf clubs and appropriate togs so that he could take advantage of Muncie's fine public course and the lessons offered by the clubhouse manager.

Employing One Arm again, he stole a car, complete with registration papers in the name of Waldo W. Miller.

Aware that his photograph had been featured in press coverage of his escapes from Warden Wyche's penitentiary and Sheriff W. H. Hall's watchdogs at Nurse Simpson's hospital, Chapman altered his appearance by growing a bristly mustache, then sent One Arm to the Woolworth five-and-ten-cent store to buy a pair of all-purpose eyeglasses with tortoise-shell frames. He knew that the elegant clothing that had been his hallmark as the Count of Gramercy Park wouldn't do when he left Mulberry Street for a place in the country, he resigned himself to workshirts, dungarees, and "clodhopper" boots. After three weeks Spickermon pronounced him fit and took him to the farm of Ben and Mary Hance. South of the town of Eaton, and close to the Mississinewa River, the hideout seemed ideal.

Amiable and unquestioning, the Hances might have deserved a paragraph, or at least a footnote, in the Lynds' report. Their reception of Chapman showed an indifference to his notorious history and dubious future that portended public mythologizing of such Midwestern desperadoes as Bonnie and Clyde, "Baby Face" Nelson, John Dillinger, and others a decade later.

Indiana-born Dillinger would also have a Muncie connection, robbing the Bide-a-Wee roadhouse on July 10, 1933, and, a week later, the Commercial Bank in nearby Daleville, which put the Muncie Police Department on full alert. After waiting for an hour in a car across from the bank until they were certain that twenty-two-year-old teller Margaret Good was on duty alone, Dillinger and his associate, Harry Copeland, marched in, guns drawn. "This is a stickup, honey," Dillinger announced as he jumped the railing. Good handed over $3,500. The leap would launch Dillinger into folklore, as Chapman's escapes had done for him a decade earlier.

Although it is likely that the Hances knew the true name of the man delivered to their doorstep, Chapman appropriated the name Waldo W. Miller, but asked to be called Tom. Writing to Betty Bales at her clandestine address in Providence, Rhode Island, he used the name Miller. He signed the letters with a bold "W" at the bottom of the page. To assure Chapman that her replies were genuine she signed them with a name known only to Chapman and Dutch Anderson: "Betty Beeswax."

An igratiating guest, Chapman soon volunteered to help Hance with light chores, feeding chickens and gathering eggs, learning to milk a cow, carrying pails of well water, and tending the pair of plow horses. "You know, Ben," he declared one day as they worked side by side, "the only thing I ever knew about farms and farming was the nursery rhyme 'Heigh ho, the derry oh, the farmer's in the dell.' My mother used to recite it when I was a tyke. I never even knew what a dell was! But I know now that farming is damn hard work." To help Mary Hance, as well, Chapman frequently washed the dishes, hung out and brought in the washing, and swept floors. Evenings, in the glow of oil lamps, he read books, sometimes doing so aloud if Mary asked him to.

On Sunday afternoons he went fishing with Ben in the muddy meander of the Mississinewa, or target shooting with Hance's shotguns on the farm.

Although these activities proved quaintly diverting, as Chapman approached full recovery, he felt a growing restlessness and a need for the old excitements.

Borrowing a gun from Spickermon, he drove into Eaton and robbed its two banks. A week later he broke into Stillman's Department Store in Muncie and burglarized its safe. Ranging across Indiana, into Ohio, and down to Kentucky, he hit banks, post offices, and other rewarding-looking targets.

Then, nothing less than a miracle occurred.

Out of the blue, Dutch Anderson appeared at the Hance farm.

Hardly the dashing, daring, and debonair figure that the nation's newspapers had discovered and relished in Gerald Chapman, Dutch carried out his escape with scant attention from the papers, except in Atlanta and New York. Yet it had been a spectacular achievement—a tunnel under the wall, months in the digging. Anderson delighted in describing it all to his astonished partner, whose deep-set eyes glowed at the idea of renewing Enterprises Unlimited.

"But to hell with the past," Anderson said. "It's the future that matters. I've been thinking about it, Chappy, and there's a hell of an easier way to earn a living than pulling stickups, with all the dangers they involve."

He paused, his eyes alight with excitement.

"What I have in mind is—counterfeiting. But not the simple paper-doctoring that we did in New York. I'm talking about currency. Phony greenbacks. Of course, this will take a lot of planning and work to set up. I always had a knack for the art of forgery, but I've learned a good deal more about it from from our pal John Gray and a few other residents of our recent domicile. What do you say? Are you in?"

Chapman paced the room excitedly. "Hell, yes, I'm in, all the way."

"I knew you would be, Chappy," Anderson said, beaming with pleasure.

"The only problem is," Chapman said, "I don't know a

thing about counterfeiting! That's always been your specialty. What can I possibly contribute?"

"You've always been an excellent student," Anderson replied. "Learn! Get yourself some books and read up on the subject. Find out all you can. And if there's something that's not in the books, I'll tutor you. It will be like the old days in prison!"

Rising to the challenge, Gerald Chapman proceeded to write a unique chapter in criminality by robbing libraries. Although he could have obtained books simply by acquiring a library card and checking them out, he set out deliberately to steal volumes containing the data he needed to become a counterfeiter. From libraries in Cincinnati, Lima, and Dayton he helped himself to tomes on paper and papermaking, inks, photography, engraving, printing presses, and counterfeiting itself.

"Getting set up to do this is going to cost," he pointed out to Anderson.

Dutch laughed. "Hey, Chappy, when did you and I ever have any problem accumulating funds? I've been giving the problem of capitalization a lot of thought. For starters, I've already been in touch with some of the bootleggers we worked with in Detroit. They've shifted their operations to running rum in Savannah and Baltimore. They're more than willing to let us have a twelfth-share that we can pay off out of our first proceeds. I checked out the operation on my way here, and it's more lucrative than bootlegging was in Detroit."

Smoking a cigar, sipping pre-Prohibition scotch, a gift from Spickermon, and basking in the unexpected presence of his mentor and cherished partner, Chapman listened intently while Dutch explained their new enterprise. "The stuff comes up from Bermuda, the Bahamas, and other islands on schooners. One of them can hold thousands of cases. They wait outside the three-mile limit. Then the stuff is put on smaller boats and brought in to be loaded onto trucks. Each of the trucks carries about a hundred and fifty cases. On their way north the trucks are followed by a car carrying armed guards. The entire transaction is done in cash. No checks, letters of credit, or any of the paperwork that we had to deal with in Detroit."

"It sounds like a sweet arrangement," Chapman said.

Indeed it was, and not only for American bootleggers. As Prohibition Commissioner Roy A. Haynes observed in *Prohibition Inside Out*, published the year that Anderson proposed joining the rum runners, plenty of money could be made by the liquor merchants of Bermuda and other islands within easy sailing distance of the United States. But the greatest windfall accrued to manufacturers of the liquor and their governments' tax collectors.

"The greatest possible measure of the traffic is written in the official records of Great Britain, France, Cuba and the other nations which are the only source of supply for smuggling traffic," Haynes complained. Pointing out that liquor importations were legal in the Bahamas, he noted that the Bahamian government collected a duty of $7.60 a case. "It is no wonder that the huge increase in liquor importations which began in 1921 is credited with having paid off long ago the outstanding indebtedness of the islands," he went on. "The law-defying American patrons of rum smugglers have made the colony a present of that sum; and piled up fortunes besides for men in the islands who have no scruples against this phase of the traffic."

However, Anderson told Chapman, there was a question as to how long this might continue. "The U.S. government is putting a lot of pressure on the governments of the islands to slap a hefty tax on liquor exports. If that happens it could mean that the price of the stuff will go so high that the profits will be eaten up. But for now, I think we can accumulate

Gerald Chapman at four stages of his criminal career. From left, the first was taken in 1907, when he was charged with jewel theft; the second is from 1912, when sentenced to ten years for a different theft; the third is from 1922, when Chapman was living the high life in Grammercy Park, where he lived under the pseudonym of G. Vincent Colwell; the last is from 1926, when Chapman waited on Death Row. (UPI/Bettmann Archives)

"Dutch" Anderson, Chapman's mentor and partner, in his various disguises.
(UPI/ Bettmann Archives)

During the arraignment for the 1922 mail truck robbery.
From left (seated): Gerald Chapman, Charlie Loerber,
and George "Dutch" Anderson. (UPI/Bettmann Archives)

Gerald Chapman in Muncie, Indiana, after his arrest
in 1935. (UPI/Bettmann Archives)

Chapman with his lawyers, 1925. Chief counsel
Frederick H. Groell is on his left, C. W. Murphy on
the right. (UPI/Bettmann Archives)

Gerald Chapman in his cell during his final trial in
Hartford, Connecticut. (UPI/Bettmann Archives)

Gerald Chapman in his cell during his final trial in Hartford, Connecticut. (UPI/Bettmann Archives)

Gerald Chapman in his cell during his final trial in
Hartford, Connecticut. (UPI/Bettmann Archives)

sufficient cash to more than finance our counterfeiting venture. We go into the rum-running business just long enough to make a killing and then move on to *greener* pastures, pun intended!"

The atmosphere reminded Chapman of romantic novels about high-seas brigands of a bygone century. On nightly dashes to sea, he enjoyed the swaggering freebooters who plied the ocean from exotic Caribbean ports to rendezvous in the dead of night, knowing that at any moment the long arm of the Prohibition Unit might speed out to capture what Commissioner Haynes called a "pack of sea vermin preying on the self-respect and decency of a people."

Chapman found the rum fleet to be a curious flotilla. Among the ships on which he stood guard while burly men unloaded cases of liquor was a former Spanish cruiser, once the pride of haughty Dons. Another turned out to be the former yacht of a captain of American industry. But most were blunt-nosed and weather-beaten old fishing schooners from the Grand Bank.

As Commissioner Haynes reported, it was not all risk and laborious work. "There are also many well-authenticated tales of wild parties out aboard the hovering rum ships, of nights of vivid doings on those rolling decks and of visitors from shore, including women, carried out by the mosquito fleet in attendance on the floating storehouses of liquor."

Relishing all of it, Chapman and Anderson thrived, paying off the cost of their twelfth-shares in the first month, living in the high style to which they had become accustomed in Gramercy Park, and setting aside the rest of their earnings to finance of Dutch's counterfeiting scheme. But in March the lucrative smuggling business, in Chapman's words, "blew up." As the rum runners had feared, pressures brought to bear on the governments of the islands resulted in dramatic rises in the cost of doing business. Taxes imposed on the liquor being shipped made it unprofitable to employ the small ships that made the run to southern destinations. Larger ships began transporting bigger cargoes to the ports of New York and northern New Jersey.

Because of the notoriety conferred upon him by the press, and proudly aware that he ranked at the top of the New York Police Department's and the federal government's rosters of wanted men, Chapman proposed establishing their counterfeiting headquarters in New England, perhaps Boston.

With a mischievous look, Dutch said, "I know why you want to go there. It's because Beantown is close to Providence, Rhode Island. You'll be near Betty!"

Highwaymen

FIRST THERE WAS A DEBT to be paid to Dr. Spickermon. In assisting Chapman to escape from the hospital and caring for him as physician and friend, he had assumed great risks and paid out money. Although the funds had been reimbursed out of Chapman's forays into banks and other establishments, Chapman wished to reward the doctor further by sharing the money he had made in bootlegging. And he wanted to do something for Ben and Mary Hance. Accordingly, he persuaded Anderson to accompany him on the long drive to Muncie.

Arriving on Tuesday, April Fool's Day, he treated Spickermon and One Arm to a lavish dinner at the Braun Hotel. The following afternoon he shopped at the department store he had burglarized only a few months earlier. Purchasing several shirts, overalls, and boots for Ben Hance and an assortment of everyday and Sunday dresses, shoes, and hats for Mary, he filled the trunk of the Cadillac that had clocked thousands of miles since he stole it in Indianapolis.

Standing at Chapman's side as he opened the trunk to unload the gifts, Hance could not miss seeing its other contents—two sawed-off shotguns, a rifle, an automatic pistol with silencer, an electric drill, a toolbox jammed with screwdrivers, chisels, a Stillson wrench, short and long crowbars, objects that might be employed to jimmy windows or doors and, couched in a thick blanket, a small wooden crate with EXPLOSIVES painted on all sides.

As was Hance's custom in dealing with Dr. Spickermon's associates, he asked no questions. Had he, it was unlikely that Chapman would have told him that the crate contained a carefully cradled vial of Dutch's favored material for opening other people's safes—nitroglycerine. Nor did Hance object when Chapman and Anderson unloaded the tools of their trade and stored them in the barn. Neither did he inquire as to the details when Chapman informed him that he and Anderson would be leaving the farm for an unspecified period, but would be back soon to collect their property.

Stopping in Muncie, they said good-bye to Spickermon and picked up "One Arm" Wolfe, hired to help out with the driving and any other purpose that might arise.

Their destination was Massachusetts. In reading the books on counterfeiting paper money, Chapman had learned that the firm that manufactured the paper for the greenbacks turned out by the United States Bureau of Printing and Engraving was located in the Bay State city of Dalton. Might it be possible to hijack or otherwise appropriate a supply of the specially made sheets of paper for their own print shop?

Situated in the Berkshire Mountains, five miles from Pittsfield, Dalton claimed a population of about six thousand and had been in the papermaking business for as long as anyone could remember. Quaint though it was, the little town offered none of the anonymity required. Staying in a hotel in the bigger community of Springfield, the partners scouted the

Crane paper mill in Chapman's Cadillac, followed paper-laden trucks and noted their routes. But after two days of observation, they left Dalton without learning which of the trucks hauled exactly the sort of paper they would need. They realized that they would have to cultivate someone who worked for Crane—a man who might prove to be just as penurious and larcenous as Jeremiah Savelli had been.

Determined to move to Massachusetts immediately, they set out for Ohio to retrieve their belongings from the Hance farm. Nearing Steubenville on Saturday evening, April 5, 1924, they had car trouble. With a cloud of steam gushing from the radiator, the Lincoln touring car sputtered, shuddered, and ground to a stop. Leaving Anderson and One Arm to guard the car and the contents of the trunk, Chapman hitchhiked into the city.

While anyone else faced with a broken-down car would have looked for a garage with a tow truck, Chapman sought a different resolution of his dilemma. He found it in the Stanton Motor Company, a Ford and Lincoln dealership owned by James H. Snyder. In its showroom stood two black Fords and a yellow Lincoln sedan.

Chapman encountered a young woman seated at a reception desk. "That Lincoln sedan is a beauty," he said as he strode toward the car. "May I have a look at the interior appointments?"

"We keep it locked," replied twenty-seven-year-old Catherine Bourne, the firm's bookkeeper. "We've found that when someone wishes to buy a three-thousand-dollar automobile they don't like to find the upholstery soiled. Most of the people who come in here are not as cleanly dressed as you."

As always, even when he had been standing guard on ships of the rum fleet, he was elegantly dressed, wearing a stiff black hat, black Chesterfield coat with satin lapels, a white silk muffler, and white gloves. The lights that reflected off the gleaming Lincoln also glinted from his monocle and the silver top of his ebony walking stick.

Never having seen his like in Steubenville, Bourne wondered if he were a millionaire.

"You get lots of farmers in muddy overalls, I expect," he said, smiling and stroking his mustache. "People with Lincoln tastes and Ford pocketbooks?"

Bourne chuckled. "If you're really interested in buying that car, sir, I have the keys."

"Just looking at the moment," he said, tipping his hat. "I may come by tomorrow. I live nearby." He smiled again. "This is a purchase I wouldn't dare make without first talking it over with the little woman at home. Are you open for business on Sundays?"

"Mr. Snyder, the owner, usually comes in after church," she said. "That would be around noon."

"It's a fine machine," Chapman said, kicking a tire. "If the wife likes it, Mr. Snyder may have a buyer."

Returning to the now-dark showroom at half past four in the morning, he had no difficulty in picking the lock of the front door. Searching the drawers of Bourne's desk, he found the keys to the Lincoln conveniently tagged. Seconds later, he had the wide side door of the showroom open. As he expected from such a fine vehicle, the Lincoln moved through it almost silently. The gas gauge, he noted, showed a full tank.

Abandoning the Cadillac, they proceeded westward for forty miles before Dutch expressed a need to urinate. As he did so, near the town of Hibbens, Chapman stepped out to stretch his legs. One Arm was asleep on the rear seat. The time was 7:15 A.M., and bus driver William D. Allison of Bergholz, Ohio, was following his usual route between Canton and Steubenville. Always ready to help stranded motorists, he stopped the bus. "Can I give you a hand or a lift to a garage?" he asked.

"There's no trouble," Chapman snapped. "Move on."

CHAPTER SIXTEEN

The Pushover

IN SPRINGFIELD, MASSACHUSETTS, in the summer of 1924, no family exceeded the Sheans in prominence. Charles T. Shean owned the Hotel Cooley and the larger Hotel Kimball. His wife managed them. Of his sons, Arthur owned the Springfield franchise of the Eastern Baseball Association, and Howard and Walter were in the family's thriving advertising agency, specializing in billboards. But it was Howard who ran the business, for thirty-nine-year-old Walter had turned out to be anything but a chip off his father's block. He had been incorrigible growing up, and at least one doctor said the boy suffered from "brainstorms." All his life he had caused his parents worry and heartache.

In 1921 he proved too much for his wife, as well. She divorced him after she learned that, in company with eight others, Walter had stormed into the People's Trust Company in Wyomissing, Pennsylvania, at high noon, producing guns and departing with $180,000 in securities. Eighteen thousand dollars' worth of these were discovered in Walter's possession sometime later, when he tried to use them as collateral for a bank loan in Springfield. Although he was indicted, he did not come to trial, thanks to sharp lawyering that cost his father $40,000.

The incident had cemented Walter Shean in the memories of the Springfield police. Presently, they heard inklings that Shean had abandoned bank robbery in favor of bootlegging, primarily as a go-between for those in Springfield with a thirst and individuals in Boston eager to quench it. Picking up Shean in the act, however, proved far more difficult than picking up the talk around town about Walt Shean's activities.

When Gerald Chapman heard his name for the first time in June 1924, he wondered if Shean might come in handy to himself and Dutch in other ways, bootlegging having been left behind, along with Dr. Spickermon, One Arm Wolfe, and the Hance farm hideout. In pursuit of Anderson's greener pastures, they had packed personal possessions and as many tools of their varied trades as the Lincoln could hold and returned to the Bay State, selecting Springfield, "the Metropolis of Western Massachusetts," as their base for further reconnoitering.

Conveniently situated about two-thirds of the way between Boston and the Crane company's paper mills in Dalton, Springfield appealed to them in several ways. In terms of their business, it offered an ideal spot from which to conduct a search for the remote house they needed to set up their counterfeiting operation. Long a bastion of culture and learning (it was the birthplace of Webster's Dictionary), the pleasant city provided attractions for men of their intellects and sensibilities that included educational institutions, a well-stocked public library, art museums, concerts, and theaters. And should Chapman wish to work on his golf game, there were several courses on which to tee up.

Springfield also provided a diverting nightlife—always a convenient means of discovering individuals to whom an illicit proposition could be made without worrying about the consequences.

Fascinated by what he was hearing about Shean, Chapman called the Hotel Cooley and asked to speak with him. "I've been referred to you by George Brown of Philadelphia," he explained. "He told me that you're the man to see in Springfield about placing a shipment of very high-quality Canadian Scotch. If that is so, I should like to meet you."

"I'd be happy to," Shean whispered. "Come to the hotel."

"Might I suggest that you come outside? My car is parked across the street. You will find a yellow Lincoln touring sedan in front of a furniture store. I'll be with an associate. Don't be alarmed. We are not the authorities."

Cautiously approaching the automobile, Shean noted two well-dressed men. "Are you the party who called me?" he asked.

"Miller is my name, sir," Chapman said, extending a hand. "My associate is Dr. Johnson. As I know you to be a busy man, I shall get down to business. We are passing through your fine city and wish to sell some liquor to big customers. It is in lots of two- or three-hundred cases. I understand that you may be in a position to help us. We'll pay a handsome commission, naturally."

"Something might be arranged," Shean said. "But it will take me a little time to make inquiries."

Chapman smiled. "You'll hear from us presently."

As Shean departed, Anderson said, "What Scotch?"

"That man may prove useful to us," Chapman said, starting the car. "He's obviously a pushover for any proposition that will bring him money. He is the embodiment of a nursery rhyme my mother used to recite to me:

The Pushover

139

There was a crooked man, and he went a crooked mile,
He found a crooked sixpence against a crooked stile;
He bought a crooked cat, which caught a crooked mouse,
And they all lived together in a little crooked house."

"Speaking of crooked houses," said Dutch, "need I remind you that we still haven't found the right one for us?"

They had scouted several, but Dutch had ruled them out, either as too small, dangerously close to others, or not up to his aesthetic standards. Between excursions to assess real estate, they motored northwest to Dalton to trail Crane Paper Company trucks and strike up casual, touristy conversations in a coffee shop frequented by the firm's employees. When not looking at houses and fishing for information, they ranged far and wide in Massachusetts and southward to Connecticut, always with a keen eye out for likely burglary targets, going as close to the dangers of New York City as New Haven. "Who knows?" Chapman asked wistfully. "If I'd had the right breaks when I was growing up, I might have been a student at Yale. Who can explain Fate?"

Anderson grunted. "Fate had nothing to do with it, Chappy. You chose to be a criminal. You're like me. You longed for the excitement."

On the way back to Massachusetts they passed through New Britain, Connecticut. Driving along Main Street, Chapman pointed to a department store. "Davidson and Leventhal," he said to Dutch. "Make a mental note. It looks prosperous."

Returning to Springfield, he wrote a long letter to Betty in which he asked her to write to him in care of the Cooley Hotel. When she did not reply promptly, he brooded.

"It's summertime," Dutch suggested to his downcast partner. "Perhaps she is away for the season, possibly in Europe. She is a rich woman now. She can afford to take time off."

There was no respite for Enterprises Unlimited. Astonished Springfield police noted an epidemic of safecrackings—six in two days, July 19 and 20—all blasted open with a charge of nitroglycerine. Another identical feature of the robberies, they noted, was the skillful means of breaking into the offices, the silence in which the robbers worked before setting off the blasts (no one could have pulled the robberies alone, the police decided), their speedy escape, and the absence of fingerprints.

"There's no question that these were experienced yeggs," declared the chief of police, "They're probably a gang that came up here from New York, did their work, and headed straight back."

Meanwhile, having heard nothing more from the two men in the Lincoln with liquor to sell, Walter Shean assumed that he would never see them again. But he was wrong. Chapman phoned at the end of July. "My associate, Dr. Johnson, and I would be pleased if you would join us for dinner this evening," he said. "We have reservations for three for seven o'clock at the Little River Inn. Are you familiar with it?"

"I've dined there often. I know the owner, Ed Buckley."

Chapman had discovered the inn early in his excursions to Dalton. Nine miles west of Springfield, the city of Westfield, Massachusetts, got its first tavern in 1672, opened by Captain Aaron Cook, hoping to capitalize on a tremendous increase in travelers following the opening of a road four years earlier. Formerly famed for whip manufacturing, the city had established itself as a center for making bicycles, boilers, machinery, and, like Dalton, thirty miles northwest, paper.

Remembering that the two men in the Lincoln had been dressed elegantly, Shean appeared at the inn suitably attired and with an apology for not having brought them the names of potential buyers for their liquor.

"Forget that," Chapman answered. "I've got other business in mind. There could be big money for everybody. If you think you'd be interested, and if what I'm planning develops, Dr. Johnson and I would be happy to have you come in with us."

Again, weeks passed before Shean heard from Chapman. Then it was not a phone call, but a letter, sent to the Cooley Hotel. It asked Shean to look out for and save any mail that arrived at the hotel addressed to Waldo Miller, the name by which Shean knew Chapman. The letter bore a Springfield postmark. Soon after Shean received it, Chapman phoned again, inviting Shean to dine with him once more at the Little River Inn.

When they finished the meal, Chapman opened a briefcase. "See what I've got in here?" he asked, pushing aside a sheaf of papers to reveal a pistol. "I show it to you so that you'll understand that we're serious."

Shean replied, "I never doubted it."

Closing the case, Chapman placed it on the floor. "If you'll recall, I promised you that I'd let you know what Dr. Johnson and I were planning." He paused, then whispered, "Counterfeiting." After another pause he asked, "Interested?"

Shean did not hesitate. "Hell, yes!"

Chapman handed Shean a cigar. "I like your attitude, Walter. We're going to get along fine, I'm sure. What do I want from you? Right now we need your assistance in buying a house. Frankly, Dr. Johnson and I have been looking everywhere and have found nothing around here that fits our special needs, if you get my drift."

"I think I can help you," Shean said. "I happen to know of a house for sale up in South Hadley. I spotted it a week ago when I was checking the condition of some of my firm's billboards. It's north of Holyoke, where Routes Nine and One Sixteen fork."

The property of the Reverend Arthur W. Bailey, pastor of

the Pawtucket Congregational Church, the house stood at the end of a long driveway and had windows facing in every direction. From the roof rose a lighthouse cupola, ideal for scanning the horizon. Presenting the delighted minister with $500 in cash as earnest money toward a purchase price of $15,000, Chapman agreed to meet him at the offices of the pastor's Holyoke lawyers, with a $5,000 down payment, to draw up a mortgage. At the meeting he identified himself to attorneys of Avery, Gaylor and Davenport as George Lawrence Shelburne and said his associate was Waldo Miller. "We would like to take possession of the house by the end of October," he noted. "Meanwhile, we will be reachable at the Hotel Cooley in Springfield, Room C31."

Having found a suitable base, at last, Chapman began making arrangements to bring to Springfield the property he had left at the Hance farm. His problem was storage, until they were ready to move into the house. He turned to Shean.

"That's no problem," Walter said. "I have a shed in back of my house. There's plenty of room for whatever you have in mind. I hardly ever use it myself."

Sent via American Express, the items bore labels addressed to Waldo Miller in care of Shean. Because the shipment arrived at the Springfield railroad depot while Chapman and Anderson were out of the city, Shean took it upon himself to claim them. Waiting for the heavy bags and boxes to be fetched by the clerk, he decided to while away the minutes by examining the clutter of notices posted on a bulletin board. Because one was larger than the rest, he read it first: WANTED FOR ARMED ROBBERY OF AMERICAN EXPRESS TRUCK AT NIAGARA FALLS, N.Y.

As his eyes drifted down to a photograph of the wanted man, he gasped in astonishment. The sloping forehead, the deep-set, piercing eyes, the high cheekbones—except that the man in the photograph was clean-shaven, the individual whom the poster identified as Gerald Chapman appeared to be the mysterious Waldo Miller.

In addition to the facial resemblance, everything about the two men matched: age, height, weight, haircut—even the part in the middle.

Reading fine print below the picture, Shean felt a surge of excitement: "Chapman, alias Bryce, alias Colwell, alias Miller, alias Chartres, alias Sherbourne, alias the Count, is also wanted for the 1921 robbery of the U.S. Mail in New York City and for escaping from the United States Penitentiary, Atlanta, Georgia."

Convinced that Chapman was Miller—there was the name among his aliases—and thrilled as never before, Shean realized that he was the only person in the world who knew Chapman's whereabouts. But also on his mind as he collected Chapman's goods was the fact that for some reason this desperado, this daring criminal mastermind, had selected *him* as an ally. The only question for him now was whether to reveal what he knew to Chapman.

By the time Shean reached the storage shed behind his house, he had decided that the answer had to be No. Here was a man with a price on his head, after all, and there was no telling what Chapman might do—possibly murder him. He would gladly become an accomplice in whatever Chapman proposed, but prudence dictated that he conceal what he knew. Meanwhile, he would wait. The next move, whatever it might be, belonged to Chapman.

On October 10 Chapman telephoned the Hotel Cooley, asked switchboard operator Ethel Fielding if Shean were at the hotel, and was put through to the office.

"Walter, are you free for dinner this evening?" he asked. "My pal Dr. Johnson is away on business and I'm feeling lonely. I have no business on my mind. Just a sociable evening of good food and conversation."

Regrettably, Shean answered, he was not available. "I've got a date with a childhood friend, Martha Wilgus. She's visiting from Atlantic City, and I promised to take her to dinner at the Red Tea Room in West Springfield. If you'd care to join us, we'd be delighted to have your company."

"Yes, I would like to join you," Chapman said gaily. "Shall I pick you up in my car?"

"That will be fine," Shean replied.

Mrs. Wilgus found Shean's friend charming. "You're English," she gushed. "I do love English accents!"

Escorting the trio to his best table, the manager of the Red Tea Room took careful note of Shean's well-dressed male companion and the fact that he spoke with an English accent. But to John Kelly, it did not sound quite authentic.

At the end of the pleasant evening, Chapman and Shean took Mrs. Wilgus home. As she left, Chapman turned abruptly to Shean. "I have something planned for the weekend," he said. "Dr. Johnson will still be away. I'd like very much to bring you in on what I've got planned. It will be an out-of-town trip."

"No problem," Shean exclaimed. "I'll clear the decks."

The Man in the Doorway

"YOUR MAGNIFICENT MOTORCAR is good as new, Mr. Miller," said Springfield garageman George Bedore as he handed the keys to Gerald Chapman on the morning of Saturday, October 11, 1924. Chapman had left the car at noon on Thursday.

"I'm sorry it took this long to do the work," Bedore said. "I hope you weren't inconvenienced."

"Not at all," Chapman said. "I had no need of it."

"She was way overdue for maintenance, and it took a little longer. But now the motor's tuned up, the valves burned clean, oil changed, tires checked, and the dents in the headlights are all smoothed out. And she's been washed and waxed," Bedore added, smiling as proudly as if the car were his own. "No charge for the wash and wax on account of the delay."

"Would it be possible for you to send the bill to me at my hotel? I prefer to settle my accounts by check," Chapman said, patting the pockets of his topcoat. "I'm never very comfortable carrying cash. There's so much crime these days.

If you have any concerns, Mr. Walter Shean of the Shean Advertising Company can attest to my trustworthiness."

"No need for that, Mr. Miller. I'll be happy to take a check from a gentleman like you. Send it along at your convenience. But there is one thing, sir."

"What is that, my good man?"

Bedore stroked a gleaming fender. "You really should take a little more care of this beauty. I recommend a monthly tune-up."

"I promise to bring it in faithfully," Chapman said, putting on a pair of yellow leather gloves, "I'll entrust her to no other mechanic."

A few minutes later he parked the car in Walter Shean's driveway and proceeded to transfer various items from the storage shed to the trunk of the Lincoln. Finding that Shean was not at home, he drove to the offices of Shean Advertising, gave one quick toot of the horn, and waited for Shean to come out.

Barely able to contain his excitement as he settled into the front seat, Shean asked, "Where are we going?"

More confident than ever that Walter Shean was a crooked man, Chapman replied, "We're going to Connecticut, where we are going to swing on a peter."

Shean blinked with bewilderment. "Excuse me?"

Chapman smiled. "It's crime lingo. To swing on a peter is to crack a safe."

Shean shifted nervously. "Where are we going to swing on this peter? In Hartford? One of the big insurance companies?"

"You'll find out when we get there, so settle down and relax. Enjoy the ride and the scenery."

On a perfect afternoon for football, beneath a brilliant blue October sky and with fall foliage at its colorful peak, the Lincoln proceeded at a leisurely pace down Route 159. It passed Enfield, on the west side of the Connecticut River, went through Hartford and West Hartford, took U.S. Route 6 to Farmington, then turned west and south to the place known as the "Hardware City of the World."

Besides the mills that turning out tools, nuts, and bolts, New Britain, Connecticut, could boast of Walnut Hill Park, designed by Frederick Law Olmstead, the planner of New York City's Central Park and the finest green spaces of Boston. Downtown were impressive and elegant nineteenth-century edifices, including City Hall. Designed and built in 1885 by the principal assistant to architect Stanford White, Joseph Morril Wells, the hall contained the police department and stood on Main Street, near the city's largest merchandising emporium, Davidson and Leventhal.

Chapman parked the Lincoln two blocks away from the department store. "Stay in the car, Walt," he said, getting out. "I won't be gone long."

Like most downtowns on Saturday, New Britain's had been thronged since before stores opened at nine o'clock by shoppers who were still spending money at midafternoon. The aisles on all floors of Davidson and Leventhal were busy. Moving through them, Chapman blended in well, pausing to examine display cases with apparent interest, investigating the goods in the menswear department, and asking to see jewelry of all kinds. Buying nothing, he browsed and fingered merchandise while his eyes drifted about in a searching manner. Presently, he noticed a stairway that could lead only to the establishment's offices.

The next item on his mental checklist was examining the locks of the front entrances. Salesgirl Edith Larsen wondered why the well-dressed man lingering in a doorway did not come into the store. But when she looked for him after she had tended to a customer, the man had gone.

Returning to the Lincoln, Chapman found Shean standing

beside the car and smoking a cigarette. "Well?" Shean asked. "What did you find out?"

"I merely proved that an impression I had awhile ago was correct. Davidson and Leventhal turn a good buck."

Leaving New Britain, they headed south on U.S. Route 5 to Berlin and beyond to Meriden, called the "silver city" because it was home to the International Silver Company.

"What are we going to do now?" Shean asked with a chuckle. "Case a place where we can pick up some sterling plate?"

"Patience, Walter. Patience," Chapman said. "All shall be revealed to you."

"Why not tell me now?"

"Because I don't want you worrying. That's my job."

As they entered Meriden, the blue sky had long since turned a star-spangled black. Tugging at a gold chain with a gold medal inscribed with his initials, Shean drew his pocketwatch and noted the time—8:30 P.M.

As Chapman turned the Lincoln off the road, a sign in front of the Old Colony Inn glowed invitingly. "This looks good," he said. "We'll have dinner and stay here for the night. I'll take an inn over a hotel anytime."

At the registration desk they were greeted by Frank Kubeck, the owner.

"We'd like two rooms for one night," Chapman said, "but I'd like to look at them first, please." Satisfied, he returned to Kubeck. "My associate and I have had a long trip today and are rather hungry. I trust it's not too late for dinner?"

"It is a little late," Kubeck said, "but if you'll step into the dining room, Miss Knell will be happy to serve you."

"May I pay her for the meals and the rooms?"

"As you wish, Mr. Miller," said Kubeck, glancing at the signature in the registration book.

Employed as a waitress, Lillian Knell was used to doing

other tasks that might be required of her. On this occasion she took two servings of roasted chicken from the icebox, heated them, and served them with French fried potatoes and tossed salad. The dinners cost $1.75 each, and Chapman paid with a twenty-dollar bill. When Knell brought the change he tipped her half-a-dollar.

"Oh, that's much too generous, sir," she protested.

"My associate and I have troubled you far too much already," he said, "but we have one more request, please. We have to be on the road rather early in the morning. Might the inn have an alarm clock for me to borrow?"

"While you gentlemen enjoy your coffee, I'll bring the clock to your room," Knell said with a smile, as she dropped the fifty cents into her apron pocket.

Going to their rooms fifteen minutes later, Chapman said, "Go right to bed, Walt. I'll be waking you at four o'clock."

Shean groaned. "Cripes, that's the middle of the night."

"Early to bed and early to rise," Chapman said, "makes a man healthy and wise but especially *wealthy*."

Still not certain what Chapman had in mind, Shean tried to sleep but could not. Nor could Chapman in the next room, although it was not nervous anticipation that kept him awake. Rather, he spent the hours going over what he had observed in the department store, what would be required of him and Shean and, as always, what might go wrong.

The alarm went off at four. Half an hour later later they were in the Lincoln, heading north.

That Sunday also started early for Edward Johnson. Working across the alley behind Davidson and Leventhal, he was in a trade that was being relegated to history—hostler in a stable, for in central Connecticut in 1924 the horse still had a place. Johnson had been at work for an hour and was busy with a broom and shovel, cleaning up the alley. When Chapman's Lincoln glided silently to a stop at seven o'clock, opposite Davidson and Leventhal and in front of New Britain *Herald* newspaper office on Main Street.

"It's pretty chilly this morning," Shean said. "Is it okay if I put on a coat?"

Chapman nodded.

As Shean reached into the back seat for a raincoat, a milk delivery wagon rattled past the car. When it was gone, Chapman also reached into the back for a coat. But instead of putting it on he removed a pistol from each pocket. "This one's for you," he said, dropping an automatic into Shean's lap. "My advice is, stick it in your belt and then tighten the belt one or two notches. I once dropped a gun because it fell through the belt. And here's an extra ammo clip." He stepped from the car. "You wait here and keep an eye out while I take care of business inside."

Shean pouted. "I'm not coming in?"

"I can handle this myself. You're the lookout. If you smell trouble, blast the horn four times and skeddaddle. Then drive round the block until you spot me and pick me up."

From the trunk strapped to the rear of the Lincoln he drew a black briefcase and a bag containing the accoutrements required to swing on a peter—electric drill, screwdriver, a chisel, a ball-peen hammer, an eyedropper, a roll of cotton, a spindle of fuse wire, and, thickly wrapped in a blanket, a small brown vial of nitro.

Turning from Main Street into Church, he walked to an alley behind the store. Entering it, he discovered Ed Johnson. Pausing only for an instant, he smiled. "Good morning, sir," he said with a tip of his gray fedora. "Isn't it a grand morning? Alas, some of us have to work, eh?" Looking round at the littered alley, he added, "It appears that the wind has played havoc with the trash bins. Look at all the paper strewn about!"

"It's the hoboes and cats," Johnson replied. "They rummage around at night."

"Well, you have your work to do," Chapman said, striding on. "I won't delay you."

Bypassing the rear of Davidson and Leventhal, he turned at the other end of the alley and waited on Chestnut Street until the cleaning man entered the stable a few minutes later. After dashing to the store's back door, he deftly picked the lock and entered a small hallway. Finding the next door unlocked, he stepped onto the main sales floor, adjacent to the stairway up to a mezzanine containing displays of radios and the store's offices. Behind an easily jimmied door, he found what he had come for.

Familiar with the first and smaller of the two safes, Chapman worked quickly, drilling into the metal at three and nine o'clock of the large round combination lock. With all the solemnity of a priest celebrating Mass, he filled the eyedropper with nitro and squirted the liquid into the holes. Gingerly, he squeezed a wad of cotton into each boring, then inserted long strings of fuse, lit them, and scurried to safety behind an oak file cabinet, his hands pressed hard against his ears.

Exploding simultaneously, the charges jolted the furniture, shook a snowfall of plaster dust from the ceiling, and popped open the safe's heavy door. Looking inside, he found stacks of ledger books but a mere $126 in cash.

With the money tucked into the briefcase he turned to the second safe, certain that it contained thousands of dollars. He recognized the manufacturer, Shaw-Walker—one of the best safes to be had. He knew its specifications: outer angle steel frame, two-by-two-by-an-inch-and-a-quarter thick, and outer and inner 14-gauge steel shells with 10-gauge armor plate. The manufacturer claimed that the safe was drillproof and had never lost its contents to fire. It would have been a challenge even for Dutch Anderson. Chapman decided the task needed two men to spell one another. Leaving through the rear door to summon Shean, he encountered Ed Johnson but did not address him.

At the Lincoln, he said, "I'm having trouble with one of those suckers. Come along, Walt, and lend me a hand."

Returning to the alley with Shean, Chapman found Johnson at work again. Irritated at his presence, he grumbled, "You'd better get these papers cleaned up pretty soon, or you'll lose your job."

When efforts to crack the Shaw-Walker proved frustrating, Shean worried about the noise. "Maybe we should forget about it," he pleaded. Having found Shean useless as a safecracker, Chapman snapped, "Take my briefcase out to the car. I'm going to give this baby one more try. If I can't crack it in fifteen minutes, I'll give it up."

With the briefcase hugged against his ribs, Shean exited to the alley. Encountering Johnson, he ducked his head and dashed toward Church Street, ran to Main and, sweating and shaking with fear, scrambled into the Lincoln. Opening the briefcase, he felt sick. Shaking his head, he muttered, "A lousy hundred-and-twenty-six bucks!" and stuffed the bills under the front seat, along with his gun.

In the alley, Ed Johnson figured that something was wrong. Never had he seen such activity in his alleyway on a Sunday morning. Nor had he ever seen the two men who had appeared there this morning, both of them acting peculiarly. Supposing they could be employees of Davidson and Leventhal, he resumed his sweeping. Then he heard a loud bang that seemed to come from the store. Considering this suspicious, he went into the stable, picked up the telephone, and got the operator. "Please connect me with Mr. Samuel Davidson of the Davidson and Leventhal store. It's very important, and I don't have his home number."

Davidson himself answered.

"It's Ed at the stable," Johnson said. "Sorry to bother you at home, Mr. Davidson, but do you have anybody working at your store this morning? 'Cause if you don't, I think you should know that there's two men been lurking around, and they could have got into the store."

In all his years as a merchant, Davidson had never demanded that anyone work on a Sunday. Therefore, he told the police officer who took his call, Sergeant Matthias Rival, that it seemed likely that a person or persons had entered the premises with illicit intent.

When Davidson phoned, five policemen were available for duty at headquarters: James Skelly, Alfred Atwater, Clarence Lanpher, John Liebler, and Walter Malona. All went to the store to investigate. While Skelly and Atwater checked the rear of the building, Malona, Liebler, and Lanpher talked to Johnson and obtained a description of the two suspicious men, one of whom, Johnson speculated, was still in the store.

A veteran of seventeen years with the New Britain police, Skelly directed Malona and Liebler to stay with Johnson. "Al, you come inside with me," he said to Atwater as he opened the unlocked rear door. "Clarence, you stay here," he told Lanpher.

Barely inside, Skelly saw the figure of a man silhouetted in the doorway at the end of the short hall. He yelled, "Police!"

Chapman shouted back. "Get down or I'll kill you."

As Skelly reached to draw his revolver, one of three shots from Chapman's gun ripped into his chest. Driven backward, he fell into Lanpher's arms.

Meanwhile, Officers Liebler and Malona had left the alley and gone round to Main Street, where they spotted a man who matched Johnson's description of one of those he had encountered in the alley.

At that moment, Johnson, who had taken it upon himself to go to Main Street also, "to keep a lookout," was approaching the front door of the store. As he reached it, the door swung open, and a well-dressed man stepped out. "I think someone has been shot in there," he said calmly.

Astonished, Johnson could only blink in amazement as one of the men he had seen in the alley brushed past him.

Noting that Shean was not in the Lincoln, just across the street, Gerald Chapman walked briskly toward Chestnut Street.

Leaving Atwater to look after Skelly, Clarence Lanpher had run to Main Street in search of Malona and Leibler, but as he reached the corner, Johnson dashed up to him, shouting. "That was him!" He pointed after Chapman. "That's one of the men that was in the store."

Observing all of this unusual activity as he waited for a bus to Boston, Henry Heller, an automobile mechanic, had also seen the man come out of the department store. Noticing a silver-toned pistol in the man's hand, he froze with fear as the gunman approached the corner of Main and Chestnut.

Saying nothing, Chapman stared into Heller's eyes for a moment, then turned into Chestnut and continued walking.

Although Lanpher sprinted in pursuit, Chapman had had a good head start and, finding a fence, had climbed over it and escaped.

Walter Shean enjoyed no such luck.

Having returned to the Lincoln and stowed the briefcase and his gun, and unaware of what had transpired since he had left Chapman to work on the second safe, Shean sauntered along Main Street in search of a cup of coffee.

Suddenly, he felt a hand grabbing the collar of his coat and a gruff voice declaring, "We want you."

Facing two policemen, Shean did his best to look and sound innocent. "What for?" he asked meekly.

"You know what," Malona snapped. "For burglarizing Davidson and Leventhal's department store."

Shean laughed. "That's ridiculous."

A search of the Lincoln turned up money—a paltry $126—Shean's gun and, in the trunk, burglar's tools.

Placed under arrest, Shean denied having been in the store. "I don't know anything about a policeman being shot, either," he stated.

On the scene now and taking command of the investigation was Chief of Police William Hart. "What the hell's your name?" he demanded of Shean.

"I'm George B. Clark, address, One Eighty-two West Seventy-sixth Street, New York City," Shean replied.

"Is that so?" Hart replied. "A call to the New York City police will clear that up, won't it?" Jerking Shean's watch chain into his hand and dangling its gold charm, engraved with Shean's name, before Shean's eyes, Hart asked, "Did you steal this from Walter Shean? Or are *you* in fact Mr. Shean? You might as well come clean, because we're going to find out the truth sooner or later. In the meantime we'll see what Jim Skelly has to say about you."

When the wounded policeman collapsed into Lanpher's arms, he had groaned, "they got me in the leg." But upon Skelly's arrival at New Britain General Hospital, Dr. George Dunn recognized the seriousness of Skelly's wound. Hitting him immediately below the ribs, the bullet had punched sixteen holes in his intestines, severed the main artery carrying blood to his legs, and lodged in his hip.

Though mortally wounded, Skelly was conscious when Sergeants Rival and William McCue brought Shean to the hospital.

Bending over Skelly, McCue asked, "Do you know who I am, Jim?"

Skelly nodded. "You're Bill McCue."

Sergeant Rival pushed Shean forward.

"Do you know this man?" McCue asked.

"He's the one who shot me," Skelly replied.

"Are you sure, Jim?"

"He's the one."

Although Dr. Dunn struggled valiantly to save him, Skelly died on the operating table, the first member of the New Britain police force to be shot and killed in the line of duty. "Not for a long time has New Britain been stirred to a depth of feeling such as it was yesterday," said the *New Britain Herald* on its front page on Monday, October 13, 1924. "All over the city, wherever people gathered, in the churches, and homes, the murder was the sole topic of conversation. Sympathy for the family, respect for the memory of the deceased policeman and indignation at the crime were expressed."

The newspaper also reported "a general air of sorrow" at police headquarters. But overshadowing the grief among the men who had to find Skelly's killer was the irrefutable reality that in identifying the suspect who had been brought to the hospital, Skelly had been wrong: when the fatal bullet ripped into his body, Walter Shean had been on Main Street, seconds away from being placed under arrest.

Until the death of the policeman, Shean steadfastly held to his claim of innocence, but when he was informed that he would be charged with Skelly's murder, defiance disintegrated into tears. "I didn't shoot that cop," he blurted. "It was Gerald Chapman."

CHAPTER EIGHTEEN

The Hick Dicks

"ARE YOU ASKING US TO BELIEVE," said Chief Hart, "that the man who pulled the Leonard Street mail robbery, the man who escaped from federal prison in Atlanta, the man whose face is on wanted posters all over the country and even in Europe, was in that department store to pull a second-rate burglary?"

"Yes," Shean sobbed. "It was Chapman."

"*The* Gerald Chapman! Now what in blazes would Gerald Chapman be doing with the likes of a small-town punk like you?"

"I am not a small-town punk," Shean retorted. "I told you, I am George Clark of Philadelphia. I'm a federal agent, and I've been on Chapman's trail for months. I finally tracked him down in Springfield."

Hart snorted a contemptuous laugh. "In all my experience as a cop I have never heard such a ridiculous yarn. If you're a federal officer, why didn't you arrest Chapman the minute you found him? How come you didn't notify the Springfield police?"

"I intended to. This week I was going to notify my boss in Philadelphia, George Brown of the Justice Department. Meantime, I kept up my pretense of being crooked so I could stay close to Chapman. When he asked me to go with him on a trip this weekend, I played along. He said he was thinking of buying a house down here and wanted my opinion. When we parked the car on Main Street I had no idea he was going into the department store. He told me to wait, and I waited."

"That's a lie," blared Chief Hart. "And we have a witness to prove it."

Escorted into the interrogation room, Ed Johnson did not have to be asked if he recognized Shean. "That's one of 'em," he exclaimed, shaking a finger at Shean. "He was in my alleyway with the other one, the one who practically bowled me over coming out the front of the store and telling me somebody was shot inside."

Still dubious about Shean's claim that Skelly's killer had been Gerald Chapman, Chief Hart all but snarled as he demanded, "Now tell us the truth, Shean or Clark or whatever your name is—who was the other man in that store with you?"

"I told you the truth," Shean cried. "It was Chapman."

"Yeah, and you're a federal officer," scoffed Hart, "and you were going to bring him in next week. Why not *last* week, huh?"

"I had to be careful. You have no idea what a dangerous man Chapman is. You don't know what it was like. It was as if he had me hypnotized. I was a damned fool."

Scorched with rapid-fire questions from Hart and others, and confronted with a detective from Springfield, who identified him as Walter Shean, "a real bad apple," Shean broke down.

But through his tears he still insisted that the second man had been Chapman. In a rambling monologue, he related the history of their association from their first conversation, with him standing beside Chapman's Lincoln—"He said his name was Miller"—to discuss bootlegging, to seeing Chapman's picture on a wanted poster at the railway depot, to seven o'clock Sunday morning across Main Street from Davidson and Leventhal.

"He had a companion, name of Dr. Johnson," he continued. "They were a couple of strange birds, believe me! Always on the move. Slipping in and out of Springfield. Talking about plans for setting up a counterfeiting scheme."

Elements of Shean's story that could be checked were, and over the next few hours Chief Hart and his men slowly came round to believing that Chapman, indeed, had been in New Britain, and not only that day. Employees of Davidson and Leventhal looked at pictures of him and said they had seen him on other occasions.

Persuaded, at last, that Chapman was the killer of Skelly, Hart recognized that he had a case with ramifications extending far beyond New Britain, one which would require money and manpower not available to him and his department. Accordingly, he contacted Connecticut's chief law officer for Hartford County.

Immediately, State's Attorney Hugh M. Alcorn ordered Shean transported to jail in the city of Hartford. To take charge of the investigation and the manhunt for Chapman, he despatched his top cop, Edward J. Hickey, who arrived in New Britain on Monday. Then thirty-four years old, he had served in the Third Naval District of the Bureau of Naval Intelligence during the World War, joined the state police as a trooper in 1921, and was named a county detective the following year. (He would be appointed Police Commissioner of Connecticut in 1939 and serve until stricken by leukemia in

1952, dying a year later.) On October 13, 1924, he was a robust and capable policeman, outraged at the murder of a fellow lawman and astonished to hear that the prime suspect in Skelly's murder was the most sought-after criminal in the country.

"I promise the grieving family of Policeman Skelly and the citizens of New Britain and Connecticut," he declared to reporters at police headquarters, "that neither I nor any of my men will rest until Gerald Chapman is tracked down and brought to justice. As of now, Chapman is public enemy number one."

No one had ever been called that before. The phrase made for great headlines. And Chapman's life offered reporters a chance to write colorful leads to their stories. A front-page backgrounder in the *New Britain Herald* was typical: "A mild-mannered, flashily-dressed, luxury-loving, gentleman yegg, with a hair trigger brain and devoid of any conscience whatever—such is the description acquaintances give of Gerald Chapman, notorious denizen of New York's underworld, escaped convict, mail robber and gunman for whom nets have spread in every city in the east in an attempt to bring him here to answer for the death of Policeman Skelly."

Colorful adjectives notwithstanding, one astute New Britain merchandiser, Adkins Printers and Stationers of 66 Church Street, took out an advertisement in the *Herald* on the day after Chapman's assault on the two safes. It pointed out that his attempts to crack a Shaw-Walker vault had been stymied. Above a photograph of the safe, a bold headline boasted, "The Safe That Protects Its Contents." Of course, the ad noted that Adkins Printers and Sationers stocked that very safe.

To hasten Chapman's arrest, the *Herald* offered a reward of five hundred dollars, adding to a three-thousand-dollar bounty already announced by Governor Charles A. Templeton at the request of State's Attorney Alcorn. Reporting the reward offers, a *Herald* writer turned a new phrase to describe Chapman: "the Beau Brummel yeggman."

Next to the story on the rewards in Tuesday's local paper was an account of the "impressive obsequies" for Officer Skelly: "Fifty uniformed policemen stood with heads bared and heads bowed at the entrance to St. Joseph's Church," the article reported. The pews were filled. Among those present were representatives of all branches of the city government. Scores of people stood in reverent silence across the street. Davidson and Leventhal remained closed for the day.

While the Skelly family dealt with their loss, the Sheans of Springfield were coming to grips with Walter. After a visit to their brother in jail, Howard and Arthur said that they would provide Walter with all that was required to ensure a proper defense but would also cooperate fully with the police. Arthur then told reporters about his brother's peculiar behavior growing up and wondered if "a kink in the brain" had led Walter to take part in a murder.

After conferring with police, embittered Charles Shean said of his son, "I've done all I can for him. But now that he has got himself mixed up with murder, I don't feel that it is up to me to do any more. In fact, I will not lift a hand to help him."

"Father Washes Hands of Young Shean," headlined the *Herald*.

In beginning to construct a criminal case that State's Attorney Alcorn could present with confidence that a jury would convict Gerald Chapman of murder, Ed Hickey was aware that as of October 14, the only link to Chapman was Walter Shean—a man of dubious character and mentality and a thorough-going liar. If Shean's claim that Chapman had killed Skelly were true, what Hickey needed was corroboration. That could come only through physical evidence linking Shean to Chapman and showing that Chapman had been in the Davidson and Leventhal store with a smoking gun in his hand.

Three bullets had been retrieved, two that had been dug out of a wall and one that had been surgically removed from Skelly's body. But no matching gun had been found. Burglary equipment had been left behind, but none of the objects yielded fingerprints. And there was the Lincoln, only cursorily searched when Shean was arrested.

"Go through that machine again," Hickey ordered. "Strip it down to the chassis if you must."

Of immediate interest was the car's odometer, indicating that the Lincoln had been driven more than nineteen thousand miles.

Assuming that the Lincoln had been stolen, Hickey solicited assistance from a team of Hartford insurance investigators in tracing the car's ownership through serial numbers engraved in its various components. Immediately, the detectives reported that the numbers had been skillfully altered— so expertly that they had to use a jeweler's magnifying glass to spot the changes. But one of the numbers, they reported triumphantly to Hickey, had been overlooked by the thief.

Located under the woodwork at the rear of the Lincoln, the unscathed serial number permitted investigators to trace the entire history of the car from the Ford Motor Company assembly line to a dealer. In a long-distance phone call to the Stanton Motor Company of Steubenville, Ohio, Hickey learned the circumstances of the car's theft. From Catherine Bourne he obtained a description of the well-dressed man suspected of the crime—a description that matched Chapman's. The description was confirmed in questioning Edith Larsen about the man she had seen hanging around the store's front door the day before the killing, Ed Johnson about the man he had seen in the alley and leaving the store after the shooting, and Frank Kubeck and waitress Lillian Knell regarding Shean and the man with him at the Old Colony Inn on Saturday night.

While the insurance men traced the origins of the Lincoln, Chief Hart's men had assembled the contents of the car's trunk for Hickey's inspection: two vials of nitro; a pistol holster designed for concealment inside trousers; an assortment of items that appeared to be loot from other burglaries; pince-nez of the type Chapman was known to wear; road maps of Ohio, Indiana, Illinois, Pennsylvania, New York State, Massachusetts, and Connecticut; and a membership card from an Ohio auto club.

Examination of the car's Massachusetts license plates showed that the numbers had been deftly changed. Because this indicated that the original plates probably had been stolen, Hickey requested that Massachusetts authorities search their records on reports of stolen plates—a process that would take a great deal of time on the part of employees of the Massachusetts Department of motor vehicles.

Having learned all that he could in New Britain, Hickey invited Sergeant Bill McCue to join him on a visit to Springfield to investigate the places named in Shean's confession: the shed in which Chapman was said to have stored many belongings and Chapman's room at the Cooley Hotel. "Who knows, maybe we'll find Chapman in his room," he joked.

Where was he?

The last person known to have seen Chapman in New Britain on Sunday morning had been Henry Heller, who would never forget the look on Chapman's face as he stared into his eyes at the bus stop before turning into Chestnut Street.

The next to come into contact with Chapman after he climbed a fence and escaped was a Springfield boy who delivered a note to the Cooley Hotel. Addressed to Walter Shean, it read, "Arrived O.K. Will call you every half hour."

True to his promise, Chapman spoke several times on Sunday to the switchboard operator at the Cooley, but by early afternoon the calls had stopped. Soon the hotel swarmed with policemen. Obviously Chapman had made his way back to Springfield. The Lincoln had been abandoned, so how had he gotten there?

As Hickey and McCue left for Massachusetts, they had one indication that a third man might have been involved in the aborted burglary, despite Shean's story that only he and Chapman had been in the store. Dr. David Waskowitz had told New Britain police that on Sunday morning he had been driving down Church Street shortly after four o'clock when he observed a high-powered car with two men in it and another with a lone occupant, and that the three men were conferring. Though the timing in the doctor's story conflicted with Shean's account, the doctor could not be simply dismissed. Shean himself had spoken about a Chapman associate called Dr. Johnson, and everyone knew that Chapman had a long criminal association with Dutch Anderson, including the Leonard Street mail truck robbery.

Might Anderson have been in New Britain? Could he have been Chapman's means of escape? Were they now long gone?

Even as Hickey and McCue traveled to Springfield, police in Pennsylvania were rushing to the state bank at Abbottsville, near the historic Civil War town of Gettysburg, where a gunman had gotten away with twelve hundred dollars and shot and killed a pursuing state policeman, Francis A. Haley. A fairly good description of the killer provided by the bank's cashier, H. F. Stambaugh, proved to be chillingly similar to Chapman's.

On the strength of the description, New Britain detectives and post office investigators went to Pennsylvania. When a man resembling Chapman was detained by police in Hagerstown, Maryland, they crossed the Mason-Dixon Line. But the suspect soon proved that he was not Chapman and that he had not been in the Abbottsville bank.

Two days later, Philip A. Hartman walked into the police station in Annville, Pennsylvania, to confess that he had shot Trooper Haley. Furthermore, he said, he had planned the robbery himself and was alone when he committed it. Of the twelve hundred in loot, he had spent only a hundred for silk shirts and two suits. He was a family man, he explained, but had lost his job and needed money for his wife and child in Palmyra, Pennsylvania. He had also robbed gas stations in Columbus and Canton, Ohio, and a man in Canandaigua, New York. The Abbotsville bank job, he said, was to be his last crime. Hartman bore little resemblance to the nation's number-one public enemy.

"The manhunt for Chapman is fast resolving itself into one of the most intensive ever conducted in the country for a criminal," observed the *New Britain Herald* on Thursday, October 16, invoking yet another term to describe him: "super bandit."

Unswerved by the Pennsylvania sideshow, Ed Hickey and Bill McCue had arrived in Springfield on Monday afternoon, going first to police headquarters to confer with Chief W. J. Quilty and receive a report on the activities of his men in securing room C31 at the Cooley and the storage shed at 26 Hampden Street, Shean's home. "Wait till you see what's in there," Quilty said. "This guy was prepared for anything! There was enough nitro in that shed to blow up half of Springfield. I took the liberty of having the stuff removed, of course. And there's enough stolen goods in the place to open a department store!"

In addition to the nitroglycerine, two sawed-off shotguns had been found, each wrapped in heavy paper, along with a rifle and boxes of ammunition, an electric drill, an Oriental carpet, four large English kit bags containing dozens of pairs of women's silk stockings, four expensive fur coats, including a mink and a sable, jewelry, and a number of suitcases containing men's clothing and other personal effects.

Hickey and McCue examined all of it, but one of the suitcases attracted Hickey's special attention.

"What do you make of this, Bill?" he asked, pointing to an American Express shipping tag tied to the handle.

Addressed to Shean, the tag bore the name and address of the shipper.

McCue read it aloud. "Dr. H. Spickermon, Muncie, Indiana."

"We've seen all there is here," Hickey said, pocketing the tag. "Let's check out the hotel."

Room C31's most likely value, Hickey figured, was as a source of fingerprints. A man might don gloves to break into a safe, but he would not wear them in his hotel room. Stepping into C31, he saw that when its occupant left it, he had had every intention of returning. Clothing still hung in the closet. Toilet articles stood on a shelf in the bathroom. A clock ticked on the nightstand. Beside it lay a deluxe volume of *Echo de Paris* with a bookmark inserted halfway through. On the small desk lay a Waterman fountain pen that was far too fine to be hotel property or to be left behind. Under it was a sheaf of Cooley Hotel stationery.

"Apparently Chapman takes time to correspond with someone," Hickey said. Seated at the desk he opened drawers but found nothing except more letter paper, envelopes, and a Gideon Bible. Riffling its pages, he found nothing hidden inside. When he picked up a wooden wastepaper basket, he muttered, "Ah, what have we here?" It was a pile of torn paper. Heaping the scraps on the desk, he noted several interesting points. It was not Cooley Hotel stationery. There were numerous pages—as many as ten, he guessed. The handwriting was a woman's. Picking through the fragments, he found a signature.

"Beeswax!"

"What's that?" asked Sergeant McCue.

"The name on this letter," Hickey said. "Beeswax!" As he spread out the bits of paper, they resembled the parts of a jigsaw puzzle. Piecing them together would require considerable patience, but for now he was searching for one part, if it existed. Presently, he whooped in delight. In the right-hand corner of the letter's first page was a return address: a mail box at the Biltmore Hotel in Providence, Rhode Island.

A failed attempt at burglary that had taken a murderous turn in Connecticut had developed into an investigation that involved the most daring criminal and escape artist in memory, a shed and hotel room in Massachusetts, a Lincoln auto that had been stolen in Ohio, skillfully altered serial numbers and license plates, bags crammed with stolen goods shipped from Indiana by a doctor, and a woman in Rhode Island. Chief Hall of the New Britain police found himself, understandably, out of sorts. The Chapman case had been taken over by Hickey, and federal agents were invading his city, along with a horde of newspapermen demanding to be informed of each development—and asking how Chapman had managed to kill one of his men and elude four others. Asked to confirm a statement by Chief Quilty concerning what had been found in the shed and the hotel room, Hall snapped, "I didn't say so."

The conduct of the five policemen who had responded to Samuel Davidson's telephone call about a possible burglary in his store had been questioned by Hall himself on Sunday. "If a man had stayed at the front door on guard," he told reporters, "we might have had another dead policeman, but we would also have had a chance to get the murderer of Jim Skelly."

Now questions of procedure were being raised by the public and the city's board of police supervisors. Announcing a meeting wherein members hoped to "familiarize" themselves with "all the circumstances," the board summoned the four officers who had accompanied Skelly to the department store. The meeting would not be an "official inquiry," the board pointed out: it was to determine what procedures might be adopted to prevent a repeat of the tragedy. Clearly, the city of New Britain had been embarassed by the entire episode.

Meantime, the investigation continued, but without further local activity on the part of the federal agents who had rushed to New Britain upon learning that the most-wanted man in their files might have surfaced in Connecticut. Declaring that they had all the evidence obtainable, they decamped. Asked where the federal headquarters might be located, Chief Hall said, "I haven't the slightest idea."

Hickey's base of operations remained in New Britain but its tentacles were stretching far beyond, and not without surprises. Among Chapman's effects, a pair of automobile license plates had been found. Issued by the State of Indiana, they had been reported stolen by a respectable resident of Indianapolis with a familiar name: Waldo W. Miller. "It looks like Chapman steals more than people's property," noted Hickey. "He also steals their names!" It was the second Indiana connection of the case.

Pursuing Walter Shean's account of Chapman's search for a house in which to set up his counterfeiting plant, Hickey located the Reverend Bailey. The Pawtucket clergyman confirmed Shean's story and made a positive identification of Chapman as the man to whom he sold the house, which was searched. From all indications, it had never been occupied by Chapman.

Upon reassembling the letter found in Chapman's room, Hickey was disappointed. Two sets of fingerprints, a man's and a woman's, were smudged and useless for purposes of comparison to Chapman's fingerprint records. And the letter revealed nothing valuable beyond the curious name of its female author and her hotel convenience address.

More in hope than expectation of success, Hickey requested that post office officials in Providence be on the lookout for the woman at the hotel, for her discreet perusal of letters received there, and for letters mailed anywhere in the state of Rhode Island addressed to *anyone* at the Cooley Hotel in Springfield. He also asked whether postal authorities could determine if anyone in Providence or their state went by the name "Beeswax," silly as it sounded.

Then he sat down to correspondence of his own, addressed to the police force of Muncie, Indiana. In October 1924 the department was thirty-one years old, decreed into existence by the Metropolitan Police Board on March 21, 1893, to replace an elected marshal. Pay for the 12 new cops (6 Democrats and 6 Republicans) was set at $600 a year for a patrolman and $1,000 for the superintendent, James Miller, a fifty-seven-year-old Civil War veteran and the marshal whose job the new department replaced. Patrols were established in two shifts, from 7:00 A.M. to 6:30 P.M. and 7:00 P.M. to 4:00 A.M., leaving three-and-a-half hours when the city went unpoliced. Uniforms, paid for out of each man's pocket, cost $45—almost a month's wages.

Strapping men were required. "Each policeman had to be able to lift two big bullies by the necks, knock their heads together and survive at least long enough to devise some type of transportation for the culprits," recalled John Seldomridge, one of the twelve hired when Gerald Chapman was five years old.

For Captain Fred W. Puckett, finding a means of transport for culprits presented no problem in 1924. As a plainclothes detective who had served on the force for better than half of its existence, he drove around town in an unmarked city automobile. He had been involved in the investigation of crimes Dr. Spickermon had described for Chapman and Anderson when they dropped in on him during their 1919 swing through the Midwest—the unsolved sniper slaying of the alleged philanderer Norman Black, Charles Taylor's running amok and slaughtering five citizens, and the thirty-three drug-related homicides of 1914–1915. But no case on record excited Puckett more than Ed Hickey's news that Gerald Chapman might be resident in or around Muncie. Hickey's suggestion that Chapman might have connections with Dr. Spickermon was hardly a surprise, since the Mulberry Street physician had a dubious reputation. But lacking reasonable cause to justify hauling Spickermon in for questioning—and maybe scaring off Gerald Chapman—the only course open to Puckett and his men was to wait and watch.

Suddenly, the alert to the Muncie police seemed to have been unnecessary. Police in New York City shocked Hickey and everyone who had been following the national manhunt for Chapman by blaring the news that Policeman Skelly's murderer had been arrested.

His name, they announced, was George Stuyvesant. The suspect had been born in Troy, New York, in 1896, and had chalked up a long criminal record in his hometown. He was the prime suspect in the Detroit murder of two men and in the shooting and crippling of a New York cop. Stuyvesant had lost an eye in a gun battle in Harlem in 1923. He had an artifical eye and wore glasses in which one of the lenses was clouded. Spotted by a Manhattan detective who thought he resembled the man who had stuck up a Times Square subway station a few days earlier, he was arrested on "suspicion" and taken to police headquarters. Immediately, someone remarked that he bore a striking resemblance to Chapman. Consequently, a call was placed to New Britain police on

Saturday night, November 16, to inform Chief Hart that the killer he was looking for was under arrest. Calling Bill McCue, Hart ordered him to pick up stableman Ed Johnson and head down to New York.

With an emphatic nod of his head as he looked at Stuyvesant in a police lineup, Johnson said, "Yesirree, that's the man I saw coming out of Davidson and Leventhal's. He's Chapman."

McCue was dubious. There was a strong resemblance between Chapman and Stuyvesant, but Johnson's identification was on the basis of photos of Chapman, and not very good ones.

News of Stuyvesant's arrest hit New Britain like a bombshell and left Ed Hickey in a quandary. In five weeks of investigation, the keystone of his efforts had been the presumption that Gerald Chapman had killed Skelly, based on Walter Shean's confession and Ed Johnson's positive identification of photos of Chapman. Every bit of physical evidence that he had accumulated pointed to Chapman.

Was it possible that three men had been involved, the third man being Stuyvesant? Information from McCue lent credence to the notion. "It appears that Stuyvesant and Shean know one another," he reported to Chief Hart and Ed Hickey. "They were together in the robbery of that bank in Wyomissing, Pennsylvania. Stuyvesant served two years for it."

"Now there's a hell of a coincidence," Hickey remarked.

Insisting that since being released from Sing Sing he had not left Troy until two weeks previously, when he came down to New York, Stuyvesant swore that he had never been in Connecticut and had had no dealings with Shean in Springfield.

Sharing Hickey's doubts about Stuyvesant, Chief Hart held back on requesting application for the extradition of Stuyvesant to Connecticut, telling Prosecutor Joseph Woods that he preferred to wait until other witnesses positively identified Stuyvesant as the man they had seen with Shean on the night before he and his companion raided the department store. Accordingly, he asked the New York police for photographs of Stuyvesant, which were shown to the staff at the Old Colony Inn. Asked if the man pictured had dined with Shean on October 11, Lillian Knell replied, "He looks like the one but he isn't him." The inn's owner, Frank Kubeck, agreed.

Springfield residents who had seen the man who called himself Waldo Miller were certain that Miller had both his eyes and that the lenses of his eyeglasses were clear.

Reverend Bailey and his legal advisers in the sale of his house said that a photo of Stuyvesant certainly looked like the person who had bought the house, but they were unequivocal in stating that they had never seen Stuyvesant in the flesh.

Chapman's handwriting and Stuyvesant's differed.

Finally, his fingerprints did not match those lifted from Room C31 of the Cooley Hotel.

In its Tuesday, November 19, issue the *New Britain Herald* headlined: CHAPMAN, WITNESSES SAY FINGER OF SUSPICION SWINGS BACK TO FUGITIVE FROM ATLANTA PRISON.

Speaking long-distance to Muncie, Indiana, Ed Hickey told Captain Pickett, "I still think this bird is going to come to roost in your yard sooner or later."

"Well if he does," Puckett replied, "we've got a cage to put him in. I guarantee you that he's not going to fly the coop the way he did in Atlanta!"

⊠

Dangerous Cargo

WHEN 11,290 DAILY READERS of the *New Britain Herald,* who paid three cents a copy for the newspaper, picked it up from doorsteps and newsstands on January 15, 1925, they were shocked by the headline: GERALD CHAPMAN, ALLEGED SLAYER OF POLICEMAN SKELLY, IDENTIFIED AS LONG ISLAND MAIL CAR BANDIT.

Two days later, readers of the New York *Evening Graphic* saw the headline CHAPMAN WIDELY SOUGHT. In the ranks of city newspapers, the *Evening Graphic* was a newcomer, first published on September 15, 1924. Founded by "the father of physical culture" and publisher of *True Story* and other magazines, Bernarr MacFadden, the zesty tabloid hit New York just in time to cash in on Chapman's sensational reappearance in a New Britain department store eighteen months after his headline-grabbing escape from Atlanta. But if it were Public Enemy No. 1 who had held up mail clerk John Green on Tuesday night, January 13, and gotten away with more than ten thousand dollars in cash, Chapman must have traveled fast, because he visited the Hance farm the next day.

Scaring the wits out of Ben and Mary, Chapman drove up to their house in another stylish automobile. He stepped out wearing as fine a suit of clothes as the Hances had ever seen, tipped his fedora, and asked if they had heard from Dutch Anderson lately.

"I ain't seen him since the last time you two was here," Hance said nervously. "I figured he was with you."

"Unfortunately, we became separated a few weeks ago," Chapman said, half-smiling. "You may have read about it in the papers or seen it in a newsreel."

"We don't go to picture shows much," Mary Hance said. "All that jumping around gives me the headache."

"Have you received any mail addressed to Mr. Miller since I've been gone?"

Hance shook his head.

"Should you hear from Dutch," Chapman said, getting back into the car, "tell him I'm staying at the Braun Hotel in Muncie. And he's the only one you tell. Understand?"

"No need to worry about that," Ben said. "We don't talk to nobody about nothin'."

"A very wise and healthy policy," Chapman said, tipping his hat to Mary as he drove away.

The Braun offered comfortable rooms, efficient service, satisfying meals, and an atmosphere of quiet discretion. It was only a few doors north of Dr. Spickermon's house on Mulberry Street. For activities unbecoming to the sedate Braun, such as playing cards for money, Chapman favored the St. John Hotel.

It may have been at the St. John that Chapman struck up a conversation with the fetching daughter of a prominent local businessman. Her name and the details of her background are obscure, but there is evidence that before meeting

Chapman she had become acquainted with members of the California underworld during a visit to San Francisco. Perhaps she enjoyed rubbing elbows (and who knows what else?) with people who exuded an air of mystery, excitement, and danger. Or she may have recognized the true identity of the charming gentleman who recited poetry and claimed to be a professor of something or other. It is not clear whether it was this woman, the Hances, or someone else who tipped the Muncie police about Chapman's presence in town, but they learned of it on Sunday, January 18, 1925.

Despatched to the Braun Hotel to check out the tip, rookie motorcycle-man Mervyn Collins, dressed in Sunday-going-to-church clothes, observed the hotel from across the street, a vantage point that permitted him to see into the lobby. Near noon, a man who resembled Chapman crossed the lobby to buy a newspaper.

"I'm pretty sure it's him," Collins reported to Captain Puckett, waiting at headquarters on Jefferson Street.

"Better be sure," Puckett said. "Talk to the clerk and show him Chapman's picture. If Chapman goes out, tail him. I'm on my way over there in my car."

The clerk had no difficulty in identifying the guest who had just bought the Sunday paper as the man with the deeply set eyes and high cheekbones in Collins's mug shot.

Presently, Chapman left the hotel. He had on a long black overcoat and homburg hat. Despite the chilly air, he kept the coat unbuttoned and wore no gloves. Walking leisurely, he turned south on Mulberry Street and proceeded to Jackson, then east to Jefferson, passing directly in front of police headquarters, and east again on Charles Street.

Hanging back quite a long way, but never losing sight of his quarry, Collins breathed a sigh of relief as an unmarked car drew up behind him, carrying Detectives Samuel Goodpasture and Harry Brown, with Puckett at the wheel. As Goodpasture and Brown got out to join Collins, Puckett said, "Take no chances. Get him before he gets you."

"How do we take him?" Goodpasture asked.

"Go to the mat square," Puckett said. "Don't take advantage of him from the rear. But he'll have a gun, so play it safe."

While Goodpasture, Brown, and Collins quickened their stride and gained on the unsuspecting Chapman, Puckett pulled the car even with him. Chapman's stroll brought him to a spot directly in front of Spickermon's house at the very moment that Puckett veered his car to the left, pulling up to the curb on Chapman's right side.

"Pardon me, Mister," Puckett said, leaning out the window and playing the lost traveler, "does a Mr. Henry live around here?"

Instinctually wary, Chapman slipped his right hand under his overcoat and continued walking, wordlessly.

Puckett got out of the car looking confused. "What number is that house there?" he asked, squinting.

Chapman hesitated but a moment. For Puckett, the second was enough. He drew a gun and grabbed Chapman's right arm.

Wrenching free at once and drawing his nickel-plated revolver, Chapman fired, barely missing Puckett's head.

In the same instant, Detective Brown leapt forward and threw a haymaker punch, catching Chapman squarely on the chin and knocking him flat. As he hit the pavement, Brown, Collins, Goodpasture, and Puckett piled on, wresting away the gun and pinning him.

When Puckett snapped on the handcuffs, Chapman snarled, "Damn the man who turned me up for blood money."

Frisking Chapman, Captain Puckett fished out of his overcoat pocket more money than he and his detectives had ever seen in one place—$4,600. There was more in Chapman's room in the Braun Hotel: $4,000 in currency and $3,000 in Liberty bonds. Opening a suitcase, they discovered fistfuls of watches and women's jewelry—pickings of no-telling-how-many burglaries. With dry mouths and steady hands, they removed from the crowded hotel a pair of bottles containing one and one-half pints of nitroglycerine, more than enough to blow them all to Kingdom Come.

Acutely aware of Chapman's reputation as an escape artist, and of the fact that he was likely to have sympathetic, dangerous friends in the vicinity, Captain Pickett set aside the professional pride that had led him to boast to Ed Hickey that Chapman could never fly the coop in Muncie. With a small army of heavily armed police, he conveyed Chapman to Marion County jail in Indianapolis and into the custody of U.S. Marshal Linius P. Meredith.

In an explosion of headlines, newspapers across the nation heralded the capture of Public Enemy No. 1. A photo of Chapman and a page-wide headline, MILLION-DOLLAR BANDIT IS RUN TO EARTH AGAIN, led off an extensive article by James C. Young in the following Sunday's *New York Times*, which began: "For two years the police intelligence of the world has sought a certain slight man with a limp, about 5 feet 7 inches tall, age 36, blue eyes tending to gray, the most striking figure that has stood forth in a generation from the dark drama of crime. No other Raffles of real life has ever typified so well the dandy cracksman. Although murder is written opposite his name on one police blotter, and although he is wanted for greater crimes than any lawbreaker of this time, and every description sent abroad has carried the line, "Dangerous man, always armed, shoots on sight"—although all of these things are true of him, he was captured easily by officers in a little Indiana town last week. The capture was easy because his pistol failed him."

The *Evening Graphic* and other papers featured a picture of Chapman in a stylish coat and homburg hat chained between law officers. It was a telling photograph. *Evening Graphic* reporter Lester Cohen said to his ink-stained companions, "Never like to see a man in chains; don't even like chains on a car." Others who saw the photo felt the stirrings of sympathy, even admiration, for the daring bandit and escaper. Their predecessors had done the same for Billy the Kid, Jesse James, and other frontier bandits and gunmen transformed into folk heroes, as earlier generations had found romance in pirates and smugglers. Americans would continue to mythologize future criminals like Al Capone, Lucky Luciano, John Dillinger, Bonnie and Clyde, 1950s bank robber Willie Sutton, and the "Teflon Don" of the 1990s, John Gotti.

Detecting the tide of public admiration for the dapper and apparently intelligent Chapman, the *New York Times* offered readers an admonishing editorial. It conceded that Chapman was a robber of a superior sort, "very different from the petty pilferers that pass in endless procession through the police courts," and that he differed "from many criminals, too, in his ability when he chooses, to be good-mannered and so notably courteous to women that one who was nurse while he was seriously ill remembers him as in every way a perfect patient." Nevertheless, Chapman was a man of "evil ways" who had "demonstrated an amount and a kind of stupidity which is absent from many who lack his good qualities."

So great was the power of Chapman's reputation, Young wrote in the *Times,* that almost every robbery of recent years had been laid against him. "As he has said of himself," Young concluded, " 'the game is up' unless he can contrive a new escape by some super-human effort. Chapman will be watched every future hour of his life. But he has been watched before."

Who would do the watching?

Hartford County Attorney Hugh Alcorn claimed the people of Connecticut had the right. "We have enough evidence to hang Chapman," he told reporters, "and we will bring him back here if we have to take the case all the way to President Coolidge." Then he convened a special grand jury to return a true bill of indictment on the charge of murder.

To the profound disappointment of Connecticut, United States Attorney Alexander G. Cavins announced on January 19 that Chapman would be sent back to Atlanta to complete his twenty-five-year sentence for the mail robbery, with time added, presumably, for the offense of escaping, not once but twice.

Assigned to fetch this dangerous cargo back to Atlanta by train were Post Office Inspectors A. S. Kelly, W. C. Ela, and C. A. Callahan and Deputy Wardens W. M. Berrong and G. W. Hughes.

Waiting in his jail cell, Gerald Chapman, who had escaped from a post office window, tricked his way into a prison hospital and gone over the wall, then slipped away from another hospital bed with three bullet holes in him, informed his guards that he had not slept well that night and was feeling rather ill.

The guard was promptly increased from three to seven.

CHAPTER TWENTY

The Dapper Defendant

CLOSELY SURROUNDED BY ARMED GUARDS, and shackled with leg irons and handcuffs, Gerald Chapman began the journey back to Atlanta at Indianapolis's Victorian-gingerbread Union Station, whisked down to a train on a baggage elevator in the last minute before it pulled out. Federal agents on board and local police at every stop along the route were on the lookout for "suspicious characters" and ready to thwart any attempt by Chapman's associates to free him.

Their apprehension was well founded. A few hours before the train was to leave, they were told of a plot involving concealment of a handcuff key, a gun, and vials of nitroglycerine in the Pullman car reserved for Chapman and his guards. Whether or not there had been such a plot could never be confirmed. The call may have been a prank, but it played on the nerves of already-anxious authorities, which may have been the intention of the caller.

Scheduled to arrive in Atlanta on Thursday morning, January 22, 1925, the train left Indianapolis on Wednesday, the very day that a grand jury in Hartford indicted Chapman for the murder of Policeman Skelly. Convened at eleven in the morning, the grand jury had handed up a true bill less than two hours later. With an arrest warrant in his briefcase, the state's attorney, Hugh Mead Alcorn, promptly boarded a New York, New Haven, and Hartford Railroad express train via the New York Connecting Railroad Bridge at Hell Gate to New York's Penn Station and on to Washington, D.C. He arrived at the Department of Justice in the nation's capital at about the time that Chapman returned to the cell that awaited him in Atlanta.

In the corridors of Justice, Alcorn was not an unfamiliar figure. In 1920 he had been appointed by President Wilson as Special Assistant Attorney General to prosecute (and convict) Dr. Edward Rumely, accused of treason for his purchase of the *New York Evening Mail* with $1,500,000 provided by the German government. The newspaper was to be used during the war to promote pro-German propaganda.

To assume the Chapman case, Alcorn had taken a leave of absence from the position in which he had served the people of Connecticut since 1909, known as a man with a lawyerly countenance, traditional Yankee propriety, and the fervent righteousness of New England's Puritan heritage. Confidently, he had promised to have Chapman back in Connecticut for trial by March and on the gallows shortly thereafter.

First, however, he had to pry the killer of Policeman James Skelly out of the iron grip of the federal government. The key to that enterprise was a lawyer as different from Alcorn as anyone could be. He was William J. "Wild Bill" Donovan, heroic commander of New York's famed Fighting 69th, recipient of a Congressional Medal of Honor, thoroughly Irish and, some people said, destined to be the first Roman Catholic president of the United States.

For now, Donovan was assistant attorney general in the

Coolidge administration. Appointed on August 24, 1924, by Attorney General Harlan Fiske Stone, he had been brought to Washington to help clean up the Teapot Dome Scandal of the administration of the late President Warren G. Harding and to straighten out the corruption-stained, fledgling Federal Bureau of Investigation. In response to his appointment, the Council of Churches of Buffalo, New York, Donovan's hometown, issued a statement regretting his departure. "There goes a man," the local churchmen asserted. "The Department of Justice in Washington is to be congratulated upon obtaining a man of such character and ability."

The fact that Alcorn dealt with Donovan stemmed from another aspect of Donovan's duties. He was also Assistant Attorney General for Post Office cases, of which Chapman's was by far the most serious and notorious.

Donovan wasted no time with amenities. "Show me what you've got by way of evidence," he said to Alcorn. "Prove to me beyond a reasonable doubt that Gerald Chapman murdered Policeman Skelly."

"We have the gun," Alcorn said. "Ballistics tests show that the nickel-plated .38 caliber Smith and Wesson knocked out of Chapman's hand by Captain Puckett of the Muncie, Indiana, police department fired the bullet that took Skelly's life."

Donovan shrugged. "Because Gerald Chapman had the gun in Muncie does not mean that it was in his hand in that department store, does it?"

"Certainly not," Alcorn answered, "but we have more, much more."

For the better part of two hours Alcorn laid out the web of ensnaring evidence gathered by Ed Hickey, Bill McCue, and others: Shean's confession, statements from those who had seen Chapman with Shean immediately before the killing of Skelly, witnesses who had identified Chapman after the killing as the man who ran from Davidson and Leventhal with a silver-toned pistol in his hand, the contents of the storage shed, items from room C31 in the Cooley Hotel, the contents of Chapman's room at the Braun Hotel, and evidence and witnesses concerning Chapman's hideout in Indiana.

Donovan smiled. "I see why your grand jury indicted. And I would venture the opinion that if Chapman were to be tried for murder and I were a member of the jury I would vote to convict. But you know juries! The one you present with your case might fly in the face of all the evidence and acquit. Therein lies the nub of the problem which faces me on behalf of the federal government. For Chapman to stand trial in Connecticut, he would have to be turned over to state authorities. But he is a federal felon, sentenced to twenty-five years, and must, under the law, be confined under federal authority. Connecticut has no federal prison. I am certain that neither the president nor the Congress, nor, I might add, the attorney general, will sanction the costs that would be entailed in assigning the large contingent of federal marshals that would be needed to keep Chapman under federal authority during what is likely to be a very long trial."

Alcorn could not repress a decidedly unbusinesslike grin. "I've given that thorny question a lot of thought," he said, "and I have a suggestion. It's unorthodox, perhaps revolutionary."

"I'm listening," Donovan said, also smiling.

"Attorney General Stone appoints the warden of the Connecticut State Penitentiary at Wethersfield an agent of the United States Government. He then drafts a letter transferring Chapman, still a federal prisoner, to the warden's custody."

"Mr. Alcorn," Donovan said, leaning back in his chair, "I understand now why you have a reputation as a damned smart legal eagle. I'll present your proposal to the attorney general."

"Of course I'm going for the death penalty," Alcorn said. "What's the precedent for a state hanging a federal prisoner?"

Donovan leaned forward. "I don't believe there is one. But one unorthodoxy at a time, please."

Leaving Donovan with a formal, written request for Chapman to be handed over for trial under the plan outlined, Alcorn returned to Hartford to await Attorney General Stone's decision. An agreement in principle came promptly, followed by an order for the removal of Chapman from Atlanta to Wethersfield, where he was to be kept in the custody of two officers from the Atlanta penitentiary pending issuance of a writ of habeas corpus by a federal court releasing him to Warden Henry K. W. Scott, acting as an agent of the United States Government.

Once more in handcuffs and leg irons, Chapman left his cell at Atlanta at eight in the morning of February 4 in the custody of Deputy Warden George C. Hughes and guard S. M. Leisell. At nine the next morning, he arrived at New York's Penn Station, walked to the Seventh Avenue exit, got into a taxi, and headed crosstown to Grand Central Terminal, where he waited two hours for a train to Hartford without being spotted by travelers in the busy depot as the country's most famous criminal. Stepping from the train in Hartford, he found a small crowd, but the curious onlookers got only a glimpse of him as he climbed into another taxi for the four-mile drive to Wethersfield.

Assigned prison serial number 11167, Chapman was locked into his own cell in a jail block holding several hundred prisoners whose numbers, names, and crimes have long since been forgotten. As a federal prisoner he would not be permitted to work in the state prison's shirtmaking shop, although the federals allowed him to clean floors and work in the kitchen.

When Warden Scott telephoned Alcorn to inform him that Chapman had been delivered, Alcorn was astonished. No one in Atlanta or Washington had alerted him of the transfer. But that surprise paled in comparison to the news that broke two days later in an Atlanta newspaper and then in papers across the country.

While searching Chapman before taking him from his cell in Atlanta, the papers reported, guards had discovered a makeshift handcuff key, made from wire wrenched from a light fixture.

"If he had produced that key coming up with us, there certainly would have been some trouble," said Deputy Warden Hughes to reporters. The guards were under orders to shoot at the slightest provocation, he said, adding that they had not closed their eyes on the trip, while Chapman feigned sleep.

Hughes then added to the reputation of Gerald Chapman as an escape artist. "On his record, he's the king of them all," he told the reporters. "He even had a scheme for getting away from us on the way from Indiana back to Atlanta."

As newsmen scribbled notes, Hughes revealed the escape plot that had been relayed to those guarding Chapman in the final moments before his train left Indianapolis. The *New York Times* headlined: FOIL CHAPMAN TWICE IN PLOTS TO ESCAPE.

Shortly after arriving at Wethersfield, Chapman received two visitors: Frederick Groehl, the loquacious attorney who had defended him in his 1924 mail robbery trial, and C. W. Murphy, a criminal defense lawyer practicing in Danbury. Because Chapman claimed to have no money, save for $250 on account in his name in Atlanta (the money was transferred along with him), Connecticut would pay their fees. They began earning them by complaining that press accounts in the Hartford County newspapers had prejudiced Chapman's case and demanded that the trial be moved to another venue.

Setting the tone for prosecutors in every sensational and nationally know criminal trial since, Alcorn pointed out that it seemed unlikely that there was a newspaper anywhere in America, indeed in the world, that had not devoted considerable coverage to Gerald Chapman. Nonetheless, Groehl's demand for a change of venue would have to be challenged, delaying the trial.

Alcorn had hoped for a speedy beginning, but he saw that a prompt opening would be impossible. Everywhere he turned he confronted the reality that the prosecution of Gerald Chapman would be without precedent.

For the first time in Connecticut's history, a jury would be sequestered.

Because there would be only enough seats (150) for prospective jurors during jury selection, no spectators and few lawyers were to be permitted in the courtroom during empanelment.

In the streets outside, in the corridors of the courthouse, and in the courtroom itself, armed guards would be on watch.

No accused person in the annals of Connecticut courts had been so closely guarded as Gerald Chapman. He would be taken from the state prison to court in the warden's car, its shades drawn. His wrists were to be handcuffed; another handcuff would link his right wrist to the left wrist of a guard. At least three other guards would be in attendance at all times.

Then there was the cost. Already, $25,000 had been spent in the search, capture, and transportation of Chapman from Atlanta. Investigator Ed Hickey, in charge of assembling witnesses, estimated a further outlay of at least $35,000 to bring people from Indiana, Ohio, Illinois, Georgia, New York,

Rhode Island, Pennsylvania, and Massachusetts. Complicating all of this was a phenomenon unparalleled in Alcorn's experience, or in anyone else's. As of March 22, 1925, thirty newspapermen, artists, and magazine writers had applied for seats in the courtroom. Many more were expected. To Frederick Groehl in his efforts to move the trial out of Hartford County, the influx of journalists validated his claims of widespread pretrial reporting, most of it inflammatory against his client.

The issue of a change of venue was taken up on March 17 by the judge who would preside over the trial, Newell S. Jennings. Seated at the back of the courtroom was Walter Shean. He had not seen Chapman since October 12. Indicted and being held as an accessory to first-degree murder, Shean was surrounded by jailers. Whether or not Chapman saw him in the courtroom is not recorded. If so, it seems likely that he would have found some way to acknowledge contempt for the one who identified him as Skelly's killer and agreed to testify to that effect.

Regarding the immediate issue of a change of venue, Groehl called several newspaper publishers to the witness stand to aver that the Chapman case had attained extensive news coverage in and around Hartford County. Prosecutor Alcorn produced evidence that the Chapman case had been publicized everywhere.

Denying the motion for a change of venue, Judge Jennings asked Chapman if he wished to exercise his right to a trial by jury. Chapman said he did. Jennings set the date for starting the trial, March 24, beginning with jury selection.

Asked about the presence of Walter Shean in court, Chapman's lawyer was not above using the press for his own purposes. Groehl replied that his client, while denying the charge of murder laid against him, admitted that he was acquainted with Shean and was not concerned by reports that Shean would be the state's star witness. "Shean may say what he wishes," Groehl said, "but the jury will learn that the truth is on Mr. Chapman's side."

How was Chapman bearing up?

A *New York Times* reporter asked "prison officials" that question on Monday, March 23, the day before the trial was to begin. They answered that Chapman had passed a quiet, normal prison Sunday. The *Times* man then spoke to persons identified only as "observers" and set down for posterity one more phrase intended to describe what Gerald Chapman was all about. The observers thought he had lost a little of his "sangfroid demeanor."

Another *Times* writer, James C. Young, reported that of all the principal figures engaged in "this dark drama," Chapman's manner suggested the least emotion. Pallid and intently watchful, Young noted, Chapman seemed "self-possessed in a way given to few men." For the *New York Times*'s Sunday magazine, he also drew readers' attention to a unique feature of the Chapman story: "Country folk from miles around arrive daily to stand outside the courthouse and gape wonderingly at its broad windows," he wrote. "This is the stage for a drama in crime such as the country rarely witnesses." Young observed that the trial of Gerald Chapman had brought to the home state of the world's greatest showman, P. T. Barnum, "a throng such as the city never knew except on circus days."

CHAPTER TWENTY-ONE

Lady in a Sideshow

LONG BEFORE GENE FOWLER lamented the impact of Prohibition on Broadway in his biography of criminal attorney William Fallon, *The Great Mouthpiece,* he worked as reporter for the *Denver Post.* There he wrote what may be the most inspired lead for a crime story in the blood-soaked history of American journalism: "She laid her wanton red head on her lover's breast, then plugged him through the heart."

In 1925 Fowler was writing for William Randolph Hearst's *New York American.* On March 24 he came to Hartford to cover the trial of Gerald Chapman. Lanky, hard-drinking, and bearing a remarkable resemblance to his friend John Barrymore (the flamboyant actor whose biography he would entitle *Good Night, Sweet Prince*) he took a seat in Judge Jennings's tiny courtroom alongside some of the best newspapermen of the era. Among them were Fowler's Hearst colleague and drinking buddy Damon Runyon, Algonquin round-tabler and insatiable crime buff Alexander Woollcott (another Hearst scribe), and Meyer Berger of the *New York*

Times (decades later he invented the "About New York" column, still a *Times* feature, though Berger is deceased).

A host of writers for national magazines, from *Collier's* to *The Saturday Evening Post,* crammed onto the benches behind the counsel tables with the best and the brightest from the police beats of the *New York Daily News, Sun, Mirror,* and *Post;* the *Boston Post;* the *Brooklyn Eagle;* Albany's *Knickerbocker Press; Troy* (New York) *Record; Hartford Courant; Muncie Star,* and *Evening Press;* and, of course, the *New Britain Herald,* for which this would always be a local story.

Artist S. J. Woolf had come for the Sunday *New York Times.* A famed portraitist, he had created drawings from life of Mark Twain, Oliver Wendell Holmes, George Bernard Shaw, President Calvin Coolidge, and scores of the world's prominent people. He would provide "on-the-scene" sketches of the proceedings to accompany the vivid word pictures of James C. Young, whose reference to the trial's carnival atmosphere caught the essence of such real-life dramas five decades before the television age coined the term "media circus."

"Chapman does not swagger to his seat at the counsel table," Young told *New York Times* readers. "Nor is he deviant or craven. Three officers conduct him to the table and he sits down beside his defenders with more steadiness than most men could command."

As Chapman entered the courtroom for the beginning of the juror selection process, he appeared quite pale, a circumstance Young attributed to his being in a jail cell for so long. "In frame he is extremely slender, looking even more attentuated by reason of diminished weight during captivity. His ears, for instance, have not a trace of color. His eyes are red, probably from a strong light after dark prisons."

Those who counted themselves lucky to be in the courtroom saw in the prisoner a man whose delicate face was almost effeminate. "It is hard to believe Chapman to be the dangerous man he is," said Young, "until the cold eyes turn toward the observer, a glance that chills without any intention of doing so."

Looming above Chapman at the defense table, Frederick Groehl appeared as a dominant figure with a magnetic personality, suave and confident. Formerly a magistrate of the New York Criminal Court, he had defended Chapman in the mail truck robbery trial at a time when "the Count of Gramercy Park" had access to plenty of money to pay Groehl's steep retainer fee. Now, in the Hartford County Court, Chapman was, by all accounts, penniless.

Who was footing the bills?

Courthouse rumor had it, Young whispered to Sunday *Times* readers on March 29, that "a woman" was the source of the funds for Chapman's defense. "Since Chapman went to trial rumors have had free play in Hartford," he wrote. One was to the effect that Dutch Anderson was ready to dynamite the courthouse. That proved unfounded: no one knew Anderson's whereabouts, not even Gerald Chapman. "But the rumor about the woman in the case persists." Young reported.

For Ed Hickey, the woman had entered the case when he found her letter to Chapman in the Hotel Cooley wastebasket. But she did not become a reality until he listened to a hollow, faraway voice on the telephone that left no doubt that the call was long-distance. "The stakeout of the Biltmore Hotel may have paid off," Inspector Al Leibholz said from the post office in Providence, Rhode Island, in February. "Since it was your tip that put us onto the woman, we think it's only right that you be with us when we question her."

Instantly, Hickey recognized what Chapman had seen in Betty Bales—the pretty face and comely figure that Broadway and Hollywood publicists liked to call "star quality"— but he found it hard to fathom what she could have found attractive in him. Yet he knew Chapman had had the same effect on a nurse in the Athens, Georgia, hospital. And he had witnessed a sudden influx of bouquets of flowers and admiring notes to Wethersfield Prison from scores of women who knew of Chapman only from what they read in newspapers and magazines. One writer compared him to Rudolf Valentino.

James Young wrote: "Chapman's dark hair, turning gray and combed straight back, belongs to the mode familiar among cabaret heroes." Although he did not know the name of *the* woman in Gerald Chapman's life when Chapman "used to stroll up Fifth Avenue on pleasant mornings, wearing a braided coat and lemon-colored gloves," Young said of Betty, whom he had never seen, "This woman was an especially vivid moth in the flame of Broadway."

Seated demurely opposite Hickey in a quiet corner of the Biltmore Hotel in Providence, Betty Bales was now a married woman, her husband an upstanding leader of the Rhode Island business community (her married name was never published). She told Hickey and the men from the post office that her husband knew all about her association with Chapman.

"He has forgiven you?" Hickey asked.

"There is nothing to forgive," she replied, "because I did nothing wrong. When I was with Gerald Chapman, I knew him as G. Vincent Colwell. I knew nothing of his activities. I never asked. I told him that what he did for a living was none of my beeswax."

"Ah," said Hickey, smiling, "that explains the name you used in your letters to him."

"Why did you keep in touch with him after you knew of his criminal activities?" asked a dubious post office man.

"Because I still love him," she said.

Betty claimed that she had not seen Chapman since her brief visit to him in Atlanta in 1923. If called as a witness, either against or for him, she asserted, she would be unable to offer any information about his life and exploits in crime because she knew nothing of them. She had no intention of contacting him again. "I have a new life," she said, "and I trust that you gentlemen will leave me to get on with it, quietly and anonymously."

Persuaded by Hickey that Betty Bales on the witness stand could contribute nothing toward convicting Chapman, and might have the effect of creating sympathy for him, Prosecutor Alcorn chose not to add her name to the list of people to be called. But that did not stop the rumors that she would appear. On the opening day of the trial, courthouse corridors buzzed with a story that the mystery woman would provide Chapman with an alibi, saying that he had been with her in Providence at the time of the Skelly murder, presumably in bed.

Just where all the rumors originated puzzled Hugh Alcorn and Ed Hickey, but as jury selection got underway, Alcorn took note of a man seated behind the defense table and, from time to time, conferring with Chapman.

"Who is that fellow?" Alcorn asked Ed Hickey. "He's not one of Chapman's lawyers."

"Never saw him before," Hickey replied.

"Find out who he is," Alcorn said.

With that request, the prosecution of Gerald Chapman took a turn that left Hickey more flabbergasted than any twist of the most bizarre and surprising investigation of his career.

Showing Hickey a press pass, and identifying himself as a reporter for Bernarr MacFadden's *Evening Graphic,* the man gave his name as John Gray. In fact, he was the man who had gone over the wall with Chapman in Atlanta in 1923. Having served the balance of his sentence for forgery, plus time for escaping, he rushed to Hartford in 1925 to lend a hand to his friend in whatever way he could. Forging the *Evening Graphic* identity card, he had obtained the press pass admitting him to the court.

Although Alcorn promptly ordered it canceled, there was nothing he could do to prevent Gray from becoming a conduit to a story-hungry pack of reporters clamoring for any morsel of news about Chapman. Undaunted by being caught with a fake *Evening Graphic* ID card, Gray peddled to the newspaper a long, highly colored and almost entirely bogus Chapman lifestory, signed by Chapman. To the *Evening Graphic* and any other paper who would take them—and most did—he provided bits of information throughout the trial. Much of it was true, some false, with no means of telling the difference. The most publicized and, thanks to the press, the most romanticized criminal defendant in recent memory was in the headlines again. On opening day of the trial, the *New York Times* reported: CHAPMAN USES WITS PREPARING DEFENSE ON EVE OF HIS TRIAL. The story continued, "Chapman seems to have assumed direction of his own trial," pointing out that Chapman had been reading the law and had decided to protest "the array of the jury," because the panel of potential jurors gave too much representation to people from outside the city of Hartford. The rationale was based on an assumption, in the rather insulting opinion of Frederick Groehl, "that men in Hartford are not as likely to read the papers as men from the smaller towns" and therefore could not have been prejudiced by the publicity surrounding Chapman.

In what was certainly an innovation, Chapman turned to the reporters in a blatant attempt to swing public opinion to his side. Through Groehl, he asked newspapers to publish a statement: "If any witnesses in this case testify to having seen me in New Britain at the time of this murder, these people are either deliberately testifying falsely or, to be charitable, they may be honestly mistaken, for I had absolutely nothing to do with the death of Policeman Skelly."

In a patently self-serving ploy that the newspapers went for, he challenged all identifications of him, adding that "it is easy to understand how people will identify someone whose photograph generally published has made an unconscious impression upon their minds." And he pointed out, correctly, that identifications of him had had to be retracted. He mentioned the case of his mistaken identification as the robber of the Abbottsville bank, the arrest of George Stuyvesant by the New York police, and the railway mail clerk on Long Island. "Evidently, some of these witnesses who claim to have identified me are only too anxious to secure some publicity," Chapman said, "and to have a part in the case against a man who has been painted as black as I have been by articles most of which are not based on the truth."

Fetched from Wethersfield at eight o'clock Tuesday morning, October 24, Chapman traveled in a curtained automobile, seated in the rear between two guards, with two more in front. He entered without handcuffs to find a courtroom whose main entrance was protected by "the tallest policeman in the world," retired Sergeant Daniel B. Ahern of the Hartford police, standing six feet, six inches. Under his command were uniformed cops inside and outside the courtroom.

To keep a sharp lookout for any Chapman allies who might have driven up from Manhattan to rescue him, detectives had been sent from New York City to patrol streets surrounding the courthouse.

The Post Office Department had assigned dozens of its men. The Hartford County Courthouse was a square, red-brick structure with sandstone trim, high arched windows, blue-slate mansard roof, and oak floors. It had been built to convey the solidity and probity that were supposed to be the foundations of American justice, even for Public Enemy No. 1, yet one observer that morning thought the courthouse exuded a kind of musty gloom.

No one could say whether 270 prospective jurors, all men, felt the gloom as they took their seats. "The gray-headed jury came to court in its Sunday clothes," James Young wrote, "and undertook the task like God-fearing men called to a high duty. These farmers, small tradesmen and workers did not shirk."

By the end of the day, five jurors had been agreed upon by Alcorn, businesslike and searching, and Groehl, capable of a scornful thrust during questioning of jurors, but speaking in a manner and tone that begat confidence and even sympathy. Over all had presided Judge Newell Jennings, with an easy smile and a mild eye, patient and dignified in his courtroom despite its atmosphere of an armed camp.

The focus of all, Gerald Chapman sat immobile, seemingly uninterested. "His mask is deceptive," observed Young, "hiding an intensely active mind. He matches his fingertips and thumbs with the nicety of a man engaged in a geometrical problem. Occasionally he squints at the ends of his long fingers as if to make sure that the problem has been solved. Then he glances up sharply at a juror, the judge, or one of the counsel. His is a mind that conceives and decides in flashes. But the flashes are cold light. No fire comes from his frigid eyes."

Because Connecticut was a tobacco-growing state, and because Frederick Groehl once had represented tobacco interests, Alcorn succeeded in keeping off the jury anyone who was a member of the Tobacco Growers' Association. Groehl did his best to have the entire juror panel dismissed, but failed.

So painstaking and contentious was the process that Judge Jennings ran out of potential jurors. Noticeably distressed, he ordered the sheriff to go out to the street and bring in the first five men he encountered. Of the surprised citizens dragooned into court, the second to be questioned became the twelfth juror and foreman—Samuel A. Chamberlin, a clothier.

At 3:40 P.M., March 26, Chapman rose to hear the reading of an indictment by the court clerk, Lucian H. Fuller, charging that he, as Gerald Chapman and a long list of aliases, had "feloniously, willfully and premeditatedly" shot Policeman James Skelly with "a lead bullet propelled by gunpowder," inflicting a mortal wound from which the policeman died two hours later.

Dispensing with opening remarks, Prosecutor Alcorn called to the witness chair a surveyor and civil engineer who described the layout of the Davidson and Leventhal Department Store. He would be the first of many prosecution witnesses whose purpose was to place Gerald Chapman at the scene of the crime with a smoking gun in his hand.

By the end of the next day, twenty-six had been called, among them Frank Kubeck and Lillian Knell of the Old Colony Inn, James Snyder of the Stanton Motor Company of Steubenville, Ohio, and the firm's accountant, with testimony about the man who had come in on a Saturday night to look at a Lincoln touring car.

Asked by Groehl why she remembered Gerald Chapman so well, Catherine Bourne said, "He was exceptionally well dressed."

"You do not have many well-dressed men in Steubenville"; he suggested sarcastically, "perhaps that is why you can remember so well?"

"We have plenty of well-dressed men," she snapped, "but few overdressed ones."

Even Chapman laughed.

Others took the stand and told of seeing Chapman: the bus driver, William Allison, who had stopped to assist Chapman on the road and been advised to "move on"; the Reverend

Bailey, concerning the sale of his house; Bailey's lawyer; the proprietor of the Little River Inn, Ed Buckley, relative to Chapman's association with Walter Shean; the switchboard operator of the Cooley Hotel, Ethel Fielding, about messages; librarians Alice Powers, Martha Gamble, and Frederick H. Cook, concerning stolen books; James W. Brown of the Ford Motor Company, all the way from Detroit to provide expert testimony on the subject of doctored serial numbers of parts of the Lincoln car; and Dr. David Waskowitz, making a four-in-the-morning house call when he saw three men in a car, one of whom looked like Chapman. But these were little more than a sideshow. The main stars of the extravaganza were yet to be heard from.

Policeman Alfred Atwater had still to state unequivocally that the man who shot Skelly had been Chapman, although Frederick Groehl planned to show that Atwater had been so terrified that he had ducked behind a counter.

There was a farmer from Indiana who had taken his first train ride to reach Connecticut in order to talk about Chapman's visits to his farm and everything else that he knew about Chapman and Dutch Anderson—Ben Hance.

And in court for the first time since the trial opened, seated beside his father Charles and his brother Arthur, protected by Hartford County Detective John J. Kelleher, waited Walter Shean, the biggest star witness of them all.

Aware of his presence, Chapman steadfastly ignored him.

At day's end James Young wrote in his reporters' notebook: "He is the enigma of crime, the gentlemanly desperado in real life. From whence he came and what will be his end no men can say."

CHAPTER TWENTY-TWO

Center Ring

LATE FRIDAY AFTERNOON, March 27, 1925, Ben Hance took a seat in the spotlight. Since coming to Connecticut, the farmer, with his new suit and sun-leathered face, had charmed everyone who met him. "You know, I ain't never seen the ocean," he said to Ed Hickey, "so I was wonderin' if I could get a little time off from all this questionin' so's I could go and see it." Hickey drove him to the shore. "You know, I never had a taste of oysters," Hance said. Hickey bought him a dozen on the half-shell. Hance blurted, "Ain't somebody goin' to cook 'em?"

On the witness stand, Hance answered Prosecutor Alcorn's queries about the man who had stayed at his farm, calling himself Miller. He told of the day in April 1924 when Miller had showed up in a Lincoln touring car with Ohio plates that he promptly changed to those of Indiana. Asked if he had seen the car again, Hance said that it had been shown to him by Detective Hickey and identified as the car that had been used in the commission of a murder. Three suitcases taken from Walter Shean's storage shed he identified as having belonged to Mr. Miller. Shown a small black library book on the subject of papermaking, he said he had seen Miller reading it from time to time on the farm.

"While he was there," Alcorn asked, "did he have any pistols or revolvers?"

"Objection!" boomed Frederick Groehl. "That is an outrageous and prejudicial question. What is its relevance?"

Judge Jennings shook his head. "Overruled."

"Exception," Groehl snapped.

"It may result in a mistrial," said Jennings, "but I am not going to interfere with the State's Attorney's case. If he does not connect this up later, he, you, and I will have to take the consequences."

Hance identified an automatic pistol, a rifle, and a sawed-off shotgun as belonging to Miller, that is, Chapman.

"Did Chapman engage in target practice?" Alcorn asked.

"I object to this," Groehl thundered. "It creates an atmosphere with the jury, which is just what he is trying to do."

Alcorn threw up his hands. "I can't help the atmosphere."

Permitted to answer, Hance described Chapman's target practices and proceeded, Groehl's objections notwithstanding, to relate seeing Chapman in possession of burglary tools.

Faced with Hance's compelling and unshakeable testimony, Groehl sought to undermine the farmer's character. "Have you been convicted of a crime yourself, Mr. Hance?" he asked. "Were you not found guilty recently of receiving stolen goods and sentenced to a term of from one to fourteen years?"

"True," Hance replied, adding that the case was on appeal.

Looking at the clock, Judge Jennings recessed the trial for the weekend.

Chapman said to Groehl, the former magistrate from New York, "They are lying about me, Judge, but I am sure I can break them down."

Having been set back in the courtroom, Groehl took advantage of the weekend recess to press his defense of Chapman with the army of reporters lounging in Hartford hotels and looking for a new angle to freshen the story for Monday morning editions. He announced that he would be going to New York City on Sunday to bring back evidence that would prove that, although the New York police had been wrong in thinking George Stuyvesant was Gerald Chapman, they were right about Stuyvesant having killed Skelly. His visit to New York, he said, was for the purpose of locating a witness who would testify that he had seen Stuyvesant in New Britain, running from the department store.

Asked by a reporter why this witness had not come forward, Groehl answered that he was terrified of reprisals from friends of Stuyvesant. "I will prove that my client has been a victim of mistaken identity all along the line," he said. "They are all mistaken: the Stanton Motor Company people, the people at the Old Colony Inn, the bus driver, the doctor on the housecall, Policeman Atwater and the stableman. I shall produce alibi witnesses to refute each and every one of them. These government witnesses are as unreliable as that stableman."

The prosecution had not called Ed Johnson, and did not plan to, for good reason. Rushed to New York by Detective McCue at the time of Stuyvesant's arrest, Johnson had identified Stuyvesant as the man who had come out the front door of Davidson and Leventhal, thus reversing his assertion that it had been Chapman. As a result, Chapman announced on Sunday, through Groehl's assistant, Nathan O. Freedman, that Johnson would be summoned as a defense witness. Freedman then informed reporters that Chapman was "very tired" and had been allowed to sleep late that morning. At noon he had eaten a big New England boiled dinner of corned beef and cabbage, topped off by Connecticut apple pie. "After conferring with me," Fredman said, "he went back to his cell to continue his reading of Joseph Conrad's 'Almayer's Folly,' obtained from the prison library. He then intends to begin the same author's 'Lord Jim.' Of course, it is the intention of Mr. Chapman to complete it after the trial, as a free man."

Well fed and well read, Chapman returned to Judge Jennings' courtroom on Monday morning prepared to hear the testimony of Hugh Alcorn's most important witness, Walter Shean. But first, Alcorn called Detective Thomas J. Feely to talk about two small bottles which he had found during a search of the Lincoln. "What do these contain?" Alcorn asked, holding up the vials.

Feely answered, "Nitroglycerine."

With that, Chapman's guards sprang from their chairs and stood between him and Alcorn, fearing that Chapman might leap upon Alcorn, wrench the nitro from his grasp, and either blow up the courthouse or threaten to do so in order to escape.

Startled by the sudden movement, other courtroom guards sprang forward, guns drawn.

Judge Jennings peered down from his bench through horn-rimmed glasses in wonderment and exasperation.

Leaping to his feet, Groehl growled, "I don't know what this is for, Your Honor, but these officers standing here like this is entirely improper."

Jennings pointed his gavel at the guards. "Gentlemen," he said angrily, "sit . . . down!"

With Detective Freely's account of finding the vials under the front seat of the Lincoln on the record, and the courtroom quieted, Alcorn examined Policeman Atwater. "Is the man who shot Policeman Skelly in this room?" he asked.

Atwater pointed to Chapman. "That is the man."

Cross-examining, Groehl asked scornfully if it were true that when confronted by a gunman in the store, Atwater had taken cover behind a counter.

"When the gunman fired," Atwater said, "I drew my revolver and dropped to one knee."

Groehl leaned forward, his face almost touching Atwater's. "And when you dropped," he said, "poor Skelly got the shot."

Atwater hesitated.

"Well?" Groehl demanded.

"Yes," Atwater said quietly.

Alcorn called two more witnesses who had put Chapman at the scene of the crime, though not inside the store. As they were questioned, the courtroom grew restless as everyone anticipated the next witness. Presently, Alcorn declared, "The State calls Walter Shean."

Now, for the first time from Shean's own lips, Chapman heard what Shean had blurted to the New Britain police on the morning of October 12, 1924. Expressionless and chewing gum, he sat still throughout Shean's recitation of their relationship, from their first meeting to the moment he left Chapman alone to deal with a cantankerous Shaw-Wheeler safe in the office of the Davidson and Leventhal Department Store.

Expecting an immediate cross-examination by Groehl, those in the courtroom found themselves disappointed. Groehl rose to state that he preferred to defer questioning until the next morning.

That evening in Hartford, Poli's Palace Theater showed a newsreel. When a likeness of Gerald Chapman flashed onto the screen, the audience cheered. As a picture of Walter Shean came on, they reacted to it as they did whenever a villain appeared. They hissed.

In cross-examining Shean the next day, Alcorn dwelt on the dying declaration of Policeman Skelly, naming—not

Chapman—but Walter Shean as the man who had shot him. Acutely aware that at the time Skelly was shot Shean had been seen by police outside the store on Main Street, his intention was not to accuse Shean of the killing, which was impossible, but to propose that, just as Skelly had given a wrong identification, so had each and every witness who had identified Chapman. His purpose was to plant in the minds of the jurors the reasonable doubt that was Chapman's only hope for an acquittal.

Essential to this strategy was discrediting the most damning piece of physical evidence in a case crammed with items alleged to belong to Chapman—the nickel-plated pistol taken from Chapman when Captain Puckett arrested him in Muncie and which police ballistics tests linked to the bullet taken from Skelly's body and two others found in the store. Alcorn had brought experts to the stand for that purpose. Now Groehl called his own firearms experts, John D. Petersen of Westfield, Massachusetts, a consulting engineer for the Ordnance Department at the Springfield Armory, and Harry A. Stevens, the superintendent of manufacturing for the Colt Patent Fire Arms Company of Hartford, who happened to be the boss of the state's ballistics expert, J. Henry Fitzgerald.

Petersen attacked Fitzgerald's testimony. There was nothing similar, he swore, between the fatal bullet and bullets that he had test-fired from Chapman's gun. He and Stevens stated flatly that the rifling marks on the bullet that killed Skelly might have come from "a thousand revolvers scattered all over the country."

At 10:30 A.M., Thursday, April 2, court clerk Lucian Fuller swore in the next witness.

"What is your name?" Fuller asked.

"Gerald Chapman."

"Where do you live?"

"Nowhere," Chapman said. "Just now, Wethersfield."

"Sit down," Fuller said.

Groehl stepped forward. "Mr. Chapman, you know Walter Shean, do you not?"

Chapman glanced at Shean expressionlessly. "Yes, I do."

Asked how he came to know Shean, Chapman said, "I will have to go back a little to explain this. I don't want to be verbose." He then recounted the first and subsequent meetings with Shean when he and Anderson were house-hunting.

Groehl asked, "Did you go [with Shean] to New Britain on October eleventh or twelfth of 1924?"

"No, I never have been in New Britain."

"So that you were not in the Davidson and Leventhal store at six or seven o'clock on Sunday morning?"

"No, sir. I don't know anything about New Britain. I never heard the name mentioned."

Judge Jennings asked Chapman to speak louder, "so that the last juror may hear you."

Groehl showed Chapman a nickel-plated pistol. "You had in your possession this revolver in Muncie, Indiana, did you not?"

"Yes."

"You have been previously convicted of crime?"

"Yes, three or four times."

"And your last imprisonment was at Atlanta, was it not?"

"Atlanta, yes."

"When did you leave Atlanta?"

"I left about March 26 in 1923."

Spectators tittered with amusement.

Judge Jennings stared at them admonishingly.

"How long have you known George Anderson, known as Dutch?"

"I would say about eight years."

He was wrong in this; they had met at Auburn prison in 1919.

"And since the time you met Walter Shean in Springfield, did you meet some of his associates and friends?"

"Oh, yes. Many of them."

In a few moments, Groehl had elicited from a willing Chapman the admission that he had not led an exemplary and law-abiding life, but that it did not include killing a cop—the implication being that his being named as the killer of Skelly had been a case of mistaken identity, an all-too-frequent occurrence in his life. Now it would be up to Chapman to reinforce a reasonable doubt in the minds of the jurors by withstanding the State's Attorney's questioning. Groehl turned to Alcorn. "Your witness."

The strategy that Alcorn brought to the cross-examination was hardly a surprise. In his opening remarks, he had outlined the thinking behind the State's case. In a sense, it was to be a short course in the history and geography of the recent life of the man on trial. The geography would be represented by a Lincoln touring car. "I shall trace the car," he had said in opening, "from a showroom in Steubenville to within five-hundred feet of Davidson and Leventhal's Department Store, where Skelly was killed." And he would show that the car had been stolen by Chapman.

From Chapman's autobiography, written with numerous aliases, from Chartres to Miller, he planned to sketch the slow but steady development of a criminal life, from teenage sneak thief to an experienced and consummate robber with increasing willingness to use a gun to avoid capture and the certainty of a life sentence. "Your last conviction was what?" Alcorn asked.

"Atlanta," Chapman replied.

"Not where," Alcorn said. "For what?"

"For holding up the mail truck in New York City."

"Who was with you in the holdup?"

"Anderson and another man named Loerber."

"And all of you were armed, were you? Did you have a gun at the time of the holdup?"

"No. I did not."

"Did Anderson?"

"Anderson did, yes—a nickel-plated gun."

Alcorn proceeded to Chapman-the-escaper with a gun in his hand as he kidnapped an Atlanta man, the gunman who fired at a lawman who attempted to question him on a Georgia roadside, and the man who took a shot at Captain Puckett of the Muncie Police Department.

"I shot at someone," Chapman said. "I didn't know if he was a policeman or not. He didn't tell me, but came up to me. Never said, 'Chapman, you are under arrest,' or anything like that. I had something like forty-six-hundred dollars in my pocket. I was afraid he was a robber."

"Now, then, when he got you on the ground, you still had your gun in your hand, didn't you?"

"No, it was picked up off the ground."

Alcorn turned his attention to articles shipped from Muncie to Springfield.

Chapman said he had obtained burglary equipment, not for himself, but for Shean. "On his repeated request for nitroglycerine—'soup,' as he called it—I brought it from Indiana. It was upon his repeated request," he insisted.

On the subject of the Lincoln touring car, Alcorn asked, "The car was in your name?"

"Oh, well, no, you can't say it was in my name. If there was any man who was in possession of the car, the car was in the name of Waldo W. Miller. I have been Waldo W. Miller. Mr. Anderson has been Waldo W. Miller. Whoever had it was Waldo W. Miller, because the registration of the car was made out as Waldo W. Miller. The names didn't mean anything. They were changed just as easily as a collar."

"Then you lied about it."

"Why, certainly! The car was stolen and I knew it."

When Alcorn ended his cross-examination, Groehl began a redirect examination. "Have you any notion," he asked, "about how many people have identified you for crimes you did not commit?"

"Well, there were one, two, three—five. And God knows how many in this case."

"Have you read of these incidents in the papers during your travels throughout the country?"

"Oh yes, it's a very ordinary thing. I got to not pay much attention to them after a while. They were a sort of joke between friends and myself. I'd say, 'There's another one.' "

Snickers rippled through the courtroom.

"You were never charged with murder in your life before this?"

"I have been credited with it in the newspapers. It was a sort of pastime, I think, of newspapers to accuse me."

The reporters chuckled.

Now came summations. For the State of Connecticut, the task fell to Alcorn's assistant, Reinhart Gideon. The question for the jurors, he said, was whom to believe—Chapman or Shean? "Compare the two," he said. "Which one would carry through a crime such as this? I don't believe Shean had the character. The accused could go through it without batting an eyelash."

For the second time, Frederick Groehl summed up for Gerald Chapman in a case in which the evidence appeared overwhelmingly against his client. After stressing the main point of his defense—that Chapman was the victim of mistaken identity—he posed a question that must have been in the minds of the jurors. "If Chapman had shot Skelly with that gun," he asked, "do you think he would have been such an ass as to have kept it in his possession until January eighteenth, when he was arrested?"

Center Ring
—
209

Brimming with contempt for Shean, he said, "I can't understand how a man who has done big things—big criminal things like the Leonard Street mail robbery in New York— would take a weakling like Shean with him on such an enterprise. Would he pick out a piker for a job like that?" With a stabbing finger, Groehl pointed at Shean.

"This lobbygow—that's what I call him—must have cost his millionaire father two-hundred-thousand dollars to keep him out of jail. It is a wonderful thing for a father to stand by a son this way, and I'm sorry for him."

With a flourish, he swept into his hand the nickel-plated revolver and held it high above his head.

"I tell you," he exclaimed, "that this gun did not kill Policeman Skelly."

At two in the afternoon, April 3, 1925, the case passed into the hands of the jury. In Judge Jennings's instructions, they had only two acceptable choices: guilty of murder in the first degree, or not guilty.

Chapman waited with Groehl in a basement detention room. Pacing the cement floor, he smoked cigarette after cigarette. "The longer it takes them," he said to Groehl, "the more likely it is that they will find me not guilty or will come back a hung jury."

Groehl agreed with the assessment.

Peering through a barred window, Chapman noticed the building opposite, the Hartford Casket Company. "Cheerful prospect, isn't it?" he said, smiling. "But what's the difference? The trial is over now. You know a man can die only once. But I'd like to get a square deal. I'd like to beat Alcorn. He's tried so hard to hang me."

Outside the courthouse, thousands of people lined the sidewalks. Hundreds of automobiles were parked for blocks in every direction. An extra force of police had been called in to maintain public order. Inside, deputy sheriffs and Hartford police officers guarded every door, mindful of Chapman-the-escaper and the fact that his dangerous friend Dutch Anderson remained on the loose. Scores of female spectators who had been first in line to get seats in the morning sat where they had been all day, having supper out of cardboard boxes, prepared to stay put until a verdict came in. Looking through a window into the detention room, three Wethersfield guards never shifted their eyes from Chapman.

Less than half an hour after retiring to deliberate, the jurors requested a microscope. A court officer was sent to a nearby jewelry store to borrow one.

At 3:15 P.M., a report that the jury had reached a verdict swept the courthouse—a false alarm.

"Chapman did not flinch or betray the slightest sign of nervousness," the *New York Times* reporter phoned to his rewrite editor in Manhattan.

At five o'clock there was another wave of anticipation. But this time the jury wanted a rereading of the testimony of Kubeck and Knell concerning the two men who had dined on roast chicken at the Old Colony Inn.

Then, quiet.

At 10:36 P.M., Judge Jennings sent for the jury. Counsel for both sides took their places. Heavily guarded, Chapman came in and stood in the prisoner's cage, motionless, save for a slight twitching of his lips.

"I have a feeling that you have put in a pretty full day," said Judge Jennings to the jury, "and unless you feel you are ready to report—"

The jurors shook their heads.

Chapman sighed.

"I will dismiss you," Jennings went on. "You may continue your deliberations in the morning. Is that satisfactory to you?"

Foreman Samuel S. Chamberlin, the citizen grabbed off the

street to complete the jury panel in the most famous trial in decades, said, "Perfectly, Your Honor."

Chapman turned to Groehl. "Don't worry about me, Judge," he said. "I'm all right. You go back to your hotel and get a good night's sleep."

Groehl left the courthouse to a swelling chorus of cheers from people lining the street outside.

As the jurymen were escorted to sequestration at the Hotel Heubelin, Chapman, handcuffed to two deputy sheriffs, got into a closed automobile for a swift trip back to prison, four miles away.

Awakened at six in the morning, the jury resumed deliberating at 8:45 A.M. At ten they took their first and only vote. With three raps on the deliberating room door, they signaled a guard that they had reached a verdict.

Chapman had arrived from prison feeling less confident than he had the night before. On the way back to prison, he had regaled his guards with stories of life in Atlanta. Now, silent and brooding as the car brought him back to the trial, he ignored the sounds of cheering onlookers as it turned into a heavily guarded alley behind the courthouse. When word came down to the detention room that there was a verdict, he snuffed out a cigarette and said, "About time!"

Taking a chair in the prisoner's cage, he waited for the jury to come in and noted for the first time that the courtroom was not filled. Expecting another request from the jury rather than a verdict, most of the loyal attendees had not taken seats. Now they were out of luck. Judge Jennings ordered doors closed and locked.

As the jurors came in, they glanced at Chapman.

With his head slightly tilted back, Chapman avoided their eyes.

Then he stood.

"Number 2606, State versus Gerald Chapman," intoned

Clerk of Courts Fuller. "Jurors in this case please answer to your names as called and as you answer, rise." With the jurors polled, he asked, "Gentlemen, have you arrived at a verdict?"

Foreman Chamberlin said, "We have."

"Gentlemen of the jury, how find you the defendant, guilty or not guilty, as charged in the indictment?"

Chamberlin said, "Guilty of murder in the first degree."

Hands that had been lank at Chapman's sides now rose and crossed his chest. He licked his lips. The deep-set eyes stared blankly forward.

Judge Jennings found no cause to set aside the decision.

Hugh Alcorn requested immediate sentencing.

Chapman's lawyer asked for a half-hour recess so as to prepare a written motion to set aside the verdict on the ground that it was against the law and against the weight of the evidence.

Jennings recessed until 11:15 A.M.

When Chapman returned to a now packed courtroom, he discovered familiar faces from his life, times, and crimes. Taking up a front row were the Mick dicks who had been the undoing of the Leonard Street robbery: McCarthy, O'Brien, Doyle, Coughlin, Cochrane, and all the rest. Completing the row were prison men, up from Atlanta and still smoldering about his escapes, along with the cops who had trapped him in a cotton field. In the next row sat the hick dicks. The burly, broad-shouldered Ed Hickey loomed protectively beside the skinny, traitorous Ben Hance. And all the way from Muncie had come Captain Puckett and the three who had helped in collaring the most-wanted man in the country.

Two faces were not in evidence: Betty's and Dutch's.

Guards escorted him to a spot in front of the bench.

"Mr. Sheriff," said Judge Jennings, "make the proclamation of silence while sentence of death is pronounced against the prisoner at the bar."

"Oyez, oyez, oyez," intoned the sheriff in the ancient Anglo-Saxon tongue of the progenitors of Connecticut Yankee justice, demanding attention of all to "the honorable Superior Court now in session."

Judge Jennings adjusted his eyeglasses. "Gerald Chapman," he said solemnly, "have you anything to say why sentence of death should not be pronounced against you?"

In testifying, Chapman had been ordered to speak louder several times. Now, in a tone that some observers thought contemptuous, he was clearly heard at the back of the room as he said, "I have nothing to say."

He had had nothing to say two decades earlier when another judge had looked down from a bench in a New York court and told a teenager named Gerald Chapman that he was a fit candidate for the electric chair.

There was no such device in Connecticut.

"The sentence of death is this," said Jennings, "You, Gerald Chapman, are remanded to the custody of the Warden of the State prison, to be by him forthwith conveyed to and safely kept at the Connecticut State prison at Wethersfield until the twenty-fifth day of June, nineteen twenty-five, upon which day before the hour of sunrise, within the prison walls and by the prison Warden or Deputy Warden, you shall be hanged by the neck until you are dead."

Turning away without a word or change of expression, Chapman looked at Frederick Groehl. Approaching him, he jerked his head toward a door and said, "Come on, Judge."

"I'm sorry, Chappy," Groehl said, following him out.

"That's all right, Judge," Chapman said. "You did the best you could."

When they were out of earshot of guards in the detention room and waiting for prison guards to claim Chapman, Groehl put a question to his client that went to the heart of the only really damning evidence against him—and to the core of

Gerald Chapman. "It was that silver pistol," he said bitterly. "Why the hell did you keep it?"

Chapman smiled faintly, "Because it was just too damn good a gun to throw away."

Later, in a statement issued to reporters, Chapman said the verdict had been expected. "It was inevitable," he said. "I have had to combat the ambition of the state's attorney, the wealth and influence of the Sheans, and the prejudice of the public mind, due to the word picture of the Gerald Chapman the jury was trying, not the Gerald Chapman who actually is."

He had been convicted, he proposed, because he was famous.

"The jurymen were prejudiced before they went into the jury box by the publicity I have had," he said. "The newspapers have made me out a super-bandit, an arch-criminal. The jurors have not convicted the accused, but a man named Chapman."

They had not condemned him, he said. They had convicted the fantasy figure called Public Enemy No. 1.

CHAPTER TWENTY-THREE

Country Road

THE ALARM BELL CLANGED in the hour before dawn on April 7.

Sleepy-eyed firemen saw the towering tongues of flame and the column of roiling black oil-fed smoke and heard the explosions of gasoline tanks blocks before they reached the conflagration.

A handful of the Stanton Motor Company's neighbors had done their best to get to the Lincolns and Fords and push them out of the showroom, but they managed to rescue only a few, and none of those came out unsinged. Left behind, a dozen cars burned and exploded as the flames enveloped the building and an adjoining repair shop. Deeming the structure beyond saving, the firemen could only play water on adjacent properties to keep them from going up, as well.

In the gray, burnt-smelling dawn, the owner, James Snyder, and his accountant, Catherine Bourne, estimated the total loss to be more than a-quarter-of-a-million dollars.

Judging the manner in which the fire had started, erupting in several spots at once, and finding signs that it had been fed by an accelerant, the fire marshal pronounced it a clear case of arson.

"It was them," Snyder said bitterly. "Chapman's friends did this out of revenge because Cathy and I testified against him."

Of course, there was no way to prove that somebody was out to get even on Chapman's behalf, but Walter Shean was taking no chances. Offered an opportunity for release on bail until the details of his slap-on-the-wrist sentencing under a plea bargain could be formalized, the state's star witness against Chapman chose to remain in the safe confines of Hartford County Jail until such time as Chapman hung from a gallows.

During the trial, numerous threats had been made against those who came out against Chapman, most of them in the form of anonymous letters that were dismissed out of hand as the work of cranks. In retrospect, and in the aftermath of the arson fire in Steubenville, others who might become subject to acts of revenge received hastily arranged protection, primarily State's Attorney Alcorn and his family, Judge Jennings and his relatives, Hickey and his kin, and Policeman Atwater. But how far could such efforts go? There had to be limits. Plus, there was no proof that the fire had been set by an ally of Chapman's. No one had come forward to admit that the fire had been an act of vengeance. Therefore, far less significant personalities in terms of damage done to Chapman got no protection. As time passed with no further acts of reprisal, real or imagined, so did worries about avengers.

As to Chapman, his chief concern was in appealing the verdict and having it set aside on the basis of new evidence, or any other loophole that his lawyers could find. He now had several lawyers in addition to "Judge" Groehl, paid for, according to never-ending rumors, by the mysterious and elusive Betty Beeswax.

The execution had been set for June 25, but Groehl had filed an immediate appeal with Connecticut's Supreme Court of Errors. This brought an instant reprieve from Governor John Trumbull, allowing Groehl time to prepare his argument. The new date for execution was set for any date between June 25 and December 3. But because the appeal could not be taken up until the Supreme Court's fall term, another date was announced: December 31.

In hopes of averting Chapman's meeting with the Grim Reaper on a night when the world would be welcoming New Year 1926, Groehl and his associates ranged the East Coast, interviewing people who said they could prove they had seen or been with Chapman far from New Britain at the time of the murder.

At the same time, Groehl began to mull over another approach to saving his client from the gallows should the appeal to the Court of Errors fail. His emerging strategy was that the State of Connecticut had had no legal basis for trying Chapman, because the Government of the United States had had no authority to turn him over to the state when under sentence for a federal crime.

By challenging the arrangement between the State's Attorney and Assistant U.S. Attorney General Donovan, and Attorney General Stone's deputizing of the warden of Wethersfield Prison, Groehl had in mind appealing to the federal courts, all the way up to the Supreme Court of the United States, if necessary. But first, a decision had to come down from the state court.

When not conferring with attorneys, Chapman had lots of books to read while he waited for the court's ruling. Having finished Conrad's *Lord Jim,* he found himself swamped with literature sent by Norris G. Osborn, president of the State Prison Board and, coincidentally, the editor of the *New Haven Journal Courier*. At Osborn's request, the most literary-minded condemned prisoner in the nation reviewed the books, explaining in letters to Osborn which pleased him and which did not. "Colonel" Osborn also let the public, still avid for news of the Count of Gramercy Park, know that Chapman had written some verses that were "very fine indeed." Asked to release them for publication, Osborn declined. "They are personal items," he said, denying them even to his own newspaper.

Always an avid reader of newspapers, especially if his name were in them, Chapman noted that interest in him as a news story had all but vanished after his conviction and sentencing, except for occasional items taking note of Groehl's legal maneuvers. But with no developments expected before the appeals court convened in the fall, Frederick Groehl had retreated to his summer home. Seeking respite in the cooling woods of Vermont, he left the newspapers to find other items with which to titillate their readers.

Among the news that broke on August 14 was an announcement by Professor B. N. Gorodokoff, a Russian explorer, that he had discovered "a hitherto unknown race" of humans living on the River Poora near Irkutsk, Siberia. Called "Pyan Has Sovo," meaning "forest people," the tribe consisted of five clans totaling six hundred individuals, he said.

Weighed upon the scales of 1920s American journalism, this anthropological find merited only three paragraphs in the minds of editors composing the front page of the *New York Times* for Saturday, August 14, because on Friday Mrs. J. P. Morgan, wife of the banker, had died. She passed away at noon in her home near Glen Cove, Long Island, after a two-month coma that had been brought on by lethargic encephalitis, a form of sleeping sickness. Mr. Morgan was at his

Manhattan office when the end came. They had been married for thirty-five years and had two sons, both of whom were aboard the family yacht *Corsair* when Mrs. Morgan's sleep became, in the *Times*'s word, "eternal."

Competing for city-desk attention on the same day was the disappearance from her Kew Gardens home of the socialite Mrs. Isabelle de Puy Thompson, twenty-two-year-old daughter of the prominent Gildersleeve family of Freeport, Long Island. The woman had left her home on Sunday morning after a tiff with her husband the previous evening. He told police that she had been unhappy with him because he had dined with two male friends despite having promised to have dinner with her.

As city police investigated her disappearance, police in Mineola, Long Island, had on their hands what they called "the case of the knee-pants burglars." Two fifteen-year-old boys were being held as juvenile delinquents after confessing that they had committed more than a hundred burglaries in Far Rockaway, Laurelton, Cedarhurst, and Woodmere. They had begun breaking into houses and stealing for thrills at the beginning of school vacation in July, police said. "Both had been caddies," the *Times* reporter told his city desk, "and their occupation had given them a slightly distorted sense of values. They threw away pearls and kept golf balls. They hurled a diamond-studded bracelet at a telegraph pole but hung onto an assortment of brassies and niblicks."

But before the *Times* was put to bed, all of these items would have to make room for an event that catapulted the name of Gerald Chapman back into the headlines.

Mrs. Charles Cromer never imagined that her name would be coupled with Chapman's in newspapers from coast to coast as she sat beside her husband for a drive into Muncie. Farmers, they were setting out to shop for the weekend. Enjoying the sun and the sweet smell of the thriving cornfields that flanked the main road five miles southwest of the city, Mrs. Cromer looked ahead at an approaching coupe carrying two men and bearing Ohio license plates—not unusual so close to the Buckeye State line. Following it came a Model T Ford, whose occupants, a man and woman, Mrs. Cromer took to be a farm couple. Behind them was a large red car with two men in it.

Suddenly, the red car swerved left, pulling out from behind the Ford. Mrs. Cromer feared that it was going to smash into her and her husband or drive them into a ditch. But as it pulled even with the Ford, it slowed and kept pace with the Model T. "Look at them damn fools," she said to her husband. "Must be some no-account kids talking to each other. You'd better move to the side and give them room, honey."

As Cromer dutifully turned the wheel, he heard a series of banging sounds.

"My Lord," Mrs. Cromer screamed, "that's *shooting*."

Facing to the rear of the coupe and standing, one of the men had fired a pistol into the front of the Ford, riddling the radiator and a ventilator on the hood.

As the three cars screeched to a stop, their occupants leapt out. Screaming, the woman jumped from the Ford and ran into the middle of the road in bare feet. Hit in the back of her head by a pistol shot, she collapsed to the roadway. Jumping out on the driver's side of the Ford, the man began wrestling with one of the gunmen from the coupe, then broke away. Dashing toward a cornfield, he covered about twenty-five feet before a volley of shots brought him down.

Horrified, the Cromers feared that they were about to be murdered as well, but the gunmen quickly climbed into their cars and sped away, though not without getting off several shots aimed at two approaching automobiles, one carrying a man and two small children and the other occupied by several black men.

Country Road
——

As the coupe and the red car disappeared into the distance, and the man with the children hurried toward Muncie to inform the police, the Cromers and the blacks left their cars in hopes of aiding the man and woman who had been shot. Finding the woman dead, Mrs. Cromer joined her husband at the spot where the man had gone down.

"You're shot bad, Mister," Cromer was saying as he knelt over the writhing victim. Four widening bloodstains soaked the man's denim shirt. "Don't move. An ambulance will be here quick. Can you talk? What's your name?"

Blood trickling from his mouth, the man gasped, "Ben Hance."

Fifteen minutes later Captain Fred Puckett received a phone call at Police Headquarters from the officer who had left town to investigate the report of a shooting. When he told Puckett who had been gunned down, Puckett exclaimed, "I'll be a son of a bitch, it's Chapman's people sure as hell."

Informed that Hance was on his way to the hospital, barely alive, Puckett raced from headquarters in a patrol car with its siren wailing and lights flashing.

Moments later, looking into Puckett's face from an operating table, Hance muttered, "I told on him and they shot me."

Bending close, Puckett whispered, "Who shot you, Ben? Did you see? Do you know the bastards?"

"One Arm," Hance said, coughing blood. "And Dutch."

Seething with anger, Puckett searched the grim faces around him until he found several of his men. "Charles Wolfe, known as One Arm," he growled. "Anybody know where the bastard hangs out these days?"

"Boss, if he did this," said one of the cops, "won't he be long gone by now?"

"Not One Arm," Puckett snapped. "He's too stupid. But the other one, George "Dutch" Anderson, he's the smart cookie. He's the one who's probably halfway to Chicago by now. As to Wolfe, how hard can he be to spot? How many one-armed killers are there in Muncie? In Indiana? In the whole country, for crying out loud! I'll turn them all upside down to nail Mr. Wolfe."

Wolfe had not gone far.

When Puckett himself knocked on the door of the home of Wolfe's mother-in-law that evening, One Arm opened it. Though he denied taking part in the Hance murders, Mr. and Mrs. Cromer had no difficulty in identifying him and the coupe parked in front of the house.

Convicted of first-degree murder, One Arm was sentenced to life in prison.

Puckett had no such luck in going after Anderson. As he had done so often, Dutch promptly changed his name and his locale. Ten days later, police in Drummondville, Canada, about one hundred miles from Montreal, flashed the news that they had him in custody. Rushed to the offices of Chief Dan D. Lorraine of the Provincial Police, the suspect was photographed and fingerprinted, but proved not to be Anderson, nor anyone else wanted for any kind of crime.

Informed that Ben Hance had named Anderson as his killer, Chapman said, "It couldn't have been Dutch. He is incapable of such a rotten deal."

Newspapers everywhere carried the quote, adding one more episode to a story that was burgeoning into legend. "The life of this young man is composed of episodes," wrote M. B. Levick in "The Glamour of Fear," carried in the *New York Times* on the day of the false alarm from Canada. "He is like a dodging man who runs past a row of brilliantly lighted windows, his figure vivid in one moment and lost the next. He lives in moments of terror. Living this way has some fascination for him which men have not yet measured. There is something in his head that makes him resemble a stage-struck youth, strutting. In the midst of a vast society organized with delicate machines for pursuit and communication he finds glamour in mystery, destruction and death; and though he spends a third of his life in jail, all of Chapman's free moments are shaped by this glamour."

Dutch Anderson, "One Arm" Wolfe, and others may have pulled the triggers on that Indiana roadway, Levick said, but the murderer of the Hances could be found in a prison in Connecticut.

"The story of Gerald Chapman, New York mail bandit," Levick concluded, "is stranger than any tale of road agents spun by any imagination."

The words certainly could have been an epitaph acceptable to Chapman himself.

But Gentleman Gerald's story wasn't quite finished.

CHAPTER TWENTY-FOUR

Awkward Moment

WHEN FRANK KUBECK stepped out from his Old Colony Inn in Meriden to get a breath of air on a cool September evening forty-five days after the Hance murders, a bullet whizzed past his ear and slammed into the door. It is not known who tried to kill him, but the attempted assassination was immediately attributed to Dutch Anderson, and not just by authorities.

Newspapers relished this exciting new angle to the Chapman story, which had grown exceedingly dull while America's best-known convict read and reviewed books and scribbled verses in a prison cell as a platoon of smart lawyers tried to avert the ignominy of a hangman's noose.

No one knows if Dutch Anderson shot at Frank Kubeck. Indeed, no one had known of his whereabouts since his pal Chappy's burst of gunfire in a New Britain department store, until Ben and Mary Hance ran into him on a country road. His "wanted" poster hung in post offices and police station squad rooms from Miami, Florida, to Muskegon, Michigan, and coast to coast, but Dutch, like his protégé, never had any trouble altering his appearance.

In every way he had seemed as much a gentleman as the Count of Gramercy Park, with the additional advantage of not having to fake a charming foreign accent or make up a sterling educational background. He had them. They had been indispensable in criminal enterprises that rested upon the premise that it was better to be wily than vicious. Only in the most extreme situations, he believed—and taught Chapman—must the thoughts of the brain give way to the gun in the hand.

As Chapman is not known to have killed prior to his shooting of Skelly, Anderson is not known to have murdered before he and One Arm Wolfe stalked and gunned down Ben and Mary Hance. "Best to talk your way out of a scrape," he had lectured Chapman in Auburn Prison and elsewhere. "Only in the most extreme situation should you try to shoot your way out."

Such was Anderson's philosophy on Halloween 1925, as he sauntered along a street in Muskegon. By one account, he had just passed a fake twenty-dollar bill in buying a box of chocolates at the Colonial Cafe. Wearing a stylish topcoat with a pistol tucked into a pocket, and horn-rimmed glasses, he walked slowly to avoid attracting attention. When he sensed that someone might be following him, he paused to look into a shop window festooned with orange jack-o'-lanterns and seasonal hobgoblins. None was quite as unsettling to him as a policeman peering at him from the bustling Saturday shoppers.

Anderson continued walking, a trifle faster.

Also stepping up his pace, Policeman Charles Hammond drew even with the well-dressed man with a box of candy tucked under his left arm and his right hand in his overcoat pocket.

"Excuse me, sir," Hammond said, as Anderson turned into an alley, "might I have a word with you for a moment?"

"About what, officer?" Anderson replied, politely and with a smile, as the pocketed hand tightened on the grip of his pistol.

"There seems to be a question about the money."

"What money?"

"The twenty-dollar bill you used to pay for the candy."

"Is that so?" Anderson said, stepping back. "And what is the question?"

"It may be a counterfeit," Hammond said, studying Anderson's face with an alarming intensity.

"Utter nonsense," Anderson said as the cop's eyes seemed to drill into him. "I drew that note from my bank yesterday."

"Can you show me some identification?" Hammond requested, trying to recall where he had seen the face. "What's your name, sir? What is your address?"

Before Anderson could answer, Hammond remembered a "wanted" poster. He remembered the name on it: "Anderson." Wanted for a double-murder in Indiana. Wanted for mail robbery. Wanted for escaping from the Atlanta federal penitentiary. Wanted for complicity in the crimes of Gerald Chapman.

"I think you'd better come with me," Hammond said.

Anderson bolted toward the opposite end of the alley.

Hammond shouted, "Halt!"

Tripped by uneven pavement, Anderson stumbled and fell, but quickly regained his feet, coming upright as the policeman ran toward him, empty-handed.

Crouching, Anderson fired. The bullet slammed into Hammond's belly just above the groin.

With Anderson running, Hammond wrenched his service revolver from its holster and fired one shot. It missed.

Turning, Anderson returned fire but his bullet also went wide of the target.

Trembling from the pain in his belly, bleeding profusely and gasping for air, Hammond gripped his revolver with both hands and fired rapidly, emptying it as Anderson emptied his. Ripped by bullets, both whirled in a gruesome *pas de deux* and fell dead.

Informed of Dutch's demise by Frederick Groehl, Chapman sighed deeply and said, "He was a good friend. Like a father to me, much like you, Judge Groehl," then, "Where do we stand on the appeal?"

Frederick Groehl's determination (some said obsession) in undertaking a tedious legal minuet on Chapman's behalf did not stem from a belief that Chapman was an innocent man wrongly convicted. He knew Chapman had killed Skelly. The evidence had been overwhelming. His struggle was not to get Chapman out of prison. He simply hoped to keep him from being hanged.

Although Chapman obviously shared that desire, there is no room for doubt that he basked in the prolonged attention that resulted from the legal maneuvering. With each new tactic, with every "discovery" of a new "witness" with an exculpatory story on Chapman's behalf, the nation's press put him back onto the front pages.

Consequently, an already sympathetic public that had cheered when Chapman's image flashed onto movie screens grew even more doubtful concerning the outcome of his trial. Across the nation, many people expressed the fear that the wrong man was headed to the gallows. Despite the facts, many believed Shean had shot Skelly.

Looking back on the case that had been prosecuted by his father, Robert Hayden Alcorn, in his book *The Count of Gramercy Park*, wrote that "the campaign in the press was handled with a naiveté that was astonishing."

Not really.

When Groehl announced that he had unearthed a witness who could clear Chapman, what was the press to do? Ignore the claim? Was the press being manipulated? Certainly it was and not for the first time. Before—and after—Gerald Chapman, American journalism provided men and women accused of crimes with opportunities to engage their accusers in a tug-of-war on a field called "public opinion." No great criminal trial (such as that of O. J. Simpson in 1995) has ever been conducted solely in a courtroom, nor will one be.

In what is still arguably the most famous murder in American history, what went on in the mind of the public as they read news stories proved as important as courtroom proceedings in judging the guilt or innocence of Elizabeth Borden of Fall River, Massachusetts. A vast portion of "public opinion" found Lizzie not guilty, as did the court. On the other hand, many believed a bit of doggerel coined in 1893 and still recited one hundred years later. Did Lizzie Borden take an axe and give her mother forty whacks, and when she saw what she had done, give her father forty-one? You can still get an argument either way.

Three months before Gerald Chapman took Walter Shean on an automobile ride to New Britain, newspapers had pounced upon the story of a couple of brainy, arrogant, and amoral youths named Nathan Leopold and Richard Loeb. In Chicago they murdered fourteen-year-old Bobby Franks for the thrill of seeing if they could get away with it. Appearing in their defense had been the most illustrious lawyer in the land, Clarence Darrow. Fighting to save "the boys" from the death penalty, he argued brilliantly in court, but just as vehemently in the court of public opinion, through newspapers. "While the State is trying Loeb and Leopold," he told a throng of eager reporters, "I will try capital punishment."

Two years after Chapman put a bullet into Policeman

James Skelly, newspapermen like Gene Fowler, Damon Runyon, and Alexander Woollcott would rush to New Jersey to cover the trial of Mrs. Edward Hall and her two brothers for the murder of her husband, the Reverend Edward Wheeler Hall, and his paramour, Mrs. Eleanor Mills. The chief witness was a former maid in the Hall household. Because she raised pigs, she became "the Pig Woman" in the papers. In spite of her testimony, the trial ended in acquittals, and the problem of who had slain Hall and Mills has remained a mystery. But now, as then, the case fascinates. Murder always does, and it will always make news, helped along by people in each homicide case with a point of view to sell.

During the 1920s some of the best news reporting and writing was done by former sports writers who had switched their talents to the only other subject, excluding sex, that was more interesting than athletics—murder.

In 1927 in an even more sensational homicide case than that of Gerald Chapman, tried as much in the press as in court, former sports scribe Damon Runyon began his coverage of a murder trial with a newsman's impression of the two people accused of murder: "A chilly looking blonde with frosty eyes and one of those marble, you-bet-you-will chins, and an inert, scare-drunk fellow that you couldn't miss among any hundred men as a dead set-up for a blonde, or maybe a gold brick.

"Mrs. Ruth Snyder and Henry Judd Gray are on trial in the huge weatherbeaten old courthouse of Queens County in Long Island, just across the river from the roar of New York, for what might be called, for want of a better name, The Dumbbell Murder. It was so dumb.

"They are charged with the slaughter four weeks ago of Albert Snyder, art editor of the magazine *Motor Boating,* the blonde's husband and father of her nine-year-old daughter, and under circumstances that for sheer stupidity and brutality have seldom been equaled in the history of crime."

It's not surprising, therefore, that being a connoisseur of the press, Gerald Chapman envisioned benefits in courting public opinion while his lawyers pursued legal loopholes. Both strategies aimed at sparing him from the rope. If Groehl's maneuvers succeeded, swell! If they did not, there was always a good chance that a sympathetic public would swamp politicians in general and the governor of Connecticut in particular with letters demanding that Chapman's death sentence be commuted, perhaps for no better motive than to see if he would escape again.

What Frederick Groehl probably did not know as he dashed about interviewing this "new witness" and that one was that the people who miraculously appeared to provide an alibi for Chapman were either Chapman allies eager to lend a hand by way of a persuasive lie or mistaken honest citizens.

One freshly discovered alibi was Charles W. Gregory, who swore that he had been on a train with Chapman when Chapman was supposed to be gunning down Skelly. Investigation by Ed Hickey proved "Gregory" to be James Earnest Rolland, an all-around brigand who had once tried to wreck a train in Canada in order to loot it. Rolland was a Chapman criminal associate of long standing.

As Groehl's efforts at turning up new evidence to warrant a new trial proved unavailing, so did his appeal based on claims of judicial mistakes in the first trial. Connecticut's Supreme Court of Errors found none.

Turning to the backup strategy that had been fermenting in his mind, Groehl carried Chapman's cause to federal court. If the move achieved nothing else, it meant setting a new date for the hanging, pushing back Chapman's last earthly appointment to April 6, 1926. This allowed ample time for a hearing in District Court and, if he failed there, an application to the Federal Circuit Court of Appeals. If that did not succeed, a writ of *certiorari* would be filed with the highest tribunal in the land, the Supreme Court of the United States.

In going to the federal courts, Groehl worked out a clever argument that had been suggested, inadvertently, by his thoughtful client. In a burst of anger and frustration during one their many conferences, Chapman had pounded his fist on a table and demanded, "What the hell right does the State of Connecticut have to hang a federal prisoner? Seems to me it's unconstitutional."

Hugh Alcorn had raised the same "unorthodoxy" in his meeting with Assistant U.S. Attorney General Donovan in 1924, resulting in Chapman's being handed over to the warden of the state prison, freshly and temporarily appointed a federal officer. With the question being raised formally by Groehl, Alcorn journeyed to Washington for another conference with Donovan on what, by any measure, was a thorny dilemma—unprecedented, in fact, in the history of the Republic.

In hopes of resolving the problem, "Wild Bill" and his boss, Attorney General John G. Sargent (Harlan Fiske Stone had been elevated to the Supreme Court), called upon a fellow lawyer who once upon a time had been solicitor for the city of Northampton, Massachusetts, and lieutenant-governor and governor of the Bay State: Calvin Coolidge, now president of the United States.

The red-haired, freckle-faced, sharp-nosed chief executive, called by William Allen White "a puritan in Babylon," heard the two men without interruption, thus keeping faith with his other nickname, "Silent Cal." When they finished describing the life and crimes of Gerald Chapman, and posing the prickly problem with which he had presented them, he asked, with typical succinctness, "What do you propose?"

Sargent replied, "Article Two, Section Two, Clause One

of the Constitution. The president 'shall have power to grant . . .' "

"I know," Coolidge said, cutting him off. "The president has the power to grant reprieves and pardons for offenses against the United States." He paused, pursing his lips and rocking slightly in his chair, then muttered, "Most unusual. You're asking me to turn a man loose so somebody else can hang him."

Sargent nodded. "Yes, Mr. President."

"Lincoln would never have done such a thing."

"I'm sure you're right, Mr. President," said Donovan. "But Abraham Lincoln didn't know Gerald Chapman."

As Coolidge shook his head slowly, Donovan regretted the wisecrack. The president stiffened. Donovan held his breath.

"This would not be a pardon, Mr. President," Sargent said. "You will simply be commuting Chapman's federal sentence to the time he has already served."

"Which wasn't much," Coolidge said with a frown.

"No, sir, that's true. He escaped. And while he was out he committed a crime that was infinitely more heinous than holding up a mail truck. He coldbloodedly murdered a police officer."

"It's quite possible that the Supreme Court will rule that we had no right to release him to a state," Coolidge said.

"I don't believe it will."

"I hope you're right, Mr. Sargent. We shall see. Draft the commutation order."

Delivered to the White House on November 23, 1925, the paper signed by the president asserted that "the ends of justice will be served by a commutation of sentence" in the case of Gerald Chapman "to the term of imprisonment already served."

Thereafter, it was up to the Supreme Court to decide if any

of this—the turning over of Chapman to Connecticut in the first instant, the trial, and its death sentence—were in keeping with the rights afforded to Chapman under the Constitution.

Blared the *Evening Graphic:* COOLIDGE FREES CHAPMAN FOR NOOSE.

With typical self-confidence, Chapman informed the press and the public that he did not "accept" the commutation. "The pardon is unconstitutional," he asserted. The words turned out to be more than bravado. Claiming that such a decree could be valid only if "accepted," Chapman, through Groehl, carried the contention of unconstitutionality to the U.S. Supreme Court.

On March 15 the Court brushed aside the petition.

The *New York Times* headline the next day read: CHAPMAN MUST HANG; LOSES LAST APPEAL.

The indomitable Judge Groehl said, "I am not discouraged." He had something else in mind, but did not say what it was.

His client spoke in sonnets. Released to the newspapers by Groehl, a portion of one poem read:

> I might have lured from bowers a
> modesty of wings,
> I might have struck from sorrow
> Some praise of darkling wells,
> Or rung disdain in numbers
> Against the muffled bells.
> Have made the night as tender
> As arms that fold the lost.

The title, Groehl said, was "Reward." He asserted that he had published the poetry because he did not want people "to think Chapman was merely a bandit with nothing in his head."

In a letter to Groehl, published with the poetry, Chapman explained that the verses were, for him, "a sort of interrupted night thunder in my private world, disturbing no one, I assure you." He apologized, saying that the lines were only a fragment of "what I promised as a whole." "To be plainer," he wrote, "one can't conceive in futility and expect to realize quickened creation. Don't think ill of me for the verses. They are only exercises, after all. Futility sets in at times like a tightening mold."

Although Groehl told reporters, "He [Chapman] has not lost courage; he does not expect to die," Chapman's poetry sounded like that of someone resigned to impending death.

So were others. In one of the most grotesque occurrences in a drama already crowded with macabre moments came an Associated Press story datelined New Haven, March 17, 1926: "A study of the brain of Gerald Chapman will be made at Yale Medical School should the body be delivered to it as law provides after he dies on the scaffold at State Prison on April 6."

An outraged Frederick Groehl declared, "Yale University will never obtain Gerald Chapman's body for dissection and a scientific examination of its brain." In all probability, he went on, "it will be claimed by a friend."

Intrigued reporters asked, "What friend?"

Newspapers erupted with speculation, primarily centered upon the ever-enigmatic Betty Beeswax. The theorizing was fueled by a report from Wethersfield Prison that a letter addressed to Chapman had been received from a woman. Described as "written on expensive note paper in a clear but minute script which was so fine as to make its reading difficult," it contained a line that sent tabloid newspapers into a dither of delight. "If they take this life," the woman pledged, "I will surely die."

Having lost all appeals in state and federal courts, Chapman turned to the State Board of Pardons. Convening a meeting of the panel, Governor Trumbull foreshadowed the outcome. "I am calling it so that Chapman's counsel cannot say that they have not been given every opportunity to present their side of the case," he said. But Chapman would not be allowed to appear before the board, he added.

"Why not? Are you scared he'll escape?" a reporter jibed.

"Exactly," snapped the governor.

That was on Sunday. But when the board gathered in a room at the prison on Monday, April 5, the day before Gerald Chapman was scheduled to hang, Groehl protested so vigorously about Chapman's absence that Trumbull hastily conferred with Warden Scott.

Moments later Deputy Warden George Starr brought Chapman in. Looking round, Chapman found a room crowded with reporters. The pale flesh of the high cheekbones that had been mentioned in every "wanted" poster showed a blush of pink. He wore prison denims and gray felt slippers. His hair looked freshly trimmed and he was clean-shaven.

Trumbull signaled him to speak.

"I don't know as I can control my voice long enough to make you understand," Chapman began. "I haven't been using it much for over a year." He shot a glance at the man who had prosecuted him. "In view of some of the statements Mr. Alcorn has made, I can't remain silent. Of course, I have acquired a sense of futility of the whole proceeding."

Leaning lightly against a long oak table, Chapman unleashed a barrage of criticism against Alcorn's handling of the prosecution, those whom he called lying witnesses, and the courts that had denied his appeals. But he kept coming back to the State's Attorney.

"We can't fight phantoms," he said, "and all these things are phantoms of Mr. Alcorn's rich imagination. There are things that are too rotten for me . . ."

Leaping to his feet, Reinhart Gideon, Alcorn's assistant, exclaimed, "If Mr. Alcorn will not object, I will. Mr. Chapman should confine himself to facts and not abuse Mr. Alcorn." "I thought that I had an equity in abuse," Chapman replied. "I have been called a murderer time and time again." Trumbull sustained Gideon's objection. "I did not appear here for mercy," Chapman continued. "I have done nothing for which I need to ask for mercy."

For thirty-two minutes the members of the board listened to Chapman's soft-spoken but often vitriolic review of the case against him—all lies, he said, built on questionable evidence and tainted testimony from self-serving witnesses, such as Shean. The board appeared unmoved. Some members stared out the window.

After briefly conferring in private, they informed Groehl that they rejected the appeal unanimously.

Groehl turned to the governor and asked for a reprieve to allow yet another petition for a new trial.

Trumbull shook his head.

Dejectedly, Groehl left the room to tell Chapman that the last hope was gone.

"It was no more than I expected," Chapman said, seated on his cot in his cell on the second floor of the prison hospital building. He asked for a cigarette. Groehl provided it. A guard reached through the barred cell door with a lighted match. "I had hoped to throw some light on the insidious fashion in which the prosecution coached witnesses," Chapman said, as he puffed and exhaled smoke. "But when I saw members of the board looking out the window while I made my last plea, the only plea of its kind that I have made in my life, I realized the utter futility of my words."

Three hours later, at six o'clock, dinner was served from the officers' mess: pork chops, cottage-fried potatoes, prunes, bread and butter, coffee with milk and sugar, and chocolate

Awkward Moment

237

layer cake. Chapman ate with what one his guards described as a "fair appetite."

At 8:15 P.M., the cell door opened to admit the prison's Catholic chaplain, Father Michael Barry. They talked until Warden Scott appeared at the door a little before midnight. What transpired between the murderer whose mother had prayed he would grow up to be a priest and Barry is unknown. The priest steadfastly refused to say what Chapman had talked about, or whether he had asked for the last rites of the Church. When Chapman left the cell which he had occupied since arriving at Wethersfield from Atlanta, walking under heavy guard to a cell next to the death chamber, Barry went with him.

The number of persons who were permitted to witness a hanging had been determined by law. Attendees were limited to prison officials, physicians, the condemned's spiritual advisor, three persons representing the condemned, and reporters for two Hartford County newspapers and "five other newspapers in the country."

Warden Scott had been inundated with requests. For the first time since the enactment of the statute, which came as a reaction against public hangings in Connecticut county jails prior to 1894, state officials decided to construe the law to admit more than one representative each from the county papers and as many from others as space permitted. Unknown to Chapman, Frederick Groehl relinquished three passes allotted to him to reporters from New York City papers. In all, fifteen newsmen gathered to watch the condemned man hang by the neck until dead.

Exactly how the deed was to be accomplished became a news item in itself. In the recent history of hangings in Connecticut, a sophisticated death machine had replaced the simple gallows in which the hangman sprang open a trapdoor under the feet of the noosed man, giving the English language the synonym "the drop." The newer system required the condemned party to stand upon a mark on the floor. His weight on that spot released a quantity of buckshot that rolled slowly down a slight incline until its weight released a triggering mechanism that opened the trapdoor. Outraged civil libertarians and humanists of the day protested vehemently, claiming that the contraption violated constitutional protections against cruel and unusual punishments. They pointed out that the system was not execution but compelled suicide.

The machine was abandoned, but not to return to "the drop." Gerald Chapman would be hanged in reverse. Rather than falling to his death by a broken neck, he would be placed on a designated spot, noosed, and jerked upward by the plummeting of a heavy sandbag at the other end of the rope. The sandbag was released by a lever pushed down by the warden's foot.

Of course, Chapman knew all about the mechanics by which he would be required to atone for murdering Policeman Skelly. In the manner that journalists had come to expect of him, he said, "Death itself isn't dreadful, but hanging seems an awkward way of entering the adventure."

To enable more than forty reporters to flash Chapman's last words to a waiting world, Warden Scott had set up eight special telephone operators to handle the communications, from Monday afternoon until mid-morning Tuesday. For longer and longer-distance messages, the Postal Telegraph Company and the American Telegraph Company had strung wires from the prison, connecting with the main telegraph line between New York and Boston. M. C. Hall of Postal Telegraph anticipated transmitting more than 120,000 words to evening and morning papers.

As the newsmen arrived at Wethersfield, they could not miss seeing outside the prison a growing crowd of the merely curious, Chapman haters, and Chapman supporters, in a gathering that seemed half funeral, half carnival. Nor far away, members of the Ku Klux Klan assembled. Their reason for being there was unclear, but at one point gunshots were heard, impelling state troopers to rush to the Klanvocation and restore order among the sheets, hoods, and pointy hats.

Never without bizarre twists, the story of Gerald Chapman took another one shortly before he followed Warden Scott and Father Hall to the room next to the hanging machine. At the prison gate, a few minutes before midnight, appeared two women. The younger, quite attractive, had on a navy blue hat and a squirrel coat; the older wore a dark brown outfit. She spoke to the guard at the door. "I am Gerald Chapman's sister," she said. "May we come in?"

"Yeah, and I'm Queen Victoria," bellowed the guard. "Get back across the street with everybody else."

Sensing a juicy sidebar story, reporters who had been denied entrance to the hanging itself scurried after the women, screaming questions at the younger one, the gist of which was, "Hey, lady, are you Betty Beeswax?"

Without replying, she and her companion ducked into the crowd.

Finally, the reporters checked their watches, saw that midnight had arrived, and retreated, standing as close to the prison as guards permitted, awaiting the final word from inside.

Four minutes and ten seconds past the witching hour, Chapman entered the death chamber. His demeanor was, one reporter jotted in his notebook, calm. Surrounded by one dozen pistol-toting guards, he stopped where directed and glanced around the crowded room. Among the faces he found those of Warden Scott, Deputy Warden George Starr, two prison doctors, and the man whose poking around in a storage shed and a hotel-room wastebasket had brought Gerald Chapman to this moment of pregnant pause, Ed Hickey.

The room was about 30 feet high, 25 feet long, and 25 feet wide. The walls were light green. Two high-powered lights shone down from the white ceiling. Another beamed from a wall like a theatrical spotlight, flooding the spot where Chapman's life was to come to an abrupt end.

Reporters had been brought into the room at 11:59 P.M., guided from a waiting area just inside the main gate where Chapman's sister and the woman in the blue hat had been shooed away. As they looked at Chapman in silence (they'd been warned to remain quiet at all times), they saw quite a small man for the bigness of his reputation. He wore a plain black sack suit that the Count of Gramercy Park would never have selected for himself, a white shirt with collar attached but open at the neck and, for an obvious reason, without a necktie. His hands were cuffed before him.

If he were to speak, this was the moment.

He did not: no last words.

Two guards stepped forward to strap his arms to his sides.

Another guard pulled a black hood over his head. (One can only imagine whether Chapman recalled pulling a laundry bag over Frank Haveranck's head.)

The noose was positioned and tightened.

Among the silent, barely breathing reporters, Gene Fowler looked at his watch and noted the exact moment: 12:04:25 A.M.

All eyes shifted to Warden Scott, his foot lifted and poised above the lever that, pushed down, would catapult the body of Gerald Chapman twelve feet off the floor and his soul into whatever eternity Gerald Chapman believed in, if any.

Gene Fowler's reporter's eyes and writer's flair recorded everything: "Two ropes are festooned from twin holes in the high ceiling to one side of the large room. One of them, the newer one, is to be used. If it breaks, the older cord will be called upon. The ropes do not break at Wethersfield, it is said, and as you look at the older, air-tanned rope, you regard it as you would a disappointed understudy of the stage whose star never is ill or on vacation, and you imagine it is thinking: 'I, too, am hungry for the kill. Here have I been for eight hangings; but, as usual, I haven't any chance. Chapman weighs but 134 pounds and that isn't likely to strain such a young, strong fellow as my brother rope.' "

Warden Scott's purposeful foot pushed down the lever.

The stillness of the room snapped with a loud click, as if the hammer of a gun were striking a firing pin.

For readers of William Randolph Hearst's *New York American* on April 6, 1926, Fowler wrote: "The slender new rope, as delicately yellow as a fair woman's tresses, hissed like a serpent, snapped taut and jerked its black-hooded burden ceilingward . . . So abrupt was the jerk that it seemed the head in its sable cowl either would be sundered from the body, or the rope must give way . . . Gerald Chapman underwent many convulsions while dying, and his felt-slippered feet quivered so rapidly that they seemed to be the wings of butterflies."

CHAPTER TWENTY-FIVE

Postmortems

IN THE CITY ROOM of the *Evening Graphic,* they hanged Chapman again.

Since the tabloid had gone into competition with New York City's numerous newspapers in 1924, the *Graphic* had developed a style unlike that of any other paper, including those of Hearst. Eager for all they could get on Chapman, the editors had gobbled up the "life story" of Gerald Chapman that had been peddled by John Gray. The headline of March 29, 1926, crowed: CHAPMAN TELLS HIS OWN STORY.

Along with mug shots of Chapman, the paper ran a photograph that was an out-and-out fake. Depicting a man in a dark suit on a building ledge, his arms stretched sideward and his back against a wall, it purported to show Chapman in the midst of his daring escape from the General Post Office. Anyone doubting this need only look below the ledge on which the man in the black suit stood. Clearly visible was the word RAIN, which could only be part of the post office's famous motto concerning letter service undaunted by meterological impediments.

The dramatic "escape" had been staged in the *Evening Graphic*'s offices. The paper called such faked news photos "Composographs," and always labeled them that way, in the knowledge that no one was likely to understand that the word was a euphemism for photo fraud. They were created by the Photography Department. The man who came up with the idea and the technique was Harry Grogin, also notable in mass-media annals as the first person to make a movie in China.

Because no photographers had been allowed at Chapman's hanging, Grogin's talents were pressed into service to come up with a Composograph. To play the role of Chapman, he enlisted an *Evening Graphic* employee of similar build named Gus Schoenbaechler. He stood on a chair while others pretended to be the official witnesses to the execution. A heavy rope was looped over a ceiling steampipe, then knotted into a hangman's noose and put around Schoenbaechler's neck.

At that moment, to the horror of all, the chair slipped, leaving Gus swinging.

"With immense acuteness," recalled *Graphic* memoirist Lester Cohen, Harry Grogin rushed forward, grabbed Gus's knees and held him up until the chair could be replaced. "When all calmed down," wrote Cohen, "we shot the hanging of Gerald Chapman."

In the real hanging, Chapman had dangled twelve feet above the floor for eight minutes and fifty seconds before Dr. P. B. Battey, a prison physician, pronounced him dead at 12:13:15 A.M. and Dr. E. G. Fox confirmed it. The body was placed in a wicker basket, covered with a sheet, and at 12:18 P.M., still guarded, carried to the undertaking rooms of Charles J. Dullin.

The corpse was formally claimed by Father Hall, but a few

minutes before eight o'clock that morning, the two mysterious women who had been turned away from the prison appeared at the funeral home with Frederick Groehl and two assistant counsels. The elder woman was, indeed, Chapman's sister. Her weeping companion was Betty Bales.

The plain oak coffin with its name plate left blank was opened for them. When they finished the viewing, the casket was not placed in a hearse but in Dullin's roomy black automobile, as the women and the lawyers got into another car for the four-mile drive to Mount St. Benedict Cemetery in the Hartford suburb of Blue Hills. When they arrived, two grave diggers were just completing their work. The plot, on a slope in a remote corner of the large and well-kept burial ground, was unconsecrated ground.

The coffin was opened again, briefly.

Frederick Groehl and his associates took off their hats.

The women sobbed.

There was no service, no prayers.

As the coffin was lowered into the grave, reporters and photographers arrived, a shouting, pushing-and-shoving horde rushing toward the women. Screaming, Betty and Chapman's sister ran for the car. It sped away. At 9:50 A.M., the women boarded a train for New York City, never to be heard from again.

Closing the grave, the cemetery hands worked the ground so that there would be no mound. A marker would not be erected for several years, to eliminate any chance of vandalism or desecration, but flowers were found on the grave the following day. Bouquets and wreaths would continue to be placed upon it for years, all of them from women whose only acquaintance with Gerald Chapman had been through the newspapers and who, no doubt, believed that Chapman was the innocent victim of the true villain in Skelly's murder, namely, Walter Shean.

Still confined to the Hartford County jail, Shean offered no comment on the hanging of Chapman. Charged as an accomplice, he awaited a court appearance in June, at which he expected to be allowed to plead guilty to charges of breaking and entering and carrying a concealed weapon. The penalty for such offenses was from three to five years, but given the fact that he had already been in jail for eighteen months, had been on his best behavior, and had been the state's star witness, early freedom awaited him; then, the enveloping mists of anonymity.

Chapman's other ally, Dr. Spickermon, had been convicted for selling drugs and sent to the federal penitentiary in Atlanta. He did his time, departed a broken man, and died in obscurity.

One Arm Wolfe, sentenced to life for murdering the Hances, won parole in 1943. Sixteen years later he was killed in an explosion and fire in his house in Dundee, Florida.

Of the Muncie cops who had nabbed Chapman the last to die was Samuel Goodpasture, in 1955.

Ed Hickey passed away in 1953, but for today's residents of Connecticut it is not likely to be the Chapman case for which he is remembered, for it was as Connecticut Police Commissioner that Hickey introduced radar to detect speeders on state highways.

No one can say for sure how Betty Bales spent life after her good-bye to Chapman at the cemetery. Whenever or wherever she died, she left as her legacy questions that are unlikely to be resolved. Who was she? Did she love Gerald Chapman? If so, why?

If not love, then what kept her loyalty? His money? Danger? His charm? His style? The intellect signified by his world of books?

Of all the public enemies who appeared after Chapman's four short years of publicized criminal enterprises (1921's mail robbery to 1925's arrest by Captain Puckett), he is the only one whose life, crimes, and demise commanded attention from the editors of *Literary Digest*. Two weeks after Chapman was hanged, the magazine published "Questions from Chapman's Grave." Accompanying the page-and-a-half essay in the "Religion-and-Social Service" segment was a photo of Chapman against a background of prison bars, ankle-high shoe of his left foot resting upon a cane-backed chair, his head bowed. He is reading a book. The line below reads, "At the end of the trail," and under it, the caption notes, "But it is a question among moralists whether society gained anything in hanging Gerald Chapman for murder, and whether capital punishment is ever actually a deterrent."

Thus, in death, a man whose entire life had been morally warped, and who demonstrated no hesitation in taking a life, posed a philosophical dilemma which still troubles thoughtful Americans. "Chapman swinging at the end of a rope was a supreme demonstration of the futility of crime—a sensational warning solemnly pictured in every town and hamlet in the country," said *Literary Digest*. "But two questions rise from the graves of executed felons: Was Chapman or society responsible for his life of crime? Has society the moral right to exact a life for a life?"

The *New York Telegram* thought so, declaring that Chapman "received his just desserts." The *New York Sun* found "the fault was more likely to be in him than in civilization." The *Boston Post* saw in his death on the gallows "a solemn message to the underworld." Albany's *Knickerbocker Press* said, "Not enough men are hanged for murder in the United States to make such a hanging an ordinary matter. That is unfortunate." The *Detroit Free Press* observed a "pathological finickiness over the enemies of society" that "is one of the factors that prolongs the homicide list in America."

Writing in the *New York World*, former sports writer Heywood Broun, who had witnessed the hanging, told the readers of his column: "If Chapman had been sentenced to life imprisonment his name and fame would have been forgotten within a year. But how can we forget him now? The ill-advised routine of the execution put the limelight full upon him, and in that light it was the upholders of the law who blinked and cringed. Why should there be a gallows for any man? The crime of execution is an offense against the community. Brutality is loosed into the air and clings close to the earth like a poison gas. I would not have sprung the trap and you would not, and what right have we to ask some other one to do it for us? The sorry joke was not on Chapman."

On the other hand, the *News* of Betty Bales's sanctuary, Providence, pointed out that Rhode Island had abolished capital punishment and noted "we doubt very much whether the type of man who would commit murder is likely to be dissuaded by Chapman's fate." The paper mentioned that Warden Lewis E. Lawes of Sing Sing Prison and others who were opposed to capital punishment and "are supposed to know most about it, believe that it is not an effective deterrent."

In his memoirs of Sing Sing, Lawes suggested that one good way to deter would-be public enemies was to deny them publicity. In 1932 he wrote, "In recent years we have been reminded rather forcibly of notorious criminals, as for instance Gerald Chapman and others, who were all inmates of the Reformatory in my days. They did not then display any particular viciousness. They became later in life the subjects of newspaper propaganda. Exaggerated accounts of their escapades turned them into headliners. They grew in their self-appraisment. They began to see themselves as others saw them, in large, black type."

In its postmortem of the Chapman era, *Literary Digest* also referred to him as a creature of the press: "Pages of publicity had attached a certain glamour to Chapman, but the cold analysis of the law shows him to have been merely a thief, burglar and murderer."

The *Eagle* of Brooklyn, where Gerald Chapman began life, in reviewing that life and its ending, said, "There never was an execution that gave more satisfaction to the decent people of our communities all over America."

Devoting a chapter to Chapman in his autobiography *Night Stick,* published in 1947, twenty-one years after Chapman went to the gallows, Lewis J. Valentine, Police Commissioner of New York for fourteen years under Mayor Fiorello La Guardia, wrote: "I am not unmindful of the fact that he had a keen mind, a fair education, and a strong-willed personality, . . . [But] Chapman spent fourteen years in prison. That, I would like to hammer home, was more than one-third of his entire span of life. If the outstanding 'bad man' of his era, a criminal with a conscious philosophy of crime which made him an avowed enemy of society, could not cope with the institutions of organized society which he defied, lesser criminals might profitably ask themselves how they could do better in the long run than he."

What did Chapman's life of crime gain him? At the age of thirty-eight, what earthly treasure did he leave behind?

He died without having made a will. None was needed.

The gold watch he carried when Fred Puckett captured him proved to have been stolen and was returned to its owner. Platinum jewelry and a fur coat found in his room at the Braun Hotel were also stolen and returned. His most prized possession in his cell at Wethersfield, a book of synonyms, had been borrowed from a guard.

Credited with the theft of millions of dollars, the man behind the record-breaking Leonard Street mail robbery and no one knows how many other crimes committed alone and in partnership with Dutch Anderson, owned as he walked to a modern gallows at Wethersfield Prison . . . two collar buttons.